The Cambridge Companion to the Guitar

From its origins in the culture of late medieval Europe to enormous
global popularity in the twentieth, the guitar and its development
comprise multiple histories, each characterized by distinct styles,
playing techniques, repertories, and socio-cultural roles. These
histories simultaneously span popular and classical styles,
contemporary and historical practices, written and unwritten
traditions, and Western and non-Western cultures. This is the first
book to encompass the breadth and depth of guitar performance,
featuring twelve essays covering different traditions, styles, and
instruments, written by some of the most influential players,
teachers, and guitar historians in the world. The coverage of the
book allows the player to understand both the analogies and the
differences between guitar traditions; all styles – from baroque,
classical, country, blues, and rock to flamenco, African, and
Celtic – will share the same platform, along with instrument
making. As musical training is increasingly broadened this
comprehensive book will become an indispensable resource.

VICTOR ANAND COELHO is Professor of Music at the University of
Calgary. His publications include *Performance on Lute, Guitar, and
Vihuela* (Cambridge, 1997), *The Manuscript Sources of 17th-Century
Italian Lute Music*, and *Music and Science in the Age of Galileo*. As a
lutenist he has performed throughout North America and Europe
and as a guitarist has just released a CD, *Come on in my Kitchen*,
with his blues band.

The Cambridge Companions to Music

The Cambridge Companion to the

GUITAR

·················

EDITED BY
Victor Anand Coelho
University of Calgary

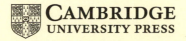

CAMBRIDGE
UNIVERSITY PRESS

PUBLISHED BY THE PRESS SYNDICATE OF THE UNIVERSITY OF CAMBRIDGE
The Pitt Building, Trumpington Street, Cambridge CB2 1RP, United Kingdom

CAMBRIDGE UNIVERSITY PRESS
The Edinburgh Building, Cambridge, CB2 2RU, UK
40 West 20th Street, New York, NY 10011-4211, USA
477 Williamstown Road, Port Melbourne, VIC 3207, Australia
Ruiz de Alarcón 13, 28014 Madrid, Spain
Dock House, The Waterfront, Cape Town 8001, South Africa

http://www.cambridge.org

First published 2003

Printed in the United Kingdom at the University Press, Cambridge

Typeface Minion 10.75/14 pt   *System* LATEX 2$_\varepsilon$ [TB]

A catalogue record for this book is available from the British Library

Library of Congress Cataloguing in Publication data

The Cambridge companion to the guitar / edited by Victor Anand Coelho.
    p.   cm. – (Cambridge companions to music)
Includes bibliographical references (p.) and index.
ISBN 0 521 80192 3 (hardback) – ISBN 0 521 00040 8 (paperback)
1. Guitar.   2. Guitar – Performance.   I. Coelho, Victor.   II. Series.
ML1015.G9 C23   2002
787.87 – dc21   2002025691

ISBN 0 521 80192 3 hardback
ISBN 0 521 00040 8 paperback

For Carina

Contents

Illustrations

Contributors

Graeme M. Boone studied at Berkeley and Harvard, and currently teaches at the Ohio State University. He specializes in early Renaissance music and American popular music, including rock music and jazz. Recent publications include a collection, with John Covach, of analytical essays on rock music, *Understanding Rock: Essays in Musical Analysis* (1997) and a monograph on the relationship between musical and verbal rhythm in fifteenth-century song, *Patterns in Play* (1999).

Victor Anand Coelho is an internationally recognized musicologist, lutenist, and guitarist. He is Professor of Music at the University of Calgary, where he teaches courses in Renaissance music and popular music, and a Fellow of the Harvard University Center for Italian Renaissance Studies in Florence. His publications include *Music and Science in the Age of Galileo* (1992), *The Manuscript Sources of 17th-Century Italian Lute Music* (1995), and *Performance on Lute, Guitar, and Vihuela* (1997). He has appeared as a commentator of rock music on the Fox Network, PBS, and the CBC, and has recorded for Stradivarius and UCM.

Banning Eyre is a professional guitarist and has written about international music, especially African guitar styles, since 1988. He has traveled extensively in Africa and has produced many programs for the public radio series *Afropop Worldwide*. In 1995, Eyre co-authored *AFROPOP! An Illustrated Guide to Contemporary African Music* with Sean Barlow. His book on Malian guitar styles, *In Griot Time, An American Guitarist in Mali*, has been recently published by Temple University Press, with a companion CD, *In Griot Time, String Music from Mali*.

Peter Manuel teaches ethnomusicology at the CUNY Graduate Center and John Jay College. He has published extensively on musics of North India, the Hispanic and Indic Caribbean, and Spain, including the award-winning books *Popular Music of the Non-Western World* (1988) and *Cassette Culture* (1993) and is currently editor of the journal *Ethnomusicology*. He is also an amateur performer of flamenco guitar, jazz piano, and sitar.

Jas Obrecht worked for twenty years a staff editor for *Guitar Player* magazine, during which time he interviewed hundreds of notable guitarists. He won the 1994 Music Journalism Award (for the John Lennon/Songwriting issue) and the Music Journalism Award for Best Interview (for his Otis Rush/Buddy Guy cover story). His books include *Masters of Heavy Metal* (1982), *Blues Guitar: The Men Who Made the Music* (1990), *My Son Jimi* (co-written with James "Al" Hendrix, 1999), and *Rollin' & Tumblin': The Postwar Blues Guitarists* (2000).

Stewart Pollens has served since 1976 as the conservator of musical instruments at the Metropolitan Museum of Art, where his duties include the restoration and maintenance of an encyclopedic collection of over 5,000 instruments. His publications include *The Violin Forms of Antonio Stradivari* (1992), *The Early Pianoforte* (1995), *Giuseppe Guarneri del Gesù* (1998), and *François-Xavier Tourte:*

Bow Maker (2001). In 1991, he helped mount *The Spanish Guitar* exhibition at the Metropolitan Museum of Art.

Gordon Ross is a professional musician and specialist in country music. As a guitarist he has shared the stage with the Everly Brothers, the Nitty Gritty Dirt Band, Don Williams, Leon Russell, and Kris Kristofferson. He is actively pursuing research in popular music and culture, and is currently working on his doctorate in music history at York University in Toronto.

Craig H. Russell is Professor of Music at California Polytechnic State University in San Luis Obispo, California, an award-winning teacher, and a noted specialist on the music of Spain and Latin America, and the music of Bob Dylan. He has published widely on Spanish and Spanish-American music, and is also an accomplished performer on the guitar. His compositions have been performed worldwide to critical acclaim.

Christopher J. Smith is Assistant Professor of Music at Texas Tech University. He is the author of *Celtic Backup for all Instrumentalists* and has published on many topics in jazz, classical, and vernacular musics. He records and tours internationally with Altramar medieval music ensemble and has performed at hundreds of colloquia, concerts, workshops, and pub sessions across North America and in Europe.

David Tanenbaum (www.DavidTanenbaum.com) is one of the most sought-after and highly esteemed classical guitarists of his generation. He has performed throughout four continents, appeared on more than two dozen CDs and has had pieces written for him by major composers including Hans Werner Henze, Terry Riley and Aaron Jay Kernis. His previous writing includes three books published by GSP as *The Essential Studies*. He is currently Chair of the Guitar Department at the San Francisco Conservatory of Music.

Steve Waksman is Assistant Professor of Music and American Studies at Smith College. In 1998, his dissertation, "Instruments of Desire: The Electric Guitar and the Shaping of Musical Experience," won the Ralph Henry Gabriel Prize awarded by the American Studies Association, and was later published by Harvard University Press in 1999. Currently, he is writing an interpretive history of heavy metal and punk rock.

Preface and acknowledgments

The history of the guitar is not only about the past, but is about how its modern traditions, covering many styles and types of instruments, cut across the lives of professional players and amateurs, and across classical and popular repertories, thus creating the need for a book about the guitar that validates not one, but many approaches. The Cambridge Companion Series offers an ideal format for such wide-angled perspectives, in which these areas can be explored on an equal basis. Surprisingly few books have attempted this kind of inclusive approach, which promotes the idea that the history of the guitar is not simply about music, but about the interactions of players and (sub)cultures of all types. Currently, information about guitar styles and players is contained in niche magazines and journals, few of which circulate outside their specific markets. This insularity has reinforced unfortunate institutional barriers between styles and approaches (between rock and classical, for example) that do not exist in the "real world" of musicians. Guitarists such as Bill Frisell, John McLaughlin, Pat Metheny, Mike Stern, John Williams, Carlos Santana, and Jeff Beck (to name just a few) have explored many aspects of guitar playing through a process of assimilating and transforming diverse styles. The influence these and other guitarists have had on thousands of musicians is incalculable, and it underscores the basic fact that guitarists find ways around the stylistic roadblocks that have been artificially demarcated by the discipline of music history.

Indeed, one of the main purposes of this book is to extend to the reader the musical collegiality that has long existed among players of the instrument. Almost every guitar style – even classical – contains some element of fusion, and this is why the instrument is a nexus for so many different approaches. Guitarists are generally respectful toward one another regardless of their own stylistic orientation or training, and guitar technique in the professional world is usually a combination of self-study, apprenticeship, and reconciliation. Much of this mutual respect is the result of the hybrid training that has come to be expected of players. The stylistic base of guitarists becomes wider by the day: rock guitar is now a bona-fide "tradition" with its own pedagogy, transcriptions, and academic curricula; contemporary classical guitar repertory calls for techniques that go far beyond the Segovia method, incorporating popular styles; and we are experiencing at present an enormous revival of interest in flamenco, Celtic, rural American, and world music styles. For many players, all of these traditions are valuable and enriching, and they form the basis for the eclecticism that is accepted as the stylistic template among guitar players today. In short, by its inclusion of guitar styles and study of players in the rock, country, world music, jazz, classical, and blues genres, this book promotes the idea that history is also created by players and builders, not just by composers.

Naturally, it is impossible to cover all guitar styles in a single book, and even more difficult to suggest that they would *all* share some common ground. Readers may not find mention (or if mention, maybe not extensive discussion) of their favorite guitar-gods or styles. Nevertheless, with the emphasis on styles that have clear crossover patterns of influence and a focus on traditions in which the guitar is the *central* instrument (with the possible exception of jazz), the selection of topics does not, I think, require more justification.

As musical training is increasingly broadened at the college and university level to include popular styles, rock, jazz, and world music, the proposed book will be a central source. The history of blues, flamenco, country, rock, and in some respects jazz can be examined through the prism of guitar technique, influences, and innovations. Moreover, an inclusive study of guitar styles and players proposes an attractive model for a modern history of music through the way the instrument can inform about issues of transmission, adaptation, revival, roots, interpretation, oral/written traditions, and the value of studying recordings.

The compiling of a book as diverse as this one is complicated but rewarding, and my first words of thanks must naturally be extended to the contributors themselves. This is a book not just about guitar styles, but about how guitarists relate to one another, toward a community of shared interests and beliefs, regardless of background or area. This book would never be mine to edit if I were not also a guitarist, and this would have been impossible were it not for my mother Rani. She was a good classical guitar player who taught me my first chords, and even encouraged my excursions beyond classical. My brother Arjun and childhood friends Chet and Poe were all influential by introducing the world of English pop to me. When my brother returned home one night in 1969 with a shard of a Gibson SG Special that he managed to catch after Pete Townshend smashed his instrument during a concert at Fillmore East, it was mounted with solemnity in a glass case and assumed the importance of a sacred relic for many years before it sadly disappeared at a yard sale. To Brita I owe the joy of having a lifelong companion who truly believes, I think, that her lutenist/guitarist husband is not just another dumb plucker; and to our daughter Carina, whose play area is constantly being intruded upon by instrument cases of many shapes and sizes, this book is lovingly dedicated.

Note on pitch

All musical examples using staff notation (with the exception of Example 2.2, which is at pitch) follow the convention of notating guitar music an octave higher than it sounds.

PART I

New guitar histories and world traditions

1 Picking through cultures: a guitarist's music history

VICTOR ANAND COELHO

Prelude: finding the guitar in history

The history of the modern guitar begins in the culture of late medieval Europe, where we find the first unequivocal evidence of the characteristic figure-eight-shaped instrument in court documents, images, and poetry of the fifteenth century.[1] By the Renaissance, the guitar had developed a sizable and idiomatic repertory written in tablature and it became standardized enough in construction, tuning, and technique to permit an explosive realization of its potential in seventeenth- and early eighteenth-century Italy, Spain, and France. By the nineteenth century, the guitar thrived in salon culture and on the concert stage, producing dazzling virtuosos and laying the foundations for what is now largely accepted as the guitar's core "classical" repertoire.

From this point on the instrument's development becomes much less indebted to its classical past. In fact, its role in Western art-music over some 600 years is but one small chapter of a much larger story concerning the enormous global impact the instrument has had since 1900. By contrast with the piano, whose developments in structure and repertoire were conditioned almost exclusively by the art-music tradition until the early twentieth century, the guitar's development is made up of *multiple* and overlapping histories. To put it another way, guitar history simultaneously spans popular and classical styles, urban and rural techniques, contemporary and historical practices, written and unwritten traditions, and Western and non-Western cultures, revealing the contributions of both formally and *un*-formally trained players.

The enormous cultural and stylistic breadth of this tradition has not made it easy for music history to digest. Consequently, because music histories have been written in a library rather than on the street, the contributions of the guitar have been relegated to little more than a few lines, a picture, and a footnote. This undervaluing, within the classical tradition, of possibly the most widely played instrument in the world is the result of several factors. Prior to the eighteenth century, guitar music was written in tablature, an immensely practical type of notation but one that continues to obscure the repertory from most non-players – the irony being that tablature was originally intended, and still is, to render guitar music more accessible.

[3]

Plate 1 French 10-franc note issued c. 1964 of composer Hector Berlioz with a guitar

Another reason has to do with the emphasis that historians have placed on the contributions of "great" composers – that is, those whose works can be arranged as links in a long chain of influence, from the Renaissance to Stravinsky, which effectively pushed guitar composers, even those baroque guitarists who were central figures during their time, to the periphery of musical developments. (One exception to this can be seen in Plate 1, in which composer Hector Berlioz was featured on a 10-franc note with his main instrument, the guitar, rather than a symbol of the orchestral works that made him famous.) Then, there is the artistic concept of musical "evolution" and compositional "worth," in which works achieve their standing and posterity through validation by musical analysis. Through this model, which has had enormous influence in the establishment of "masterpieces," the guitar works of De Visée, Gueráu, and Sor, for example, are "quantifiably" rendered "inferior" to the works of their respective contemporaries, Lully, Bach, and Schubert. Finally, and most importantly in my opinion, musicology's apprehension (until recently) to engage in the study of popular cultures (or even *culture*) has been chiefly responsible for ignoring the guitar's role within music history, even in studies of the Iberian peninsula.

Paradoxically, the unnotated, oral guitar traditions – rock, blues, world music, ethnopop, and flamenco, to name a few – have fared much better and offer the clearest map for the positioning of a guitar history. Recent popular music studies have rightly acknowledged the contributions of the guitar, with research into rock guitar, for example, now established as a bona fide academic industry on the heels of Robert Walser's and Steve Waksman's pioneering studies.[2] Similarly, many of the guitar styles active within the popular music of Europe, Africa, Indonesia, and Latin America have been studied for years by ethnomusicologists, focusing not only on style, but on their impact on culture. In other words, as much if not more has been written about guitar music that was *never* written down, rather than the other way around, a point I will return to that raises important issues about how our histories might be written.

Seen in this light, Frederic Grunfeld's *The Art and Times of the Guitar* (London, 1969) remains an admirable and durable work. Despite his denunciation of the electric guitar, which now appears outdated – Grunfeld does not even consider the instrument as a "guitar" – he was correct in his implicit understanding that the story of the guitar must be narrated by both history *and* its contemporary players; that the guitar's unique history is, in fact, the reconciliation between its past and present.

With this opening essay, I would like to continue along these lines by marking off the common ground that exists between guitar history and the modern player. Without trying to construct, reconstruct, validate, or revise the history of the guitar, I will approach the topic mainly from the standpoint of today's player of popular music, through whom history interacts with contemporary practice. Most guitarists, professional and amateur, would never see themselves as historians. Yet they are more concerned with the history of their instrument and with notions of authenticity than a piano major at a college or conservatory for whom music history is a required part of the curriculum. In fact, other than early music performers, the most historically minded players are not even the classical guitarists, who have shown only mild interest in historical practice, but the rock, jazz, country, and especially blues players, who are reverential in their respect for the older generations of players but thoroughly pragmatic as performers themselves. So although guitarists have rarely been offered speaking roles in any staging of music history, contemporary players reveal a systematic and critical engagement with historical sources, theory, and practice, whether they are pushing the technological boundaries of effects and digitalization, or dedicating themselves to historical performance and lutherie. Thus, the following discussion will focus on what guitar history has to offer and what common ground exists across guitar cultures.

The guitar across cultures

Despite the consistency in the guitar's basic shape and tuning over the past four centuries, it has accommodated more diverse players, techniques, and styles than any other instrument in use today. The guitar's universal presence in the world today testifies to its long history of crossing (and even bridging) cultures. It reminds us that the popularity of the guitar since 1900, even in the "classical" worlds, is largely indebted to the widespread dissemination

Plate 2 Keith Richards, 1999, Oklahoma City (photo courtesy of Guido Karp)

of popular music – with which the guitar is virtually synonymous – and the global seeding of guitar cultures through human migration, colonialism, post-colonialism, technology, and revival.

Even if the guitar holds a Spanish passport, it has naturalized itself uniquely throughout the world, across cultures and demographics, embedding itself simultaneously into folk, popular, and classical traditions. The classical guitar is Spanish; but the electric guitars and Dreadnought are unequivocally American; the many Latin variants of the guitar can be considered indigenous; and guitar makers throughout the world have personalized their instruments to such an extent that their guitars achieve nationalistic autonomy. This cross-cultural migration and naturalization of the instrument is a process that began in the sixteenth century, and continues to have far-reaching implications on current guitar styles and techniques. Moreover, the guitar has acted as an important conduit for the transmission of culture and ideology. If we agree with Keith Richards (see Plate 2) – and it is plausible to me – that it was the invisible but steady, subversive work of rock and roll, not politicians, that finally brought down the Berlin Wall, then the guitar figures more prominently in this landmark moment in history than Reagan's famous admonition to Gorbachev.

Guitar cultures thrive in many parts of the world, in the Caribbean, South America, Africa, Indonesia – in short, along the paths, mainly, of colonialist expansion. We will bypass the irresolvable question of the instrument's origins – whether it originates in central Asia or the Arab world – since there is just as much evidence to suggest that the guitar is European in origin. Whatever the case may be, during the fifteenth and sixteenth centuries, the guitar was cultivated in Spain, Italy, and France, mainly as a four-course *chitarrino* and five-course *chitarra*. By the sixteenth century, the Portuguese spice route and missionary expansion brought the vihuela to Asia; Francis Xavier brought along bowed vihuelas and clavichords as gifts on his missionary travels, and the "bihuela" is listed as a domestic instrument in archival documents in Goa, India and represented in early seventeenth-century paintings both in Goa and in Japan.[3] Unfortunately, we possess no information about its repertory in Asia; but we do know that native youths attending the Jesuit College of St. Paul in Goa played Portuguese "chacotas" on the guitar even during church services, causing a minor scandal and prompting reprimands by the Jesuit elders.[4] (Missionaries had introduced the guitar to assist in their evangelical activities as well as to eradicate indigenous instruments, musical styles, and idols.) Other guitar cultures, such as those that developed in western Africa, within the *kroncong* tradition of Indonesia, and, of course, in Brazil, were also seeded by the Portuguese.

The guitar (and vihuela) come to the New World during the sixteenth century. Of the three original vihuelas that are extant, one is from Quito, Ecuador, and has been dated by specialists to the beginning of the seventeenth century, suggesting the kind of instrument that might be associated with the vihuelas mentioned in India and elsewhere. The cultural doors of the guitar swing the other way as well: the guitar is the host for New World styles like the *sarabanda* that were carried back to Europe and were cultivated by European guitarists long before they were standardized as courtly Baroque ballet, at which point the works were blanched of the "ethnicity" that the guitarists had been able to preserve of the dances' origins. By the 1720s, one of the leading guitarists in Spain, Santiago de Murcia, makes an historic trip to Mexico where he leaves a fascinating trail of musical sources. Much of the repertory contained in these New World manuscripts is typically Spanish, but some pieces, of "rambunctious vitality,"[5] are clearly derived from his exposure to indigenous music in his new, New World home. The cultural openness demonstrated by Murcia – a highly regarded court musician who was once the guitarist of the Queen of Spain – in adopting music of Afro-Mexican origins is in stark contrast to the religious and military arm of most colonists, whether in Asia or the New World, who expressed little to no interest in native art forms aside from their value in trade. Despite the Euro-imperialism of his age, Murcia emerges as a spokesman for and an early example of the "inclusive" musical personality that remains a characteristic more of guitarists than of practically any other contemporary instrumentalist.

A case study in guitar migrations: the blues guitar

This short sketch of the guitar's early itineraries demonstrates the extent to which the instrument is associated with large-scale migration, exploration, and colonization. The ramifications of these travels continue to be felt in the succeeding centuries, and they are crucial to the development of popular music. Throughout the twentieth century, guitarists in the areas of jazz, blues, pop, folk, and country have assimilated, modified, and personalized styles of astonishing cultural diversity, partly because they are (blissfully) ignorant of the classical hierarchies – promoted more, to be honest, by performers like Segovia than by musicologists – that constructed an "impenetrable" firewall around the Western art tradition.

The blues guitar offers a fascinating example of cross- and even *crisscross*-cultural exchange, highlighting Mississippi as a crucial nexus for guitar cultures. As is generally known, the history of the blues guitar as it evolved out of the Delta in the early twentieth century is indebted to distant traditions of west African instruments and styles, which were combined with the underpinnings of Western harmony. At the same time, from deep in the Pacific, the Hawaiian slack-key tradition provided the same Delta blues players with a repertory of open tunings that had a formative influence on their guitar technique and compositions. Country, hillbilly, vaudeville, Spanish, and even cowboy guitar styles were soon added to the mix. By the end of the 1940s blues musicians had largely migrated north to cities like Chicago, where the electric guitar was firmly established as the blues guitarist's instrument of choice. The increased availability of blues and R&B records issued by major companies like Imperial and Chess, found a hugely receptive, eager, and most of all *white* audience on the other side of the Atlantic, especially in England. The resulting English blues revival in the hands of devotees such as John Mayall, the Rolling Stones, Eric Clapton, and others proved to be seminal in the development of a central rock language in the 1960s and 1970s. It provided an "authenticity" to rock and legitimized it as a musical style with a profound and engaging historical past, rather than as a music that was crude, unimaginative, and hastily manufactured, as many critics then claimed. (One of the many stories about the Beatles' "Nowhere Man" is that it is about one of their earliest critics, a musicologist who wrote for one of the London dailies.) Many of the vocal inflections from the old blues masters are instantly recognizable in the rock generation's mimicry of singers Jimmy Reed (listen to the Stones' "Spider and the Fly," for example), Howlin' Wolf, and Muddy Waters. But it is safe to say that the most influential borrowings – the "core" of the revival – were taken from the guitarists, including Muddy Waters, Elmore James, T-Bone Walker, Buddy Guy, and R&B players Matt Murphy and Albert King. They exerted a deep and lasting influence on young guitarists like Eric Clapton, Jeff Beck, Jimmy Page, Keith Richards and Brian Jones, and the incomparable Jimi Hendrix.

Africa to Mississippi to Chicago to London: the guitar's role within a single genre, blues, reveals a migration that cuts across widely diverse cultures and peoples; Third World to G-8; African to Afro-American to European; colonized to colonizer; poor to rich. It is a history that runs fully contrary to the patterns of transmission that shape Western music history. In the latter, courtly cultures and economically privileged classes are the primary patrons and first consumers of music. Only later, through the democratization of print culture and technology, and for the profit to the publisher (and sometimes artist), does the music reach a wider audience.

During the 1960s and 1970s, the blues migration we have just described, guitar in tow, veers off into two new post-colonial directions. The first leads us back to America, where the English blues revival in the guise of the Rolling Stones, The Animals and, later, blues-based bands like Deep Purple and Led Zeppelin, returns a harder, virtuosic version of the blues that was first exported to them a decade earlier. The second path leads us further back to Africa, where a number of thriving guitar cultures begin to incorporate American blues, R&B, soul, funk, and reggae, along with indigenous elements and occasionally French lyrics. An exploding popular music scene in Africa during this time resulted in several important electric guitar traditions flourishing in central Africa, particularly in the Congo. By the late 1960s, a traditional predisposition toward Cuban music gave way to American influences, thus completing a unique and important cultural circle.

The influence of rock

If the role of the guitar prior to the twentieth century has been ignored by music histories, it would be difficult to over-emphasize its importance in music from the 1950s on. Although purists might disagree (on emotional rather than realistic grounds), it is really impossible to deny that it is the enormous, unstoppable influence of rock that has made the guitar perhaps the most widely played instrument in the world. Here, one must distinguish between rock music itself and its influence. As music, rock is both worthy of study and easily dismissed. It has deep roots in American genres like country, blues, R&B, and rockabilly, all of which were already skillfully amalgamated by rock guitarists of the 1950s, such as Elvis's great sideman, Scotty Moore. Indeed, rock is essentially guitar-driven, and the best players employ the latest technological advances in effects, recording, and instruments while maintaining a strong interest in authenticity through sustaining old styles and techniques. They often use vintage equipment as well in order to preserve "that sound," inspiring Fender's decision a few years ago to reissue its famous 1959 Bassman amplifier – "The most legendary amplifier ever built by any company" according to the instruction manual. At its best, rock can be complex, virtuosic, layered with styles ranging from Indian classical music to techno, and unrestricted by *a priori* rules of form and harmony. It is unnotated; but a clear notion of "composition" emerges through the various stages of the often complex and lengthy recording process. In short, rock music offers much to study, and this is why it now holds its own in academic circles.

The trajectory of rock's influence, however, reaches far beyond its music, impacting on practically all other styles, including jazz, country, folk, and classical. It is ironic that while Segovia denounced rock, the overwhelming profile of the modern classical guitar student at college or conservatory is one who began as a rocker. In fact, it is difficult to see how the classical guitar could have maintained its presence without the many rock-trained students who began flocking to guitar programs since the middle 1970s, successfully transferring some aspects of their self-taught rock training (particularly left-hand technique) to classical guitar. Similarly, the greatest influx of new jazz players also occurred during the 1970s when rock guitarists poured into jazz (including established players like Jeff Beck and Carlos Santana), inspired by fusion groups like John McLaughlin's Mahavishnu Orchestra and Chick Corea's Return to Forever which combined modern jazz styles and modes with rock rhythms, virtuoso playing, and volume.

Rock and its pedagogy

Why, and how, can rock be so influential on so many different styles? One answer lies in the well-kept secret that rock guitar offers one of the most successful, though unrecognized, pedagogical programs for learning music. Using the basic principle that playing one's favorite tunes, however simple, can unlock innate musical expression, rock guitar has introduced music to many students with absolutely no prior musical experience. They are never as musically "rounded" as the pianists or string players, but many music majors in classical guitar and composition began precisely in this manner. Even if guitarists do not "graduate" from rock to classical or jazz, the stylistic breadth of rock is so wide that guitarists are challenged by the many diverse styles and traditions within the genre itself, such as classical music, world music, a variety of fusion styles, bluegrass, folk, and country.

Finally, rock today is no longer an exclusively oral tradition. Guitar playing and learning have been transformed by the many tablature transcriptions of solos, lessons, pieces, and entire repertories that are published in editions and in magazines like *Guitar Player.* Consequently, rock playing is moving ever closer to a text-based, or score, tradition. While the majority of players still learn by ear and through observing other guitarists, the increase in the use of tablature scores reveals a closer alignment with classical methods, coupled with a more standardized process of learning. The difficulty in telling guitar players apart these days is already an indication that rock guitar pedagogy has become more organized, more systematic, and more efficient. It is only a matter of time before rock guitar is accepted as a soloistic "classical" tradition, taking its rightful place next to the violin, cello, and classical guitar.

Postlude: classicizing rock guitar

That this trend is already underway is revealed by the Kronos Quartet's now-famous 1985 recording of Jimi Hendrix's "Purple Haze." They transform Hendrix's signature piece into a scored composition for string quartet, and effectively move one of the most famous rock guitar anthems from the Fillmore East to Carnegie Hall. The arrangement is not in itself unusual; hundreds of works by the Beatles, Elton John, and others have been orchestrated for a variety of string ensembles for ambient easy listening and, occasionally, performance. But the Kronos's version is different in that the members of the quartet seize upon the essence of Hendrix's work: the riff, its attitude, its sound – in short, Hendrix's guitar. When a rock band plays "Purple Haze," it is called a "cover." The Kronos's version, however, becomes a "reading," an "interpretation," a performance, that the quartet approaches as they would any great work, regardless of its genre. Moreover, in choosing the work for performance, they picked one that had all of the necessary traits for a traditional masterwork: its brilliant composer died tragically young, he was a virtuoso, and in the intervening years the work had been anointed within the rock world as a "classic."

The peril we are now seeing in the classical music world – orchestras on the brink of financial ruin, the recording industry continuing their massive layoffs and the closure of their classical operations, the thrifty economics of labels selling their back catalogue rather than promoting new artists, the switch, every year, of radio stations from classical programming to popular and chat formats, the failure of orchestras to understand the cultural importance of new music – has been exacerbated by a growing culture that has positioned rock as the new classical music. It now has the infrastructure of any classical cultural institution: famous venues; a history with traceable roots; the existence of a rock élite as well as its younger anarchic adversaries;

a canon of "masterworks" that is often re-interpreted by other artists; a systematic pedagogy and training for young musicians; a strong presence in academic circles; band competitions and festivals; and the availability of transcriptions and "scores." Even the many franchises of the "Hard Rock Café," with its memorabilia hanging on the walls and from the ceiling, are rock's answer to the famous bohemian cafés like Les Deux Magots.

Of particular interest are the recent museum exhibitions featuring the guitar at the Smithsonian National Museum of American History (1996) and the Boston Museum of Fine Arts (2000), which placed the guitar in a historical context, categorizing instruments by genre, type, vintage, and purpose. The result is a rarefication and connoisseurship; the instruments inhabit the world of *objets d'art*, Les Paul's famous "Log" or the Fender "Broadcaster" (both from the 1940s) being treated as an early baroque violin. Finally, the Rock and Roll Hall of Fame provides the most visible evidence of the cultural institutionalization of rock, in which rock history has been curated and arranged, complete with "masterpieces" in the form of instruments and clothing used by rock musicians. Within this growing cultural and artistic recognition of rock, the guitar is poised to become a symbol of a new classicism.

2 Flamenco guitar: history, style, status

PETER MANUEL

Flamenco guitar constitutes an instrumental idiom of remarkable richness and contemporary vitality. As a musical tradition, its status is unique in that while its origins lie in folk music and its practitioners articulate little in the way of a standardized theory, it embodies a degree of technical virtuosity and sophistication comparable to that of a classical art form. Flamenco can be seen as comprising song (*cante*), dance (*baile*), and guitar playing (*toque*). The status of guitar music within this framework is ambiguous and contradictory. Flamenco, in its origins, basic structure, and traditional aesthetic orientation, is primarily vocal music, to which guitar accompaniment is a secondary (and occasionally even dispensable) addition. Nevertheless, the guitar has come to play an increasingly prominent role in accompaniment, and flamenco solo guitar has emerged as an independent idiom that has achieved greater international renown than vocal flamenco. This essay provides a brief historical and stylistic overview of flamenco guitar, outlining its distinctive features and its unique status within flamenco and world music as a whole.

The evolution of flamenco

The early history of flamenco, like the origin of the word "flamenco" itself, is ultimately obscure.[1] In the past, various Spanish *flamencólogos* ("flamencologists") argued that flamenco derived from an ancient and private tradition which the Gypsies brought with them when they migrated from India some six or more centuries ago. Nevertheless, it now seems clear that the genre emerged in the late eighteenth century, primarily from the corpus of Andalusian folk music, especially as stylized and refined by Gypsy professional musicians. Andalusian musical culture was itself an eclectic entity, syncretizing the legacy of the region's diverse ethnic groups (see Plate 3). After the advent of Moorish rule in the early eighth century, Arabs, Berbers, Jews, and Christians coexisted for centuries, and many Moors, or *moriscos*, remained in Andalusia, more or less clandestinely, after the fall of Granada to the Christian Spaniards in 1492. With the growth of trade with the New World, port towns of Seville and Cádiz came to host communities of black Africans, and Latin American influences established a presence in

[13]

Plate 3 Map of Andalusia, showing historical centers of flamenco

local musical culture. Last but not least, from the 1500s the region's ethnic mix was enriched by the immigration of substantial numbers of Gypsies, among whom performance of music constituted one traditional occupation. Socio-economic backwardness, relative isolation from cosmopolitan European culture, and the richness of the musical heritage itself together perpetuated the vitality of Andalusian folk music as a distinct and living entity.

Contemporary references from Seville and Cádiz in the late 1700s indicate the existence of a musical genre that would subsequently come to be called flamenco. In the following generations this idiom evolved primarily as an elaboration of Andalusian folksong styles, with diverse influences from other sources, such as Latin American (including Afro-Latin) music and, according to some scholars, Italian opera. Flamenco developed as a product especially of a Gypsy-centered subculture which comprised not only ethnic *gitanos* (Romany Gypsies whose ancestry and traditional language derived primarily from India) but also other lumpen bohemians and social outcasts. The flamenco *cantes* or song-types that coalesced in the late nineteenth century fall into two categories: those deriving directly from Andalusian folk music proper (especially the varieties of fandango), and those inspired by other local idioms (especially the *cante jondo* ["deep song"] styles). These latter, although Andalusian in a general sense, are more distinctively associated with flamenco and Gypsy subculture and lack specific counterparts in regional folk music.

From the 1830s on, flamenco rapidly developed both as private party music within this community and, perhaps more importantly, as entertainment performed by professional musicians and dancers both in public *cafés cantantes* ("singing cafes") and in wild parties (*juergas*) held by dissolute, albeit musically discriminating, playboys (*señoritos*) of the landlord class. As with other music styles, the effects of commercialization and professionalization were mixed, often obliging artists to pander to cheap public tastes, while at the same time stimulating higher technical standards and expansion of repertoire, increasing the sheer amount of performance, and attracting the talents of non-Gypsy (*payo*) performers. Throughout its evolution, flamenco has had to cater to the tastes of diverse audiences, including festive Gypsies, slumming aristocrats, purist intellectuals, an uninformed *payo* mass public, Romanticist tourists seeking "exotic" and "passionate" Andalusia, and, increasingly, international fans. The mid-twentieth-century decades were a particularly difficult period, as informal *juergas* in taverns were formally banned by the Franco dictatorship, while the public tended to favor light, commercial *cante bonito* ("pretty song"). However, veterans of that period note that the ban on flamenco fiestas was widely ignored in smaller towns, and that the period sustained several outstanding artists. Fortunately, since the 1960s the genre has rebounded with great dynamism, whether in traditional, commercialized, or innovative avant-garde forms. Guitarists – especially but not only Paco de Lucía – have played an essential role in this revitalization.

The guitar in flamenco history

While the guitar was somewhat slow to be recognized as an instrument fit for classical music, by the seventeenth century it was widely used in Spain and Italy to accompany a variety of popular and courtly songs and dances, both in informal contexts and in professional theater. Scholars, however, disagree regarding the presence of the guitar in early flamenco. During the formative era, guitars were beyond the means of most lower-class musicians, and the early Gypsy *cante jondo* songs – which were thoroughly modal and monophonic in character – were often performed *a palo seco*, that is, accompanied only by hand clapping (*palmas*) or perhaps rhythmically striking the knuckles on a table. Accordingly, some *flamencólogos* have argued that the guitar's usage did not become standard in flamenco, such as it existed, until around the 1830s. Others, however, cite contemporary sources attesting to the ubiquity of the guitar from the late 1700s in accompanying folk songs and dances, including Gypsy songs and fandango variants that would become central to the flamenco repertoire.

While skilled flamenco guitarists may not have abounded until around the 1930s, many of what would become basic aspects of flamenco guitar technique were present, in however rudimentary a form, in earlier guitar styles, both vernacular and learned. Some of these techniques can be traced to the mid-seventeenth century, and the dance-oriented music played on the new five-course guitar. In this style, vocal verses would be accompanied by strumming (*rasgueado*), while instrumental interludes would feature plucked (*punteado*) or arpeggiated passages derived from lute style, sometimes played with the thumb. Eighteenth-century *jácaras*, as stylized and refined by classical composers like Santiago de Murcia, foreshadow other flamenco techniques as well as some of the distinctive syncopated rhythms of modern flamenco. In a more general sense, the variations or *diferencias* on popular *romance* tunes composed by vihuela-players like Luis de Narváez in the sixteenth century can be regarded as precursors of the flamenco *falsetas* performed between sung passages.

In general, the guitar's incorporation into flamenco seems to have developed fairly rapidly from the mid-nineteenth century. By the 1850s–60s, guitar accompaniment had become standard in the *café cantante* context. In the wake of Francisco Rodríguez (El Murciano, 1795–1848), the first flamenco guitarist to be known by name, other distinguished guitarists, such as El Maestro Patiño (1830–1900) and Antonio Pérez (1835–1900) earned renown as skilled accompanists; some of Patiño's *falsetas* are still performed. Patiño's student Francisco Sánchez (Paco el Barbero, 1840–1910) is believed to have been the first to perform flamenco guitar solos, which he interspersed with classical pieces by Arcas, Almagro, and Verdi. Sánchez's successors, especially Francisco Díaz (Paco Lucena, 1855–1930) and Javier Molina (1868–1956) continued to enrich the solo style by adapting certain techniques from classical guitar music, which were suitably "flamenco-ized" (*aflamencado*). In 1902, one Rafael Marín published the first flamenco guitar method book, *Método de Guitarra por Música y Cifra*. This volume, which sought in its own way to further refine and popularize the art, illuminated the state of contemporary technique (much and varied use of *rasgueado* and thumb patterns, limited use of arpeggio and two-fingered tremolo), and indicated that most of the conventional association of individual *cantes* with particular guitar keys were established by this time.

A crucial development during this period was the standardization of the modern guitar itself by Antonio de Torres Jurado (1817–92), who enlarged the body, fixed the string length, added modern braces, and introduced the use of lighter woods. He also standardized the distinction between the flamenco guitar and the classical guitar. Torres's flamenco guitar, as subsequently adopted by Manuel Ramírez and other makers, used light cypress instead of rosewood on the back and sides, and old-style rear tuning pegs as opposed to mechanical horizontal ones. While these features made the instrument more affordable to impecunious flamenco players, the light wood also provided a louder, brighter sound suitable for accompanying song and dance, and facilitated the traditional practice – subsequently abandoned – of holding the instrument in a near-vertical position. The flamenco guitar also retained slightly smaller dimensions and came to incorporate a plastic tap plate on the face to protect it from rhythmic *golpes* (fingernail-strokes). The bridge and saddle are also set slightly lower than on the classical guitar, facilitating left-hand techniques like hammering-on and pulling-off while occasionally generating a slight buzz, which is not regarded as objectionable.

By far the landmark figure in the consolidation and refinement of the modern flamenco guitar style was Ramón Montoya (1880–1949), whose contributions are also the first to be well documented on recordings. Montoya established a new standard of virtuosity by supplementing the flamenco techniques inherited from Molina with classical features he learned from the music of Francisco Tárrega and Miguel Llobet. According to some *flamencólogos*, he "dignified" the flamenco guitar by introducing arpeggios, intricate left-hand work, varied and fast *picado* passages (single-note runs), and the four-fingered tremolo. (Other commentators believe that these techniques must have been present in the playing of nineteenth-century soloists.) Some further credit Montoya with standardizing the association of particular guitar keys with particular *cantes* (e.g., as discussed below, F♯ Phrygian with tarantas). Montoya also popularized the use of alternate tunings of the guitar, particularly for rondeña, a new creation in C♯ Phrygian, in which the sixth and third strings are lowered to D and F♯, respectively. Montoya's rondeña (not to be confused with the fandango variant rondeñas) is also unique in being the only exclusively guitar-based idiom in the flamenco repertoire. Similarly, his practice of playing in G♯ Phrygian for his version of mineras also took on its own life among subsequent guitarists. While regularly accompanying seminal non-Gypsy singers Juan Breva (1844–1918) and especially Don Antonio Chacón (1869–1929), Montoya further popularized the solo flamenco guitar idiom, even performing abroad on a few occasions.

Manuel Serrapi, a non-Gypsy better known as Niño Ricardo (1909–72), also helped establish flamenco guitar as a sophisticated virtuoso idiom, with his own somewhat busy and rough, but highly inventive style.

Among their younger contemporaries, Sabicas (Agustín Castellón, 1913–90) brought the style established by Montoya to new levels of refinement and virtuosity, and also became the first flamenco guitarist to enjoy genuine international success. In his wake Mario Escudero (b. 1928) promoted a somewhat formal, classicized version of flamenco solo guitar. Meanwhile, guitarists like Diego del Gastor (1908–73, see Plate 4), Melchor de Marchena (1907–80), and Perico del Lunar (1894–1964) perpetuated a more traditional and less showy style, which was preferred by those purists who regarded the modern virtuosos as sacrificing soulful expression (*duende*) in favor of flashy technique.

Around 1970, flamenco guitar was revolutionized as never before by the appearance of Paco de Lucía (b. 1947), a non-Gypsy genius from Algeciras who is perhaps the most brilliant and influential flamenco artist of the latter twentieth century (see Plate 5). De Lucía's contributions in some respects defy analysis or enumeration. One may note such elements as his extraordinary technique, his enriched harmonic vocabulary, and his innovative use of left-hand slides, bent notes, right-hand *tirando* (unsupported) chords, and other details. Ultimately more important and ineffable, however, is the general brilliance which pervades his music, reflected in a dramatically greater degree of variety and richness, and an unprecedented technical virtuosity which, however, generally remains within the balance and good taste essential to the flamenco aesthetic. De Lucía's sources of inspiration are at once cosmopolitan and firmly rooted in flamenco tradition. On the one hand, he has grown up listening to all manner of musics, has recorded renditions of Manuel de Falla's classical compositions, and has performed extensively with jazz-rock guitarists John McLaughlin, Al DiMeola, and Larry Coryell. On the other hand, by his own admission, he reads music with difficulty and does not really know or play jazz *per se*, and most of his flamenco remains firmly within the inherited repertoire of *cantes*. As might be expected, the ranks of flamenco fans include many purists who profess outrage at de Lucía's innovations and accuse him of bastardizing the genre. Fortunately, in recording and concertizing so extensively, he has been able to offer something to everyone, whether in the form of acrobatic collaborations with other "guitar-heroes," innovative, pop-tinged *flamenco nuevo*, or more or less mainstream flamenco; his straight-ahead flamenco comprises both solo and accompaniment playing – the latter especially with the brilliant but ill-starred vocalist Camarón de la Isla (d. 1992).

Aside from his own performing career, de Lucía has inspired a new generation of technically dazzling imitators, along with some genuinely

Plate 4 Diego del Gastor (photo by Steve Kahn)

original and gifted junior artists, among whom Vicente Amigo is perhaps the most outstanding. Despite the grumbling of purists, there is no doubt that flamenco, both in traditional and innovative forms, is flourishing and that flamenco guitar has attained unprecedented heights of sophistication, artistry, and recognition.

Plate 5 Paco de Lucía (photo by Paco Sanchez)

The flamenco guitar scene

In terms of function, pedagogy, and personnel, the flamenco guitar world
can be seen as spanning a continuum, with the intimate, private Gypsy community at one end, and the international concert scene at the other. The
primary crucible of flamenco performers continues to be the Andalusian
(and to some extent, Madrid) Gypsy neighborhoods (which have always
included fair numbers of *payo* families, such as Paco de Lucía's). If many
Andalusians are indifferent to flamenco, Gypsies regard it as a cultural patri-
mony (see Plate 6). Alongside flamenco's professional, public or semi-public
performance contexts, the art has always thrived as an entertainment music
within the Gypsy community itself, whether for rowdy dance parties with
tangos and bulerías, or more serious sessions devoted to *cante jondo*. Hence
the ranks of passionate amateur singers, dancers, and guitarists are legion.
Most guitarists learn informally by imitating elders and, increasingly, by
copying recordings. Given the casual pedagogical techniques and practice
methods, it is quite surprising how many virtuosos continue to emerge from
the communities of Gypsies and lower-class *payo* flamenco fans.

A skilled guitarist, aside from accompanying neighborhood fiestas and
dance classes, may find work in a *tablao*. These are latter-day versions of the
café cantante, presenting glitzy flamenco shows to tourists. In the *tablaos* –
as in other contexts oriented toward outsiders – dance sets are the main
focus, and *cante jondo* is kept to a minimum. Nevertheless, guitarists get

Plate 6 Unidentified Gypsies (photo by Steve Kahn)

their licks in, and might even be allowed a short solo during the course of an evening.

The better guitarists graduate to the level of professional flamenco performances, in which they accompany singers at private clubs (*peñas*) and public concerts – especially night-long, open-air festivals held in Andalusian towns during summertime, attended by hundreds of rowdy Gypsies. Guitarists regard the all-night concerts as less than ideal venues, with their often poor sound systems and disruptive audiences. Nevertheless, the festivals can also be rewarding for musicians, as guitarists have ample space between vocal strophes to demonstrate their skill, and audiences are in their own way discriminating and likely to roar with approval at a particularly expressive vocal melisma or guitar passage. Also popular are the formal *concursos* in which singers and guitarists compete for prestigious awards.

It is only a select handful of guitarists who manage to become recognized as soloists. These may get occasional solo slots alongside their more regular work as accompanists, and a tiny handful are able to support themselves as soloists, often supplementing their incomes by teaching.

Meanwhile, ever since Ramón Montoya successfully performed in Paris in 1931, a few of the most gifted or fortunate guitarists have been able to establish themselves on the international concert scene. This circuit affords money, the opportunity to reach foreign flamenco fans, and also the particular sort of prestige gained from playing in opulent concert halls to élite Western audiences who may or may not know much about flamenco. In the foreign concert circuit the traditional flamenco hierarchy is often reversed, with guitar music – which is "pretty" and presents no language barrier – taking precedence over flamenco singing, which strikes many outsiders as hysterical, histrionic, and generally incomprehensible. (Similarly, for example, it was sitarist Ravi Shankar, rather than equally gifted vocalists, who brought North Indian music to the West in the 1960s–70s.) The perversities and peculiarities of playing for international audiences generate their own anomalous standards of success. In Europe, and especially in the glitzy Riviera hotel-club scene, the most conspicuous flamenco star throughout much of the latter twentieth century was French Gypsy guitarist Manitas de Plata ("Silver Hands"). Since Manitas paid little heed to the basic *compas* patterns, his music, although flashy in its own way, was pseudo-flamenco at best. However, as American *flamencólogo* Brook Zern wryly noted, in his playing and flamboyant personality Manitas masterfully perpetuated the traditional Gypsy *guasa* art of conning gullible *payos* to his own advantage. Meanwhile, in the United States during the same period the field of flamenco guitar was largely dominated by Carlos Montoya (1905–95), a nephew of Ramón Montoya. Carlos was an unpretentious man and a respectable guitarist, and he certainly succeeded in bringing flamenco to the nation's most prestigious concert halls. At the same time, aficionados would agree that his renown was somewhat incommensurate with his talent, especially in comparison to that of Sabicas and Mario Escudero, who, although also living in New York since the middle of the century, enjoyed less popularity outside of the circle of serious flamenco fans.

With the arrival of Paco de Lucía on the international scene in recent decades, the crown of flamenco guitar-god has rested on a more unambiguously deserving head. However, his hard-core flamenco fans are far outnumbered by guitar-technique fetishists who hoot and howl after every lightning sixteenth-note run. De Lucía himself, who is among other things an intelligent, humble, and articulate man, has no illusions about the refinement of such musical tastes, although he has found the art of improvising in such contexts to be challenging in its own way. He has also commented on the contrast between such ecstatic international reception of the shallower aspects of his music, and the ambivalence or even indifference with which flamenco often continues to be received in Andalusia itself, the cradle of the art form. Indeed, it is worth observing that most Spaniards, and even most Andalusians, have little interest in flamenco, and some regard it scornfully as a decadent low-life music; outside Gypsy society it has flourished as a music for aficionados, somewhat like jazz in American society.

Serious international students and fans also constitute a significant, if numerically small, aspect of the flamenco scene. In contrast to the informal learning methods predominating in Andalusia itself, American and northern European flamenco guitar students avail themselves of formal lessons, pedagogical books, videos, websites, and internet chat-lists. Several foreigners have become fine players, and a few, such as the American David Serva (David Jones), have enjoyed moderately successful careers, performing in Spain as well as the United States.

Flamenco and flamenco guitar: style and structure

The flamenco repertoire consists of around a dozen basic *cantes*, and a few dozen more subsidiary or obscure variants of these. A *cante* (or *palo*) is a song-type, identified by a particular poetic meter, characteristic vocal melody (or melodies), in some cases a *compas* (rhythmic structure, which may include typical chordal patterns), and – last and perhaps least in terms of structure – a distinctive guitar key and set of conventional accompaniment patterns. The so-called *cantes libres* or "free" *cantes* – notably Malagueñas, Granaínas, tarantas, and *fandango libre* – are performed in free rhythm, that is, without metered *compas*. Most of the basic *cantes* appear to have been informally codified by the early twentieth century, and continue to form the basis for modern flamenco.

In more general terms, flamenco itself is distinguished as a genre by various formal features (aside from lyric content and other less strictly musical aspects). Much flamenco harmony is in the form of what is generally called "Phrygian tonality," in that it roughly coheres with the "E" mode (or transposed versions thereof). Thus, in the common chord progression Am–G–F–E, the E major chord functions not as the dominant of the tonic A minor, but as the Phrygian tonic; the role of the "dominant" – that is, the chord that demands resolution to the tonic – is played by the supertonic (F), or the sub-tonic (Dm). The chordal vocabulary thus derives primarily from the Phrygian mode, with the exception of the tonic E major chord, which uses not G, but G♯ (the raised third degree). The use of this note, especially in melodic lines, reflects Andalusia's Arab heritage, and in particular, the affinities with the Hijaz or Hijazkar *maqams* (modes), with the distinctive augmented seconds in their lower tetrachords (i.e., E–F–G♯–A). Typically, chords – and especially the "dominant"-function chords – are enriched by the inclusion of non-triadic tones, which most often are played on open strings. Thus, for example, in the key which uses A major as the Phrygian tonic, the "dominant" function chord – which could be analyzed variously as G minor, B♭ major, or some combination of both – could appear in the following forms:

Example 2.1 "Dominant"-function chord in A Phrygian

Meanwhile, simple major or common-practice tonality also occurs in several *cantes*, sometimes in juxtaposition with Phrygian tonality.[2] Most flamenco musicians, of course, lack formal training in Western music and employ their own idiosyncratic terminology, by which, for example, vocalists might indicate key preferences to accompanists. Thus, the key of E Phrygian is referred to as *por arriba*, or "above," referring to the placement of fingers in an E major chord, while the fingering of the A major chord has led to the key of A Phrygian as being designated *por medio* – "in the middle."

Flamenco rhythms are also distinctive in their own way. The most characteristic of these use elaborated forms of the hemiola or *sesquialtera* pattern which has pervaded Spanish music for centuries. In its most rudimentary form, this could be regarded as a bar of 6/8 followed by one of 3/4, affording the stress pattern: ONE-two-three-ONE-two-three-ONE-and-TWO-and-THREE(-and). As indicated below, however, this pattern generally does not appear in such a straightforward form. Flamenco vocal style is also distinctive, with its pronounced use of melisma, its sob-like falsetto breaks and guttural effects, and its generally histrionic, impassioned delivery. Also unique, of course, is the guitar style, to which we may now turn.

Flamenco guitar, as mentioned, evolved primarily as an accompanimental idiom, secondary to the vocal *cante* itself. In this capacity, the most basic requirement of the guitarist is to provide the correct *compas*, which, in the metered *cantes*, comprises an isorhythm (that is, a repeating rhythmic-harmonic scheme) and a more or less pre-determined chordal pattern, to which are added various improvised flourishes and adornments. Preceding and in between the vocal strophes (*tercios, coplas,* or *versos*), the guitarist plays solo interludes called *falsetas.* These are invariably pre-composed, and in general, flamenco guitar playing contains little or none of the sort of free improvisation encountered, for example, in jazz. However, the choice of *falsetas* and the ongoing extemporized flourishes and varia-tions lend the guitar playing an essential flavor of looseness and spontaneity.

The guitar introduction to a song serves, on a basic level, to set the pitch and tonality for the singer, to establish the mood of the *cante,* and, in the case of metered *cantes,* to set the rhythm. Although this introduction tradi-tionally consists of a straightforward *falseta,* many modern guitarists (to the annoyance of some purists) play extended, meandering preludes in which the identity of the *cante* only gradually becomes evident. In general, how-ever, the accompanist's main job is to support and follow the singer, and to make him or her sound good. This involves sensitively complementing the vocalist in various ways, by anticipating phrases, tailoring dynamics, inten-sity, and even tempo to particular passages, knowing when to be assertive and when to lay back, and generally intensifying the vocalist's mood.

Accompanying dance is an art form in itself. In the *tablao* or dance con-cert context, much of the time the guitarist is accompanying not a singer, but a dancer, who is setting the dynamic structure of the piece with his or her own choreography, whether spontaneous or pre-arranged. As with vocalists, the guitarist must accompany with sensitivity and flexibility, and be able to adapt to performers of various degrees of competence. The *tablao* context also has its own conventional structures, such as the *escobillo* part of the alegrías – a section in minor key and slower tempo – which would not be heard outside of the dance format.

As noted, the idiom of solo flamenco guitar, although extant from the late 1800s, did not become a widely popular and recognized art form until the era of Ramón Montoya. Even today, the typical flamenco performance at an Andalusian all-night conference is unlikely to include a guitar solo. However, *tablao* shows and formal dance-oriented performances often do include guitar solos, partly in order to vary the pace of the evening. The traditional guitar solo would generally consist of a series of *falsetas* – such as would normally punctuate vocal strophes – without any particular over-arching formal structure or design. Within this loose format, the guitarist would naturally try to introduce a measure of variety, perhaps, for example, by including an extended melodic passage played in tremolo style. Since the 1970s, however, guitar solos by leading artists like Paco de Lucía are generally presented as extended compositions, with evocative titles, which are rendered in more or less the same fashion in successive performances. (In order to be a top-ranking guitarist today, one must not merely play well but also compose original and striking *falsetas*.) Even these pieces, however, continue to consist essentially of strings of *falsetas*, which are freely disembodied and copied by imitators. Moreover, fanciful titles notwithstanding, modern flamenco guitar solos invariably adhere to the inherited body of traditional *cantes*; thus, modernization and innovation have consisted not of adding to the repertoire by the creation of new *cantes*, but of expanding and enriching the *cantes* from within, by using more varied, adventurous, and eclectic styles and harmonies.

The relation of guitar solos to the *cantes* themselves, however, is often flexible and loose, since the *cante*'s foremost distinguishing element – the vocal melody – is absent in instrumental performance. A rendition of a metered *cante* (such as soleares, bulerías, or siguiriyas) will naturally adhere to the distinctive *compas* of the *cante* in question. It will also generally employ the most conventional key used to accompany that *cante*. Thus, for example, siguiriyas, tangos, and bulerías are most typically played *por medio* (in A Phrygian), both by accompanists and soloists. However, they are not always played in this way. Quite commonly, for example, an accompanist might choose to perform a bulerías not *por medio* but *por arriba* (in "E", perhaps with a capo) in order to match the range of a singer, or simply for variety; by extension, a soloist might render a bulerías in various keys, including the distinctive F♯ Phrygian otherwise associated with tarantas. The relation to the traditional *cantes* is even more ambiguous in the case of *cantes libres*, such as Granaínas and tarantas, that are essentially free-rhythmic. Here, since neither vocal melody nor *compas* is present, it is only the conventional guitar key (Granaínas in B Phrygian, and tarantas in F♯) and, perhaps, the use of a few typical *falsetas*, that identify the *palo* as such. In effect, guitar solos in these *palos* have the character of free fantasias exploring the possibilities of a given guitar key.

Much of the distinctive character of flamenco guitar comes from its colorful stylistic conventions. As mentioned above, guitarists since Ramón Montoya have freely adapted classical-style *picado*, tremolo, and arpeggio techniques to the flamenco idiom. For example, *picado* runs (generally played with the first two fingers) most typically consist of scalar passages which descend, sometimes circuitously, to the tonic; in this sense they cohere to the descending nature of the most typical flamenco vocal melodies and chord progressions (e.g., Am–G–F–E). Competent flamenco guitarists are able to play *picado* with dazzling speed and power, although they strive to use such passages sparingly, as part of achieving a general balance between strummed and plucked textures. The most common tremolo, as popularized by Montoya, combines thumb arpeggios with four sixteenth quintuplets on the other fingers, as shown in Example 2.2, a fragment of soleares. Other guitar techniques used are more unique to flamenco. *Rasgueado* patterns

Example 2.2 tremolo pattern

are particularly important and diverse; some of these, as shown below, may be used either to produce a machine-gun-like percussive effect, or a more constant, unbroken roll. (To cohere with staff notation, a downward arrow henceforth indicates an upward physical stroke, and vice versa.)

Example 2.3 Rasgueado patterns
(a) (b) (c)

(a)   ↑↑↑↑↓ ↑↑↑↑↓   (b)   ↑↑↑↓ ↑↑↑↓   (c)   ↓↑↑ ↓↑↑
    c a m i i   c a m i i   a m i i   a m i i   p m p   p m p

Alzapúa (*alzar*: to raise; *púa*: plectrum) is a basic traditional technique, in which the thumb is used with both up- and downstrokes, to generate forceful and often fast passages. A typical *alzapúa* in tangos is shown here:

Example 2.4 Alzapúa

Flamenco guitar style is further distinguished by the use of hammering-on and pulling-off techniques, of *golpes* ("blows," or fingernail strokes) on the face of the instrument, and of a generally more vigorous and forceful touch than would be considered appropriate in classical playing. Traditional flamenco guitarists play mostly in first position, which allows them to take best advantage of open strings. It should also be noted that the traditional flamenco guitarist rests the instrument on his right thigh, twisting his right hand downward in a position which other guitarists would find awkward.

The *cantes* themselves may be classified in various manners, for example, by region, degree of profundity, ethnic origin, or musical features. One useful approach in the latter vein divides most of the *cantes* into four groupings:

(1) soleares, alegrías, bulerías, and variants, all of whose *compases* use a form of the 6/8-3/4 hemiola/*sesquialtera*, stressing beats 3, 6, 8, and 10; these *cantes* are regarded as the most distinctively Gypsy in character and origin.

(2) the stately and solemn siguiriyas, whose *compas* resembles a displaced version of that of the preceding group.

(3) traditional duple-metered *cantes*, of which tangos and tientos are the most important.

(4) the members of the fandango family (including Malagueñas, Granaínas, tarantas/taranto, and the numerous varieties of fandango *per se*); most of these feature vocal strophes in common-practice harmony punctuated by guitar interludes in Phrygian tonality; they are variously free-metered (*libre*) or in 3/4.

While a thorough description of the *cantes* is neither possible nor appropriate in this space, a brief look at a few of the most basic *cantes* may serve to illustrate some of the ways in which they are rendered on guitar. Both soleares (typically in E Phrygian) and alegrías (in E, C, or, often by soloists, A major) feature a twelve-beat *compas* (imperfectly notated below as four bars of 3/4) in slow or moderate tempo, with accents on beats 1, 3, 6, 8, and 10; guitar phrases generally end on 10. *Falsetas*, such as this typical introductory passage in soleares, will generally reflect this isorhythm:

Example 2.5 Soleares

The bulerías *compas* is similar, except that its *aire* (tempo, spirit) is fast and festive, and most typically set to A Phrygian (*por medio*); guitar *falsetas* often begin on beat 12, and the first beat is de-emphasized and often essentially silent (while retaining a certain ineffable structural significance). A typical *compas* rendering of bulerías is as follows ("g" represents a fingernail *golpe*):

Example 2.6 Bulerías

The rhythm of the slow and serious siguiriyas may be seen as a displaced version of the same hemiola, schematized below:

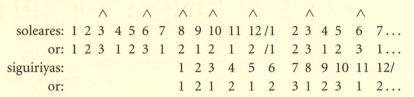

```
                     ^       ^      ^  ^      ^          ^         ^
soleares:  1  2  3   4 5 6   7  8  9 10 11  12 /1   2 3 4 5   6   7 . . .
       or: 1  2  3   1 2 3   1  2  1  2  1   2 /1   2 3 1 2   3   1 . . .
siguiriyas:                  1  2  3  4  5   6    7 8 9 10 11 12/
       or:                   1  2  1  2  1   2    3 1 2 3   1  2 . . .
```

Its *compas* might be rendered in passing as follows:

Example 2.7 Siguiriyas

In the family of duple- or quadruple-metered *cantes*, tangos (which has only a very general musical and historical relation to its Latin American namesake) is typically rendered *por medio* in moderate or fast tempo, with a basic *compas* ostinato figure as below:

Example 2.8 Tangos

Tientos is a slower counterpart of tangos, with more of a triplet-sub-divided feel.

Members of the fandango family derive not from Gypsy subculture, but from Andalusian folk music. They generally follow a specific harmonic progression, which played *por arriba* (as in Malagueñas and fandangos *per se*) is roughly as follows:

	guitar ostinato	verse	guitar ostinato
Chords:	Am G F E	C F C G7 C F E	Am G F E
E Phrygian:	iv III II I	II I	iv III II I
C major:		I IV I V7 I IV	

In the guitar ostinato of the metered fandango de Huelva, the fingernail *golpes* play particularly important roles in marking the downbeats:

Example 2.9 Fandango de Huelva

Tarantas and its metered counterpart taranto are played in the key of
F♯ Phrygian (with verses in D major), which offers particular possibilities to guitarists. The tonic chord is typically rendered with non-triadic
open strings; when first sounded it is often followed by a legato ornament
as shown:

Example 2.10 Tarantas

Granaínas offers its own guitaristic potential, being played in B
Phrygian, with verses in G major. Again, the tonic chord may include
non-triadic open strings:

Example 2.11 Granaínas

In the nineteenth century this key appears to have been popular in the hilly
regions of western Andalusia, and thus came to be the conventional accompaniment key for the fandango variant named after the nearby town of
Granada. Granaínas is the only fandango type to regularly conclude on the
"common-practice" tonic – that is, E minor – perhaps because of the resonance of that chord as played on the guitar. The convention of ending on this
chord illustrates how flamenco's chordal vocabulary has in many respects
evolved in direct connection with the guitar, rather than developing as an
abstract harmonic repertoire along the lines of Western common practice.

Flamenco guitar enters the new millennium

Over the course of its meteoric trajectory in the last century and a half, flamenco has been able to evolve, thrive, and adapt to changing circumstances
while retaining a relatively stable and coherent stylistic core. This healthy

continuity is quite evident in flamenco guitar, if understood as a set of conventional techniques applied to a standardized repertoire of song-types, or *palos*. The technical vocabulary codified by Ramón Montoya, however enriched by innovators like Paco de Lucía, still constitutes the essence of the style, and guitarists continue to work largely within the inherited *cantes* standardized by the early twentieth century. Even the current eclectic excursions into various pop styles can be seen as perpetuating the tradition, established since flamenco's origins, of interacting with contemporary vernacular idioms, be it folk fandangos, Cuban *campesino* music, or disco.

While flamenco continues to thrive in its quintessential context of Gypsy *juergas*, guitarists have recently led the way in experimenting with a variety of international genres. Such syncretic endeavors have encompassed rock and blues (as by the group Pata Negra), Latin and North African musics (notably Ketama), jazz-rock (Paco de Lucía's forays with John McLaughlin and others), and modern jazz itself (as in Tomatito's Grammy-winning CD with pianist Michele Camilo). Perhaps most familiar in today's modern flamenco sound are the lively crossover recordings produced by de Lucía, Vicente Amigo, and others. These combine flamenco solo and backup vocals, concise guitar interludes, and bass and light percussion, in the context of tuneful pre-composed songs, usually categorizable as tangos, rumbas, or bulerías. The most successful of these recordings – such as the 1998 *Me Voy Contigo* of Amigo and singer Remedios Amaya – have become mainstream pop hits in Spain and even earned the approval of hard-core traditionalists. As in the case of jazz artists like Herbie Hancock and Chick Corea, guitarist-producers like Amigo and de Lucía can continue to gratify their more purist listeners by recording straight-ahead acoustic CDs alongside their pop-tinged forays.

Many traditional music genres worldwide have fared poorly in their confrontation with mainstream Western pop music, with its common-denominator appeal and its powerful multinational backing. The intensified processes of globalization in recent years have heightened both the challenges and the new opportunities for "peripheral" musics associated with specific ethnic, regional, or linguistic audiences. Lovers of flamenco and of world music in general can find much gratification in the way that flamenco guitarists, rather than being swamped by these developments, have ridden the crest of musical globalization, at once taking their art into exciting new directions while maintaining its traditional coherence and integrity.[3]

References

General reference books

Howson, Gerard. *The Flamencos of Cádiz Bay.* Westport, 1965/rpt. 1994.

Mitchell, Timothy. *Flamenco Deep Song.* New Haven, 1994.

Peña, Paco. "Flamenco Guitar." In *The Guitar: A Guide for Students and Teachers.* Ed. Michael Stimpson. Oxford and New York, 1988, 211–36.

Pohren, Don. *The Art of Flamenco.* Jerez de la Frontera, 1962/1972.

Schreiner, Claus, ed. *Flamenco: Gypsy Dance and Music from Andalusia.* Portland, 1990.

Sevilla, Paco. *Paco de Lucía: A New Tradition for the Flamenco Guitar.* San Diego, 1995.

Websites

flamenco-world.com

guitarsite.com/flamenco.htm

flamenco-teacher.com

guitarist.com/fg/fg.htm

Performance manuals

There are increasing numbers of performance books (with audio recordings) and videos on the market today. Particularly notable is the series of booklets containing notations and, in some cases, audio CD, published by Affedis (Paris), which includes the following titles:

Flamenco: El arte de Gerardo Nuñez. 1994

Arte Clásico: Flamenco: Ramón Montoya. 2000 (with compact disc)

Arte Clásico: El genio de Niño Ricardo. 1999 (with compact disc)

Arte Clásico: Sabicas: El Rey del flamenco. 2000

Flamenco esencias: Pepe Habichuela. 1997

Flamenco: La guitarra de Tomatito. 1999

Also see:

Koster, Dennis. *The Keys to Flamenco Guitar* (with compact disc). Part I, West Hurley, 1992; Part II, New York, 1994.

3 The Celtic guitar: crossing cultural boundaries in the twentieth century

CHRISTOPHER J. SMITH

Introduction

Ever since its incarnation in modern form, the guitar's adaptability to different musical roles has led to its use in a wide variety of indigenous music. According to ethnomusicologist and virtuoso slide player Bob Brozman, the cross-cultural impact of the guitar results from the contact between the instrument's diatonic applications (specifically, the use of chords) in the West, and the non-diatonic ideas (specifically, an orientation toward modes and drones) of indigenous music from around the world.[1] Add to this the instrument's ubiquity and portability, its players' receptivity to different musical styles, its suitability for multiple musical functions (monophonic, polyphonic, homophonic, drone-plus-melody, instrumental versus accompanimental), and its long ancestral lineage in the plucked string instrument family, and it comes as no surprise that the guitar plays a significant role in the modern history of "Celtic" traditional music.[2] This article will focus particularly on the role of the guitar in Irish traditional music, as that role is well documented historically, and has been a strong influence, through the medium of the "Celtic revival," in other Celtic guitar traditions.

The history of the Celtic guitar reflects in many ways the modern history of the music itself. Prior to the earliest Celtic recordings made during the first decade of the twentieth century, consisting of a series of wax cylinders recorded by accordionist John J. Kimmel (1866–1942) and piper Patsy Tuohey (1865–1923), vernacular instrumental music of Ireland, Scotland, Wales, and Brittany was mostly monophonic and unaccompanied. In general, instrumental playing, in public or in private, for listening or for dancing, was soloistic, and when multiple instrumentalists (pipes, flutes, fiddle, whistles) participated as a group, they played the melody together in rough heterophonic fashion; harmony was an accident or afterthought. The two notable exceptions to this monophonic emphasis in the rural Irish and Scots folk music traditions are the harp, which was associated ever since the Middle Ages with chamber music and the ruling classes rather than the rural dance music, and the bagpipes, regional variants of which used combinations of melody, drones, and keyed regulators to produce unique musical textures that are only marginally related to conventional Western ideas about harmony.[3]

Guitar was employed in art music and salon music from the eighteenth century in Ireland and the British Isles, but only enters the indigenous music tradition in the twentieth century.[4] The "English" and "Spanish" guitars (that is, citterns and forerunners of the modern six-string) in pastoral paintings and in images of bourgeois homes are essentially idealizations of a salon or light-classical tradition, heavily influenced by European chamber music and only peripherally related to the indigenous dance music.[5] There are tantalizing hints of the instrument's employment in the folk tradition prior to the advent of audio recording, but there is very little tangible information about how, or how widely, the instrument was employed.[6]

Thus, a history of the guitar's usage within Celtic traditional music is a very recent pursuit, and is most safely approached, as in jazz history, through studying specific sound recordings, organized according to various complementary historical templates. In fact, the historical use of the guitar as a "Celtic" instrument almost exactly parallels its usage in jazz: in both cases, the instrument only really exerts a presence from the 1920s. And, as was the case with jazz, the Celtic guitar's stylistic and functional evolution is similarly dense, accelerated, populated by wildly colorful and influential players, and documented on recordings that are widely available to the general public. As a result, we can trace the history of the Celtic guitar as we might that of jazz guitar, through parallel histories of the music itself, its stylistic evolutions, the instrument's function, and the recordings of seminal players.

1920s–1930s: guitar- and piano-drivers in the Golden Age

The "Golden Age" of Irish traditional music on record occurred during the 1920s, when small American labels and independent entrepreneurs realized that a viable market for indigenous music existed amongst the immigrant populations in the United States.[7] It was only with the resulting advent of audio recording, with its primitive acoustical capacities and commercial presumptions, that it was deemed necessary to provide accompaniment for the melody-oriented instrumentalists. Harmony instruments had not played a key role in the Irish tradition up to that time, and as a result few pianists or guitarists understood how the music worked harmonically.[8] Thus fiddlers like Michael Coleman, James Morrison, and Paddy Killoran, and many other recording stars of the vaudeville era, often found themselves saddled with "piano-drivers" or guitarists whose stylistic understanding of the music was woefully inadequate.[9] On those seminal early recordings, one must therefore learn to listen "beyond" the incompetent and insensitive piano or guitar stylings, the wrong chords, misunderstood modes, and clumsy rhythms, to hear the beauty and virtuosity of these legendary melody players. Yet these recordings, which were wildly popular not only in the United States but also back home in Ireland, exerted an enormous influence on generations of subsequent players and aspiring accompanists, not least by establishing an initial presence for (and, in the minds of some hardcore "pure drop" musicians, a lasting prejudice against) the instrument.[10]

Nevertheless, in America as early as the 1930s there were certain notable exceptions to this "no bleedin' guitar-players!" dictum: both Dan Sullivan (piano) and Paddy Killoran (fiddle) recorded and performed live with backup bands (the Shamrock Band and the Pride of Erin Orchestra) whose members, some non-Irish, included saxophonists, clarinetists, and swing-style guitar accompanists.[11] (There is, by the way, an interesting and as yet largely unwritten history to be told regarding the interaction of 1920s "ethnic" and jazz musicians in the ferment of the New York studios.) In addition, the Flanagan Brothers – Joe on accordion, Louis on guitar, rhythm banjo, or voice, and Mike on tenor banjo – were perennial favorites in New York dance halls and recording studios.[12] And, as early as 1939, the guitarist Arthur Darley accompanied singer Delia Murphy on recordings made in Ireland.[13] However, these were exceptions, and by and large guitarists were superfluous or actually detrimental when they did appear on the classic recordings.

The 1930s–1940s: céilí bands and show bands

Concurrently with these 1920s recordings for the immigrant market in America came the first flowerings of the céilí band movement in Ireland and England. In the wake of morally conservative new laws restricting unsupervised dancing, this music finally began to move out of kitchens, barns, and crossroads dances, and into dance halls in the 1940s and 1950s. As early as 1907 seminal ensembles like the Kilfenora Céilí Band had come together in larger combinations to produce a bigger, more exciting rhythmic sound for dance purposes, and by the early 1930s such ensembles were being featured on Radio Eireann.[14] Most often the céilí bands featured a front line of traditional melody instruments (flute, fiddle, accordion) and used a rhythm section consisting of a drummer and a pianist, the latter "vamping" on the implicit chords of the melodies.[15] The occasional guitarist, banjoist, or mandolin player would make an appearance, but was not thought essential or particularly welcome.[16]

However, with the arrival of rock and roll in the 1950s, market pressures led many ensembles to evolve into "show bands" which did feature guitarists. Saxophones now shared the front line with fiddles and accordions, and sets of traditional jigs and reels alternated uneasily with the latest rock and roll dance crazes: the Frug, the Shimmy, and the Swim. The stylistic duality (if not plurality) of this time led bands to recruit young guitarists who often shouldered double duty, backing the traditional tunes with improvised chords and then shifting roles to play the guitar licks of Buddy Holly and Chuck Berry.[17]

At the same time, and partly in reaction against the rock and roll boom, a generation of young, urban, and mostly college-educated people in both Britain and the States turned away from pop culture to seek a greater "authenticity" in rural music which their parents had either ignored or re-jected. In the States, this led to the "Great Folk Scare" of the late fifties, when youngsters from urban areas began to find their way, first to the recordings and then to the actual points of origin of the old players. Appalachian old-time music, Woody Guthrie songs, Mississippi Delta blues, and high-torque bluegrass were all stirred together into this stylistic mélange and launched the careers of folk stars like Bob Dylan, Joan Baez, and many others. By the early 1960s, this rich style had crossed the ocean and sparked the skif-fle revival, which found young Irish and English musicians singing "Rock Island Line" and "The Prisoner's Song" in Appalachian accents even more unconvincing than those of the New York folkies.

The 1960s: the Clancy Brothers, Seán Ó Riada, and the folk revival

In 1960, a quartet of young Irish actors, stranded in New York after their show closed, observed the young suburbanites in Washington Square Park singing Dust Bowl Ballads with guitars and banjos, and asked themselves if there might be gold to be mined from their own indigenous music. One night the Clancy Brothers and Tommy Makem, singing the ballads, drinking songs, and rebel songs they had learned from elderly relatives, and accompanied by American folk-style guitar and five-string banjo, suddenly found themselves lengthening their set on the popular Ed Sullivan television program when the act scheduled to follow them became stuck in a traffic jam.[18]

The next morning they woke up to find themselves national media stars. They had conquered America, capturing the prize so ardently desired by many Irish and English entertainers. Back home in Ireland, another gen-eration of young musicians playing American-influenced skiffle (blues and folk songs) looked at the Clancys and realized that perhaps there was more music in their own back gardens and family trees than they had realized. The Clancys' appearance on the Ed Sullivan Show, and a vibrant folk-song revival in Britain spearheaded by radical socialists like Ewan MacColl and A. L. Lloyd, sparked a boom in informal song collecting: young Irish players went back to their mothers, aunties, and grannies to find out what songs they knew, added "three-chord trick" accompaniments, and took them out to the earnest folk clubs and coffeehouses of the early 1960s. This development led to the guitar- and five-string-banjo-toting "ballad groups," primarily an urban phenomenon, like the Wolfe Tones, the Dubliners, and the Johnstons.

Parallel with these developments were the innovations of composer, arranger, radio commentator, and ensemble leader Seán Ó Riada (1931–71), who, though trained in the modernist Austrian music tradition which dominated the post-World War II era (Schoenberg, Berg, and Webern), was also seeking musical resources for a modern Irish art music. When asked to provide a score for a 1961 film of J. M. Synge's *Playboy of the Western World*, Ó Riada had the idea to create a chamber music-style score which would substitute traditional instruments and melodies for the modern orchestral instruments and thematic ideas typically employed. He assembled an ensemble of Dublin-based traditional musicians, including Paddy Moloney (pipes) and Seán Keane (fiddle), later of the Chieftains, and added his own bodhrán (frame drum), and later harpsichord in place of the snare drum and piano associated with the céilí band format. The musical result was so enormously popular that Ó Riada formalized the ensemble as a performing and touring group called Ceoltóiri Chualann. When he stood on the stage of the Abbey Theatre in Dublin, looked out at the packed hall full of impressionable university students, and said "This is *your* music," a crucial second phase of the coming Irish folk revival was established firmly in place.[19]

Ó Riada despised the céilí bands' sacrifice of individual melodic expression in favor of melodic unison and rhythmic lift for the dancers; he once likened their sound to "a rhythmic but meaningless noise with as much relationship to music as the buzzing of a bluebottle [large bluish fly with a penetrating buzz] in an upturned jamjar."[20] He was equally dismissive of the American-influenced guitar and banjo styles of the ballad groups, and as an educator, author, and radio presenter his dicta carried weight. In self-conscious contrast, he carefully arranged suites of tunes for his own ensembles which employed solo playing, counterpoint, and shifting combinations of melodic instruments. But like the céilí bands and the Clancys, Ó Riada also compromised with the post-traditional preference for accompaniment, and employed the harpsichord, whose sound he likened (erroneously, it turned out) to that of the old Irish lyre called the *tiompan*, to realize a chordal

Example 3.1 "Wat ye wha I met the streen" (Richard Thompson on Dave Swarbrick's *Smiddyburn*, Essential ESM 434)

accompaniment;[21] Ó Riada never employed guitar, probably because of its associations with céilí bands, show bands, and the ballad groups. This use of keyboard instruments and harp in an accompanimental role was carried on by Derek Bell in the band Paddy Moloney built on the model of Ceoltóiri Chualann, the venerable Chieftains. Together, the Clancys and Ó Riada had fired the imagination of a generation of young Irish musicians, many of them guitar-strumming college students in the mid to late sixties, and turned them away from international pop style and toward their own indigenous sources.

The 1960s: deeper into psychedelia and the tradition

By the late 1960s, and with the psychedelic era in full Technicolor swing, guitarists were moving toward a deeper, more educated involvement with traditional music, through adapting their instruments and techniques in order to keep with the tradition's own aesthetics. This led away from the use of borrowed stylistic approaches, and pushed players to try to develop more indigenously "Celtic" guitar approaches. This in turn led in two different directions, one electric and the other acoustic. Electric musicians like Richard Thompson, Jerry Donahue, and Trevor Lucas borrowed the folk-rock and occasional fuzz-tone aesthetic of the Byrds and the Beatles, and the chicken-pickin' techniques of American country guitarists, and melded them with the fiddle-based repertoire, modal vocabulary, and ornamenting techniques of Celtic traditional music. The result was a pungent, bagpipe-oriented electric guitar style (see Example 3.1). Simultaneously, acoustic guitarists like Davey Graham (a Scot), Bert Jansch, and John Renbourn (both English)

Example 3.2 "Bransle Gay" (Claude Gervais, arr. John Renbourn)

Example 3.3 "Anji" (Davey Graham)

pioneered a "folk-Baroque" finger-picking style, one that melded the techniques of the Nashville-based country guitarist Merle Travis with the songs of the English folk tradition and the counterpoint of Elizabethan lutenists (see Example 3.2).

Graham, the most musically omnivorous and far-ranging of the folk-Baroque Britons, brought back tunings he had learned and adapted from the north African *oud*, most notably the tuning known now in the tradition by the acronym "DADGAD" (after the notes employed from lowest to highest pitch). This tuning, which yields a kind of suspended-fourth D chord (that is, a chord which is neither major nor minor), was far more conducive to playing which avoided conventional triadic chords and instead mirrored the droning, modal nature of the traditional tunes themselves.[22] Graham's recordings, whose repertoire included blues, jazz, Renaissance, Celtic, and Near Eastern pieces, were immensely influential. (His standard-tuned instrumental "Anji," a litmus test for 1960s fingerstyle guitarists, shows up on Simon and Garfunkel's *Sounds of Silence* from 1966; see Example 3.3.) The great English traditional singer, collector, and guitarist Martin Carthy also employed this tuning, subsequently passing it along to the French virtuoso Pierre Bensusan, before moving to related tunings that would allow him to fashion a highly personalized, highly idiomatic style that closely imitated the drones, ornaments, and rhythmic articulations of piping and fiddle style (see Example 3.4). Jansch and Renbourn tended to focus on the

Example 3.4 "Merrily Kiss the Quaker's Wife" (trad. Irish; arr. Pierre Bensusan)

standard EADGBE tuning, with the occasional inclusion of a lowered sixth
string (DADGBE) which facilitated playing in certain sharp keys, but their
emphasis was always more contrapuntal and decorative (influenced variously by blues, jazz, and Elizabethan music) than the more modal, droning,
and idiomatic approaches of Graham and Carthy. By 1965 Carthy's first
recordings of traditional repertoire arranged for guitar and voice were re-
verberating throughout the English folk revival (and providing fodder for
Paul Simon's uncredited borrowings), and by 1967 Jansch and Renbourn
had joined forces in the "folk-Baroque," jazz-influenced chamber group
Pentangle.[23] Though Graham and his contemporaries in the late 1960s used
open tunings primarily for solo instrumental or accompanimental playing,
across the water in Ireland other guitarists were listening closely and beginning to think of ways in which such tunings could be used in chordal
fashion as backup in a band.

The 1970s: the Celtic revival

Around 1972, the Irishmen Johnny Moynihan and Alec Finn brought back
Greek bouzoukis from busking trips on the Continent, while further adapting the use of open tunings for modal sounds (see Example 3.5). The stage
was now set for the next great evolution in the "Celtic" guitar: the adaptation of the instrument to play in a fashion more truly indigenous to

Example 3.5 "Martin Wynne's #1" (Alec Finn on DAD 3-course bouzouki accompanies Frankie Gavin)

Example 3.6 "The Kesh Jig" (Mícheál Ó Domhnaill with the Bothy Band)

the tradition of the pipes, flute, and fiddle.[24] The myriad open tunings and drone-based accompaniments of players like Moynihan, Finn, Donal Lunny, and most notably the guitarists Mícheál Ó Domhnaill and Daithi Sproule, mimicked more closely the drone of the pipes, and in the 1970s interlocked with bouzoukis and keyboards to power the rhythm sections of key Celtic Revival bands like Planxty, Altan, and the Bothy Band.[25] Moving away from the standard-tuned guitar's triadic orientation and the English players' finger-picking technique, these players found ways to tune, finger, and strum the guitar so that it could function, alternately, as a source of contrapuntal bass lines, as a spooky, modal backdrop, or as a powerful "tuned drum" (see Example 3.6).

The Celtic guitar in a new millennium

As had been the case with the recordings of Michael Coleman and James Morrison fifty years earlier, recordings by these 1970s bands were enormously influential, fueling an explosion of interest in both Celtic music and the role of the guitar in that music. And since the 1970s, generations of new players have come along who have further refined, expanded, and developed the instrument's role. Some (Dick Gaughan, Richard Thompson, and Martin Carthy) have returned the electric guitar to a style much more suited to the tradition's own aesthetics, playing bagpipe-oriented fuzz-tone licks alongside rock bass and drums; others (Duck Baker, Pierre Bensusan, and Martin Carthy again) have delved deeper into the implications of open tunings in traditional repertoire, finding ways to play solo guitar that make the instrument sound as ancient and indigenous as the pipes or fiddle; still others (John Doyle with Solas, Zan McLeod with Touchstone, Mark Kelly with Altan, Roger Landes with Connie Dover, Dean Magraw with John Williams) continue to evolve and develop a droning, percussive, and contrapuntal acoustic approach in band settings.

Two recent exemplars of the synthesis, cross-fertilization, and receptivity which have always marked guitarists in general, and Celtic guitarists in particular, are the American Dennis Cahill and the Irishman Arty McGlynn. Born in Chicago of Irish immigrant parents, trained in rock and pop as well as traditional music, Cahill, along with his duo-partner Martin Hayes (fiddle), is finding ways to use his encyclopedic stylistic and harmonic knowledge to play the standard-tuned guitar in a fashion that draws on all the sounds available to the Celtic guitarist's palette, from percussive to contrapuntal, drone-based to complex jazz harmony. McGlynn, who has been a key player in numerous ensembles including Patrick Street and Four Men and a Dog, and appears on influential recordings by fiddler Tommy Peoples and flutist Matt Molloy, has years in rock and roll and country music under his belt. Employing primarily "dropped-D" (DADGBE) tuning for the flexibility it provides in a range of approaches, McGlynn is often praised for his ability, in Molloy's words, to "wait for you around the next corner" of tunes in an improvisational setting – that is, to comprehend and exploit the harmonic implications of the melodies, moment by moment as they are played (see Example 3.7).[26]

Conclusion

The guitar has never been an essential presence in the world of "Celtic" music, and its contributions – limited or ham-fisted in the 1930s, irrelevant

Example 3.7 "Miss Monaghan" (Arty McGlynn with Matt Molloy)

in the 1940s, lounge-tacky in the 1960s, and finally, gradually, more and more attuned to traditional aesthetics in the 1970s and 1980s – have often possessed a refreshing air of variability. That the instrument is not essential to the traditional sound in turn has liberated it from the restrictions of a "received style." There is not, as of this writing, a single, definitive, or regionally specific approach to the "Celtic guitar." The amorphous nature of the guitar's role in the music at this stage parallels the historical introduction of several other "non-traditional" instruments into the music, notably the concertina, accordion, and tenor banjo. In each case, given the absence of an existing style for the new instruments, players have been forced to invent and re-invent what the instrument means to the music, often borrowing techniques from core instruments like pipes, flute, and fiddle, with their only limitations being those of tradition's own indigenous aesthetics. At the beginning of the twenty-first century, and in the hands of a Martin Carthy, Arty McGlynn, or Dennis Cahill, the guitar has adapted easily and meaningfully to Celtic music as it has done in so many other times, places, and idioms.

4 African reinventions of the guitar

BANNING EYRE

Africa has nurtured a surprising array of modern and neo-traditional guitar styles. Portable, rugged, versatile, and relatively easy to construct, the guitar has thrived in African settings to the point where today it is among the most pervasive instruments continent-wide, second only to the drum. In places like Mali and Madagascar, ancient instrumental traditions have inspired distinctive acoustic guitar finger-picking techniques. Elsewhere – in Zimbabwe, Guinea, and Cameroon, for example – pre-guitar traditions have evolved into guitar-based, electric "afropop," once again engendering techniques and sounds unique in world music. In Congo in the 1950s, bands trying to play Cuban dance music substituted the handy guitar for the more rare piano, and within a few years, they developed a highly influential method of layering multiple electric guitar lines. Looking at the range and diversity of guitar innovations in Africa, one could argue that only rock and roll has so revolutionized the instrument over the course of the twentieth century. African guitarists are now beginning to earn widespread recognition, and their work is sure to have further impact around the world in years to come.

Consider these recent developments. Paul Simon drew upon guitarists Ray Phiri of South Africa and Vincent Nguini of Cameroon while creating the music for his Grammy Award-winning Graceland project. Ry Cooder also won a Grammy Award in 1994 for his collaboration with northern Malian guitarist Ali Farka Touré, *Talking Timbuktu* (World Circuit/Rykodisc 1994). That release focused attention on the connections between blues and Malian music and opened the door for other "Malian bluesmen," such as guitarist and singer Lobi Traoré. David Byrne tapped Diblo Dibala, an icon of Congolese guitar music. David Lindley and Henry Kaiser made a musical pilgrimage to Madagascar in 1991 and helped to launch international careers for a number of local guitarists, notably the incomparable finger-picker D'Gary. Whether it is Nigeria's King Sunny Ade, Mali's Boubacar Traoré or Djelimady Tounkara of the Super Rail Band, Congo's Nene Tchakou or Dizzy Mandjekou, South Africa's Marks Mankwane, or Zimbabwe's Jonah Sithole, Rise Kagona, or Joshua Dube, African guitarists with manifestly individual sounds are gaining worldwide reputations, and justly so. Their music represents the fruit of centuries of largely overlooked musical history.

When guitars first arrived in Africa – at least a century ago – they encountered far older plucked string relatives. Still, our earliest clear view of Africans playing guitars finds them for the most part performing music that originates abroad in Cuba, the United States, and also Hawaii, whose swooning slide guitar sound inspired many imitators in western Africa. During the 1950s, however, as nationalist fervor swept the continent, traditional African music came increasingly to the fore, and a period of remarkable creativity involving the guitar began.

Origins of today's plucked string instruments

Since its emergence as a distinct instrument in the fifteenth century, the guitar has taken on many forms, from the gentle, gut-strung classical guitar, to the roaring, metallic Stratocaster favored by Western rockers. In Africa, the instrument's course was inevitably shaped by older, local string music traditions. In northern Africa, the spiritual brotherhood of *gnawa* musicians were playing the *gimbri*, a big lute with a stretched-skin drum resonator and a round, fretless neck, its strings held in place by leather tuning rings. A smaller version of this lute was common among the *griots* – professional musicians and praise singers – of western Africa. This type of instrument, often called a "spike lute," is a likely ancestor of the American banjo and goes by various names, such as *halam* among the Wolof of modern Senegal, *ngoni* or *koni* among the Bambara and Mande (see Plate 7), and among non-*griot* musicians in what is now Nigeria, *molo* and *kwamsa*.[1] Andrew Kaye cites a variety of other examples of pre-guitar African lutes and harps, such as the *seperewa*, a harp-lute from the west African coast, the *ramkie*, a plucked lute from the Cape Town region of South Africa, the *kabosy*, a small Malagasy lute, and the Swahili *udi*, a local version of the *oud* (the lute-like instrument found throughout northern Africa and the non-African Arab world).[2] And there are others, such as the Luo *nyatiti* lyre of eastern Africa, and the *simbi* and *doso ngoni*, both hunter's harps found in western Africa.

These string instruments and others were widely in use at the time when Portuguese sailors began taking vihuelas and guitars all over the world during the sixteenth century. But we know little about how they may have interacted so long ago. The first hard evidence we find of Africans playing guitars goes back just over 100 years, to the closing years of the nineteenth century. This coincides with the so-called "scramble for Africa," the period during which European powers fought and finagled to claim or conquer the continent, parcel by parcel. This period naturally brought to Africa an influx of European people, technology, and, inevitably, music.

Plate 7 *Ngoni*

From that time on, guitars turn up accompanying bands in what are now the nations of Ghana, Nigeria, Mali, Guinea, Liberia, Congo, South Africa, Zambia, and Zimbabwe among others. Once recordings were made in the 1920s and 1930s, a comparative account of guitar styles from these regions began to emerge. Speaking generally, American notions of guitar playing seem to have had a greater influence in southern Africa. Ships bearing slaves from the American South are known to have arrived, and even become stranded, in Cape Town, perhaps setting the stage for South Africa's long love affair with American music, including vaudeville and jazz and, later, country music, rock and roll, soul, and hip-hop. By contrast, the west African coast had more contact with guitar cultures developing in Brazil, Cuba, and, by extension, Portugal and Spain. This contact began with sailors, but was strengthened when freed slaves from Brazil and Cuba returned to their ancestral homes.[3] In the first half of the century, recorded music out of Cuba had an enormous impact on musical tastes throughout the world. In Africa, especially the western and central regions, people heard transformed echoes of their own musical cultures in Cuban *sons*, boleros, beguines, rumbas, and cha-cha-chas, and they naturally embraced these sounds and set about re-Africanizing them.

Since there are far more African guitar styles than can be covered in a single essay, I will narrow the focus of my discussion in two ways. First,

I will concentrate on the most influential local guitar styles, those genres that seem to have genuinely reinvented the instrument in some tangible way. Secondly, I will concentrate on areas where I have had personal contact with the music culture, or at least the musicians, and have been able to get a feel for the ways that players conceptualize the instrument. I will emphasize the guitar styles of Mali, Congo, and Zimbabwe, while touching more lightly on guitar music in Ghana, Senegal, South Africa, and Madagascar.

Palm wine two-finger pickers

Much of the existing literature about African guitar music focuses on the music of Sierra Leone, Liberia, Ghana, and Nigeria. These countries shared the English language during the colonial era, and they also shared seminal guitar traditions, notably the lilting, two-finger-picking style generally known as "palm wine" music. The two-finger guitar picking technique is nearly universal in western and central Africa, and to some extent throughout the continent. It may have grown out of a European model, like the common thumb–index right-hand style, similar to European lute technique, but it has proven a natural fit with many African idioms. The opposition of thumb and forefinger allows the player to juxtapose two distinct rhythms and melodies, a fundamental feature of much African guitar music (see Plate 8). After World War II, when electric guitars came into use, and it became possible to arrange for multiple guitars and percussion, many players, especially in the Congo, began using a flat pick. But the two-finger technique persists, and anyone who has seen King Sunny Ade and his African Beats will note that Ade leads his three-guitar string section playing his own Telecaster with his thumb and forefinger.[4]

Palm wine music in particular developed in the port cities of western Africa along marine mercantile routes. In Liberia and neighboring Sierra Leone, a guitar-based song style known as *maringa* evolved. The name may have a relationship to *merengue*, which was developing across the Atlantic in the Dominican Republic.[5] Such trans-Atlantic borrowing is entirely possible. During the nineteenth and early twentieth centuries, the seafaring Kru of Liberia traveled widely, sharing recreational music over the local palm wine during layovers in port. The Kru provided a complex conduit of musical ideas from various parts of Europe, the Caribbean, and Africa, and they certainly played a role in the early transmission of palm wine guitar music. Largely through them, palm wine music reached the port capitals of Accra (Ghana), Lagos (Nigeria), and even as far south as the Congo.[6]

Maringa and other palm wine styles bear strong resemblances to early forms of West Indian pop music, especially calypso. In Sierra Leone, *maringa*

Plate 8 Right hand of Djelimady Tounkara

developed steadily, achieving widespread popularity and even recording success as performed by Ebenezer Calender.[7] In more recent times, S. E. Rogie of Sierra Leone, and Ghana's Daniel Amponsa, who goes by the name Koo Nimo, have been the standard bearers for palm wine guitar music (see Plate 9).[8] Probably palm wine's most lasting impact was its role in the early development of "highlife" music, which in turn became a model for more durable genres, such as Nigeria's *juju* and "afrobeat," and also the all-powerful guitar pop of the Congo. John Collins, a British guitarist and musicologist who has lived most of his life in Ghana, has written extensively on the early forms of palm wine guitar music in Ghana, and their roles in the formation and development of highlife. Collins acknowledges the contributions of the Kru to early palm wine forms, but he also sees a role for local village idioms from the Ghanaian interior, styles Collins refers to as "native blues."[9]

Collins and especially Waterman are excellent sources for information about highlife and *juju* music, which go back to the 1920s and 1930s, and represent some of the earliest examples of what we now call afropop styles. While these synthesized, modern genres were developing in coastal cities, the guitar was working its way on a parallel track into traditional musical settings in the interior of western Africa.

Plate 9 Koo Nimo of Ghana

Griots, hunters, and bluesmen: the guitar in the Sahel and the Guinea Coast

Any discussion of modern African culture is complicated by the artificial overlay of colonial history. The modern nation of Mali covers a substantial portion of what was once the Manding Empire (1235–1400), and later the Songhoi Empire (1400–1580). Before either of these, the region was part of another large empire called Ghana, which, confusingly, did not include the present-day nation of Ghana. After the decline of Songhoi, there was the smaller Bambara Empire and also Fulani political entities took hold, such as the kingdom of Hajj Umar Tal, who spread his power by force under the banner of Islam. Today, the Mande people are divided among Mali, Guinea, Burkina Faso, Senegal, Gambia, Ivory Coast, Liberia, Sierra Leone, and Niger. The Fulani also live in those countries. The Songhoi spread from Mali into Burkina Faso and Niger, and the Bambara into Burkina Faso, Guinea, and Ivory Coast.

There is unique guitar music associated with each of these ethnic groups, and while all of it exists in Mali, little of it can be said to be truly indigenous. Complicating matters further, Mali also has distinct guitar music traditions among the Bobo, Senufo, Tuareg, Soninke, and other peoples.

The world has come to focus on Malian guitar music in part because the centrally located country includes such a cross-section of peoples who have embraced the guitar and contributed to its repertoire. But it is important to realize from the outset that to explore any one of these guitar styles fully is to venture across national borders, and often to blur easy classifications.

One of the most extraordinary adaptations of two-finger guitar playing in Africa occurs among the Mande *griots* or *jelis* – professional entertainers and praise musicians by birthright. The praise singing practiced by *griots* is more than just flattery aimed at receiving money. *Griots'* words serve the purpose of reminding people of their ancestors' roles in history, and so feed a basic sense of self-worth and dignity that is palpable in societies where the tradition exists. According to Eric Charry, the guitar most likely spread among the Mande in Guinea when it was brought by soldiers returning from World War I.[10] It did not take long to be accepted as a part of *jeliya*, which is both the art through which the *jelis* use a base repertoire of songs, and an extensive knowledge of all the region's family histories, to ennoble individuals by "singing" them in largely improvised performances. Charry includes a 1949 photograph of a *jeli* ensemble in Kela, a major center of Malian *jeliya*. The guitar's place alongside the far more venerable *jeli balafon* (a wooden-slatted xylophone) indicates that the guitar had become a *jeli* instrument by then.[11]

Meanwhile, in the Guinean capital, Conakry, dance bands were playing the popular international styles of the day – everything from Cuban *sons* and beguines, to tangos, waltzes, foxtrots, and American swing – all disseminated by a young recording industry and radio. With few pianos around, these bands turned to a more portable harmony instrument, the electric guitar. Initially, guitarists imitated American guitar approaches and adapted piano parts to guitar. But after independence, developing folkloric guitar traditions had a defining impact on electric dance band music. Guinea's first president, Sekou Touré, created a national system of regional orchestras, and laid down an edict that they must incorporate indigenous – especially Mande – music into their compositions and performances.

This led to an amazing period of creativity with profound implications for the guitar. Charry documents the rise of such groups as Syli National Orchestra, Bembeya Jazz, Keletigui et ses Tambourinis, and Balla et ses Balladidins, and of the innovative, influential electric guitarists who infused these bands' music with ancient Manding melodies and rhythms: players like Kerfala "Papa" Diabaté, Sekou "Docteur" Diabaté, and Sekou "Bembeya" Diabaté, who still lives and performs in Conakry today. The proliferation of *jeli* names like Diabaté, Kouyaté, and Kanté among musicians in this region indicates the predominance of *jeli* tradition in the music.

Example 4.1 "Bajourou" in the style of Djelimady Tounkara

kora technique (the C note is a ringing note played with the forefinger on the B string;
the lower B note is a dead note played with the thumb on the G string)

arrows indicate first finger picking direction: ↑ upstroke ↓ downstroke

In neighboring Mali, a similar course of events led to the formation of a national orchestra, and later spin-off groups like the Rail Band of Bamako, Orchestra Badema, and Les Ambassadeurs, the group that gave Mali's most famous singer Salif Keita his springboard to international fame. In my own explorations of African guitar music, I tracked down the Rail Band's lead guitarist Djelimady Tounkara in 1992. I was so impressed with his musicianship that I later spent seven months in an informal apprenticeship with him in Bamako.[12] Because Tounkara is both a master of traditional *jeli* music and one of the most respected dance and pop electric guitarists, he was the perfect mentor. Together we moved between wedding parties where Tounkara and others performed the standard *jeli* repertoire, and Rail Band gigs and rehearsals where this music was transformed into afropop and blended with Afro-Cuban, reggae, blues, and rock idioms.

Perhaps the reason that the guitar has become so accepted in the tradition of *jeliya* is the fact that *jeli* players like Tounkara have so thoroughly reconceptualized the instrument. By and large, they use the two-finger technique, but in their efforts to make the guitar play the fleet lines associated with the *ngoni, kora,* and *balafon,*[13] they developed significant refinements. The right-hand picking finger points back toward the neck so that it can play with the inside of the nail. The finger is held straight and plays both upstrokes and downstrokes, as if the nail were a flat pick. The sound is strong, fast, and even. Sometimes the finger drags across adjacent strings to allow lines to flow seamlessly from string to string. Meanwhile, the fretting hand uses hammer-ons and pull-offs freely. The combination of these techniques allows the player to produce long, flowing melodies and to convey the distinctive character of the older *jeli* instruments (see Example 4.1). In acoustic settings, the thumb opposes these melodies with counter melodies, allowing the guitar to approach the density of sound that the 21-string *kora* can produce (see Plate 10). Incidentally, both the *kora* and the *ngoni* also use the thumb and forefinger to pick notes. The *ngoni* technique is closest to

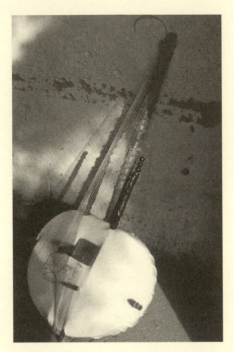

Plate 10 *Kora*

the one adapted by guitarists, since it involves this unusual use of the fore-finger to play both upstrokes and downstrokes. Manding electric guitarists easily adapt the right-hand technique, and replace the left-hand forefinger with a flat pick. For many, the pick may allow more force and precision, but Tounkara is fond of demonstrating that he can produce the same sound using either the pick or his forefinger.

A word on tunings. Most west African guitarists, especially electric gui-tarists, use standard tuning (EADGBE). Finger-picking *jelis* like to use an F tuning, raising the low E to F, and the B string to C. In regular tuning, *jeli* music usually works around a C major chord. The F tuning shifts the melodic activity one string higher, and puts the tonic (F) on the lowest string, effectively expanding the note range for a player using first position. This way, the guitar's range is closer to that of the *kora*. In northern Mali, Songhai and other guitarists raise the low E to a G and use it as a drone. There are probably other tunings in use, but in my experience these are by far the most common.

Djelimady Tounkara makes a fairly common distinction between two broad categories of Malian guitar music: (1) Manding music, which is hep-tatonic, and (2) pentatonic music, which includes a huge variety of ethnic music styles: Bambara, Tamaschek, Bobo, Peul, Senufo, and Dogon.[14] In fact, even among the Mande peoples, it is mostly the Malinke and the Khasonke subgroups that favor the seven-note scale. Much other Manding music also uses a pentatonic scale. So while this distinction is crude, it does point to the relative uniqueness of the heptatonic music favored by Mande *jelis,* and also the overwhelming preponderance of pentatonic music in this region.

In my interviews with pentatonic guitarists in Mali in 1995–96, I often tried to get players to articulate tangible differences between, say, Bambara music and Bobo music, or the music of the Wasulsu region in southern Mali, which has produced internationally successful musicians Oumou Sangaré, Nahawa Doumbia, and others. The guitarists in most of these pentatonic styles pick with a plectrum, not with their fingers. They play fast, clean melodies, often favoring cycling ostinato patterns. Saffre Coulibaly plays lead guitar in the band of singer/songwriter Abdoulaye Diabaté, Coulisse Star. The band performs a variety of pentatonic styles, and when I asked him this question, he gave perhaps the clearest answer I received: "You need to know the language you're playing," he said, "Then you can add whatever you like. That's my impression of Malian music." Coulibaly's answer highlights one of the most defining characteristics of Malian music: the deep commitment to improvisation. The expectation that a player should somehow interpret or individualize a song each time he plays it has much to do with the variety and advancement of Mali's musical genres. Coulibaly's answer also points to a striking level of codification within these musical genres. Other players later confirmed for me the notion that guitar melodies and rhythms contain "language" that marks them as plainly as do the lyrics a vocalist sings.

It takes an insider to spot all the cultural references within particular melodies, but the music itself does contain indicators that help even a naïve listener to distinguish among pentatonic styles. For one thing, there are at least three different pentatonic scales in common use in Mali. The Songhoi of the north and the Bambara of the Segu region frequently use a major pentatonic scale: GABDE. Songhoi players like Ali Farka Touré and young Baba Sallah of Gao often tune the low E string up to a G and play finger style (see Plate 11). Bambara and Wassoulou guitarists, on the other hand, play almost exclusively with a plectrum, and Wassoulou songs tend to favor a Dorian pentatonic scale – GACDF – and sometimes, the distinctive minor pentatonic scale: GB♭CDF. The Dorian scale is notable for its reflective, ambiguous character. With no third in the scale (with respect to G), it feels neither major nor minor (see Examples 4.2a–d).[15] The scale is never enough to go on, as none of these ethnic genres is limited to just one pentatonic scale. But combined with characteristic rhythms – such as the 12/8 lope of Oumou Sangaré's "Dugu Kamelemba" (Ko Sira, World Circuit 1993), or the deliberate 4/4 of Super Biton de Segu's "Malamini" (Belle Epoque, Sullart/Sono 1999) – the scale can be a clue to the ethnic origin of a song.

Plate 11 Ali Farka Touré of Mali at WOMAD USA 2000

Example 4.2a Wassoulou accompaniment melody

Example 4.2b Wassoulou accompaniment melody

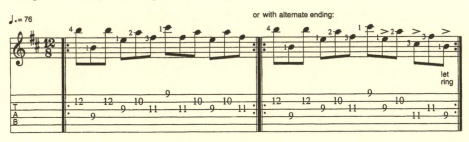

Example 4.2c Bambara accompaniment part

Example 4.2d Fingerstyle accompaniment from Gao

The pentatonic scale that American ears most readily recognize is the minor pentatonic scale, which instantly recalls the riffs and lead patterns of blues and rock music. The subject of the African origins of the blues has generated much discussion. The African contribution to blues music is self-evident to most observers: minor pentatonic styles, altered vocal pitches, prevalent use of string accompaniment, and familiar, rolling rhythms are all evidently bluesy features found in many forms throughout this region. Confusion results when one tries to make more specific connections. Given the paucity of data concerning the pre-history of blues music in America, it is difficult to go much beyond noting these general similarities. After all, many of these same characteristics also exist in Celtic music, which has certainly found its way into American musical idioms. Gerhard Kubik, one of the most diligent scholars in this area, cautions against any simple explanation of the origin of blues, arguing that the blues presents evidence of influences spread far and wide through space and time.[16] He deconstructs the "African blues" marketing hype surrounding the work of Ali Farka Touré, pointing out that Touré had listened to a good deal of Delta Blues in Paris by the time he made the recordings in which bedazzled outsiders discovered the presumed roots of that music.[17] Touré himself has made overly sweeping statements to the effect that the blues represents a diluted, half-remembered strand of African tradition, rather than a new synthesis of elements. Just the same, Kubik contends that the central Sudan, including Touré's home in Niafunke on the Niger, is the core source of African traits in American rural blues. Specifically, Kubik points to "the region from Mali across northern Ghana and northern Nigeria into northern and central Cameroon."[18]

Kubik's designation discounts the notion that music in the western Sudan (Senegal and Gambia) demonstrates the same blues characteristics as that in central Sudan. He does not find these characteristics, for example, in the heptatonic music of the Mande *jelis*. On the other hand, I would assert the music of the *jelis* does have a relationship to American plucked string music, if not the blues. While much energy has been devoted to exploring the connection between black-identified blues music and west African string music, connections between more white-identified genres such as old-time Appalachian mountain music, finger-picking banjo and guitar music, and even bluegrass seem equally evident. Few would dispute the fact that the banjo is an American instrument developed from an African concept. Constructed from a drum resonating chamber, rather than a box, the original banjos were fretless like their African forebears, and the first banjo players were black. As blues music came into its own, African American musicians increasingly abandoned the banjo, in part because it was tainted with the stigma of inherently racist minstrel shows. This fact has tended to obscure the African contribution to non-blues American folk music. While living in Mali, I observed a number of *ngoni* players picking up a banjo for the first time, and within minutes, playing Manding traditional music on it. I also saw them learn Appalachian string tunes from a banjo player by ear and play them with ease on the *ngoni*.[19] While this hardly qualifies as definitive ethnomusicology, it does suggest that this subject deserves further study.

Congo's guitar madness

No African guitar music has had a greater influence around the continent than that developed in the Congo region, that is, the former French colony that is now Congo, and the former Belgian colony that became Zaire and is now the Democratic Republic of Congo. In his survey of Congo music, Gary Stewart contrasts the capital cities of these two nations, Brazzaville and Kinshasa, which face one another "like diamonds washed up on the opposite banks of the Congo River, one cut with the precision of a lapidary's chisel, the other rough and sandy, still bearing nature's scars."[20] Despite their differences, these two cities shared in developing the most successful pop music modern Africa has produced, variously known as rumba, *kwassa-kwassa*, *soukous*, or simply *Congolais*. The unique guitar playing that emerged during the 1940s and 1950s in these two then-cosmopolitan cities is a complex blend of borrowed elements and instincts synthesized from a great range of traditional cultures represented among the local peoples, many of whom came to the city from within the vast interior.

Kazadi wa Mukuna identifies four periods in the development of Congo guitar, beginning with the "troubadour" phase, in which solo acoustic guitarists used the instrument to accompany singing, just as their predecessors would have done using a *sanza* (hand-held lamellophone) or xylophone. There is also a hint of American folk and country guitar playing in the lyrical two-finger guitar pieces of this era's greatest players, especially the legendary John Bosco Mwende, one of the first African guitarists to make a recording career.

The 1950s saw the beginning of a period in which local orchestras formed in the cities, initially imitating foreign music, especially the Cuban *son,* just as bands were doing in Conakry, Dakar, and other developing African cities.[21] In the chaotic period that followed independence in 1960, the education system faltered, and more and more youths saw music as a viable and desirable profession.[22] As bands formed, and record companies competed to create hits, the music evolved, bringing in distinctive traditional melodies and rhythms.

During the economically ruinous Mobutu era (1965–97) in what was then Zaire, music thrived in a vacuum. Mobutu discouraged expressions of foreign culture and emphasized all things indigenous in a policy called "authenticity." Even prior to Mobutu, leading guitarists like Nicolas Kasanda – a.k.a. Docteur Nico – had played cycling guitar lines that drew upon the deep rhythms of the Luba people in the interior Kasai region, and drove listeners and dancers wild. Nico's foil, Franco (Luambo Makiadi), the "Sorcerer of the Guitar," had also incorporated village music in his rugged, double-stop guitar passages. But during the 1970s, the impulse to infuse Congo music with a strong local identity grew even stronger, and the guitar was an important tool in this crusade.

Zaiko Langa Langa, the most popular youth band in Kinshasa during the 1970s, dropped horns from its lineup and used layered guitar patterns to crank out rhythm during the *seben* section that concluded each song. Veteran Congo guitarist Lokassa Ya M'Bongo told me in a 1995 interview that one inspiration for the *seben* came from the palm wine, finger-picking "coastmen" from Ghana who taught many young Congolese to play guitar during the 1940s. The Ghanaians had also been listening to Hawaiian guitar and were fond of using a dominant seventh chord to add intensity to a sweet song. "People liked that sound and they would call for it," recalled Lokassa. " 'Play seven, play seven.' But they didn't understand the word seven, so it became *seben.*" The propulsive bass playing that animates the modern *seben* is also noteworthy. Boston-based Congolese bassist Fellyko Tshikala told me that the pounding lines, often alternating rapidly between interlocking high and low melodies, was called "marche militaire" because it expressed the aggressive, militaristic mentality that Mobutu sought to encourage at all walks of life during his regime.

Zaiko's "rumba rock" songs began with rumba, but always ended with a long *seben,* where the solo guitar took center stage and the music surged to create dance frenzy. Zaiko's first soloist, Manuaku Waku, was known

Example 4.3 Excerpt from a Choc Stars Seben

for his speed and stamina. But for the lead guitarist, melody was also very important. "You can't complicate it too much," another top soloist Syran Mbenza of the Four Stars told me. "If you do, people won't remember it. It has to turn. It has to move. That creates the ambiance."[23] The light, quick flat picking of Congolese lead guitarists like Nene Tchakou, Dally Kimoko, Diblo Dibala, Dizzy Mandjekou, and Huit Kilos offers a striking balance of melodic inventiveness and rhythmic repetition. But equally remarkable is the way Congolese bands arrange for multiple guitars. During the Zaiko era, the standard line-up included four guitars: lead, rhythm, bass, and the so-called *mi-solo* guitar, which sometimes harmonized the solo, and sometimes filled in rhythmic spaces between the high and low guitars. Franco's TPOK Jazz used up to six guitars, sometimes with three playing interlocking lead lines (see Example 4.3).[24] In order to differentiate one part, older guitarists used to replace the D string with a second high E string, tuned to E. This doubled note in what was known as the *mi-composé* set up creates a ringing warmth and facilitated the characteristic parallel sixths riffs favored by some rhythm players. Lokassa says that guitarists in the Franco school rejected this technique, while followers of Nico and his rhythm guitarist brother Dechaud used it.

As life in the two Congos deteriorated steadily in the 1990s, Congo music also faded. The coalescence of recording technology and Mobutu's decision to use music to sedate his people and to promote his country abroad made Congo music the beat of Africa for decades. But today, most Congo music is recorded in Europe, and contemporary tastes have tended to favor keyboard melodies while de-emphasizing guitar. A great deal of classic Congo music was released on the Sonodisc label during the 1990s, but now that the label has folded, even these reissues are becoming hard to find.

Southern African guitar

Some of the earliest firm evidence of guitars being played in Africa comes from South Africa. Perhaps more than any country on the continent, South Africa looked more to the United States than to Europe or the Caribbean for its musical models. Early in the twentieth century, local acts like the Rhythm Kings Band and Pixley's Midnight Follies based their careers on imitating American jazz and vaudeville styles and conventions.[25] As more distinctive local styles like *marabi*, pennywhistle *kwela*, and later *mbaqanga* and *mqashiyo* developed, they maintained strong elements of American jazz, R&B, and soul. From the early music of Miriam Makeba and the Skylarks to the exuberant pop of Mahlathini and the Mahotella Queens and the Soul Brothers, these flavors are unmistakable.

By 1950, the acoustic guitar was a fairly common instrument in South Africa, and other American styles had also entered the mix, notably country music. South Africa distributed albums by Jimmie Rodgers, and his music had a significant impact on guitarists and singers not only in South Africa, but also in Zimbabwe,[26] Zambia, and other neighboring countries. As in other parts of Africa, local people were adapting the instrument to their own uses. Among the most remarkable South African reinventions of the guitar occurred among the Zulu people. The acoustic guitar became the most popular Zulu folk instrument – it even has a Zulu name, *isigingci* – and remains so today, despite the instrument's waning popularity in the nation as a whole.[27]

Nollene Davies wrote in 1994 that Zulu finger-style guitar was still being performed competitively as a solo art form, and showed no signs of decline.[28] The distinctive idiom is the centerpiece of the Zulu's *maskanda* pop music, which helped to inspire Paul Simon during the pre-Graceland days, and remains popular in Zululand. When I visited South Africa in 1988, Johnny Clegg – a white musician who immersed himself in Zulu culture in his boyhood and co-founded the legendary crossover pop band Juluka – gave me a lesson in the Zulu picking style called *ukapika* (see Plate 12). Clegg explained that Zulu players typically tune the high E down to a D and use it as a drone. The thumb plays an active pulse ostinato, derived from

Plate 12 Johnny Clegg of South Africa, Central Park, New York, 1998

Example 4.4 Contemporary Zulu approach demonstrated by Johnny Clegg

Zulu mouthbow music. In addition to keeping up a drone, the forefinger plays beautiful melodies that contrast with the pulse bass, typically working around implied A minor and G major chords (see Example 4.4). Davies writes that while the venerable mouthbow provided just one string, and typically five notes, Zulu choral music provided rich notions of harmony and counterpoint that also turned up in *ukapika* guitar playing. Indeed, players think of the low and high strings as male and female voices.[29]

The origins of South Africa's electric guitar styles are less easy to pin down. The punchy, strummed double-stop lines popularized by, among others, Marks Mankwane of the Mahotella Queens' backup band, bear some resemblance to the high melodies in Congo music. But the rhythmic character is different, more foursquare and at the same time more squirrelly. The late Mankwane's guitar introductions and solos contain rhythmic accents right out of traditional Zulu dance, which was freely adapted in the group's

live performances. Mankwane's style along with the booming, sliding bass
guitar of his band-mate Joseph Makewla have been imitated to the point
where they are now hallmarks of South African township music.

In landlocked Zimbabwe, musical influences from the Congo (and by
extension Cuba) and South Africa (and by extension the United States) met
on fertile ground, and the result, once again, was singular guitar music.
Thomas Turino provides an excellent analysis of Zimbabwe's guitar-based
pop music styles: *jit, chimurenga,* Zimbabwe rumba, and others.[30] A seminal
element in the story is the presence of itinerant guitarists who moved around
the country playing informally at parties and night spots during the 1950s
and 1960s. Turino says that they were the first guitarists to play renditions
of traditional village music, including the sacred music of the Shona *mbira,*
one of many iron-pronged hand-held lamellophones in the region.[31]

Turino finds traditional music working its way into the music of pop
bands as early as the 1960s, mostly as a way to win new fans by expanding repertoire beyond the era's pervasive South African jazz and Congolese
rumba. By the time Zimbabwe's most celebrated pop musician, Thomas
Mapfumo, began recording electric, afropop versions of traditional songs
during the country's 1970s liberation war, promoting African culture had
become a political statement. Turino puts all of this in a larger context,
and rightly corrects many oversimplifications in Mapfumo's history and
significance as reported in the world music press. Zimbabwe has produced
a great deal of original guitar music, including local versions of Congolese
rumba and South African township pop. Still, from a guitarist's point of
view, the *mbira* style music developed by guitarists in Mapfumo's band,
the Blacks Unlimited, is one of the most unusual guitar styles on the
continent.

During three trips to Zimbabwe, I interviewed and learned from a succession of Blacks Unlimited guitarists, including Jonah Sithole, Ephraim
Karimaura, and Joshua Dubé, all dead now (see Plate 13). Dubé was the
first guitarist to work with Mapfumo in adapting an *mbira* song on guitar, and after a long absence he rejoined Mapfumo's band in 1993. In the
band's early days, guitarists essentially imitated *mbiras,* rolling the flesh of
the picking hand over the bridge to dampen each note.[32] Two guitarists
playing interlocking lines mimicked the effect of two *mbira* parts. During
the 1980s, Mapfumo introduced *mbiras* into the band lineup, and encouraged his guitarists to get away from the damping technique and play more
legato lines – as he put it, to let the guitar be a guitar.

Dubé gave me a lucid description of the style, pointing out that in order
to play *mbira* music on guitar, you must start by identifying the chord
progression. Most *mbira* pieces can be thought of as a repeating set of four
phrases. Each phrase typically uses three chords distributed over a bar in

Plate 13 Joshua Dubé of Zimbabwe

12/8 time. In each bar, there are four strong beats, played by the bass drum in a band setting – in effect, a sequence of four triplets. The harmonic rhythm of the chord changes can vary. But often the first chord in each phrase covers the first six beats, with each of the other two chords covering three. Here is the chord progression for "Karigamombe," the first song most *mbira* players learn. A great number of *mbira* pieces use variations on this basic progression.[33]

C	F	Am
Dm	F	Am
C	Em	G
C	Em	Am
I	IV	vi
ii	IV	vi
I	iii	V
I	iii	vi

Example 4.5 Basic phrases from "Gwindingwe Rine Shumba"

The guitarist uses a plectrum, generally playing the on-beats using down-strokes and the pickup notes using upstrokes. The picking technique is strong and even. As in Congolese music, it is important not to lose notes by playing them too softly. The rhythmic character of the line is critical. Amid a dense ensemble sound, every guitar note must be heard equally (see Example 4.5). The recordings of the Blacks Unlimited, many of which are readily available, provide a wealth of fascinating guitar music. The growing role of keyboards and *mbiras* on the later releases does not diminish the grace and beauty of the guitar lines. As the guitar moves beyond imitating *mbiras* and begins instead to accompany them, it defines a mature, neo-traditional art form.

I conclude this introductory survey of African guitar music with a mention of a rich body of music that has come to international attention relatively recently: the guitar music of Madagascar. The Indian Ocean island is home to a diverse intermingling of African, Asian, Arab, and European peoples, and from the highlands of the capital, Antananarivo, to the forested, tropical coasts, there is a stunning array of string music, including unique guitar styles.

Salegy pop music – a fast, electric dance style from the northern coast – bears some resemblance to 12/8 pop music found in other southern African countries, such as Zimbabwe. But where *mbira* pop music puts the accent on the first beat of each triplet, *salegy* accents the second, giving the music a distinctive swing.[34] More remarkable still are the acoustic guitarists like

Solo Razaf, D'Gary, Johnny, and Haja.[35] As in Mali and Zimbabwe, these guitar styles build on much older music played on indigenous instruments like the *valiha* (a tube zither) and the *marovany* (a box zither).

Writer and musician Ian Anderson has made a preliminary study of Malagasy guitar styles summarized in an article in his own *Folk Roots Magazine*.[36] Like everything on this somewhat mysterious island, the picture that emerges is complicated. From the rowdy northern *salegy* and southern *tsapika* – both party music styles – to the stately, almost classical music of the central highlands, the guitar music is ambitious and inclusive. One player who has mastered the art of playing *marovany* music on electric bass is also adept at playing jazz fusion. Another, Ernest Randrianasolo, who uses the stage name D'Gary, has become the island's most celebrated guitarist since his discovery in the early 1990s. His precise, lacelike finger-picking is loaded with traditional references, but also with undeniable personal flair. He tells Anderson that he uses twenty-three different tunings, but does not reveal them.[37] This tantalizing fact is emblematic of the work yet to be done in exploring and explaining Malagasy guitar.

Conclusion

A new crop of serious books about African music, many cited in this essay, gives rise to hope that the story of African guitar music is at last being written. Today, the guitar is less popular continent-wide, in part a victim of widespread fascination with keyboard technology. During the late twentieth century, the guitar became in many cases a traditional instrument, and like other traditional instruments, it tends to get left aside by young musicians keen to discover something new. Just the same, most of the great guitar music the continent has engendered is still being played, if in more modest settings. For all the important guitarists who have died, many remain, waiting to tell their stories. And if the past is any guide, African guitarists will continue to surprise us with their innovations.

PART II

Jazz, roots, and rock

5 The guitar in jazz

GRAEME M. BOONE

Jazz is distinct from certain other art forms – notably Western art music – in its emphasis on performance as the primary medium of creative achievement, and many of the greatest jazz composers, such as Duke Ellington and Thelonious Monk, are also among its greatest players. For this reason, the following discussion of jazz guitar styles appropriately centers on the individual musicians who have pioneered those styles, and, from time to time, on individual recordings that epitomize them.

The history of jazz begins in obscurity around the beginning of the twentieth century at a time when much popular and folk music of oral tradition was not yet widely written about or captured on recordings. The guitar was already well entrenched as a versatile instrument for popular music: a "poor man's piano," maybe, but also a rich resource in its own right. It was one of many stringed instruments, and combinations of one kind or another – including banjo orchestras, mandolin orchestras, Hawaiian groups, Mexican mariachi groups, minstrel groups, and "Gypsy" bands, to name a few – were ubiquitous. Their sound is echoed today in the legacy of folk, bluegrass, and other string-band music, but the range and stand-alone capability of the guitar made it particularly useful for ragtime and blues, the two greatest influences in the formation of jazz.

The technology of popular guitars had also reached a significant turning point by this time. Steel strings, though not factory-installed on Martin guitars before 1922, were gradually introduced in the course of the late nineteenth century in emulation of other stringed instruments. They engendered a new kind of sound, louder and more percussive than that made by the quieter gut strings of classical and Spanish guitars. With the founding of the Gibson company in 1902, the arch-top guitar took its place alongside the flat-top guitar: having a particularly resonant and warm tone, the Gibson and other arch-tops would eventually become the instruments of choice for jazz musicians. These and related innovations set the stage for a host of new styles.

Ragtime and blues

Ragtime, which took the United States by storm in the later 1890s, is grounded in a duple rhythm (commonly transcribed or composed in

2/4 meter), bringing with it a marked alternation of strong and weak. That alternation operates not only on the slower levels of beat and measure but on the faster ones of ornamentation also. Magnified by intense syncopation and rhythmic drive, it makes the music sound "peppy" (to use an expression of the time), or bubbling with extroverted, sometimes nervous energy. The two-beat foundation of ragtime was well suited to a "boom-chick" flat- or finger-picking guitar style, as were its syncopated melodies to the percussive attack of upper-string solo lines. For this reason, the registral functions common in ragtime stride piano and wind band (bass notes for harmonic support / mid-range for chords / high notes for melody) proved equally amenable to guitar. At the same time, strumming- or tremolo-based styles, especially well suited to the four-string banjo, mandolin, and ukulele, yielded bright rhythms and full chordal sound. Guitar virtuosos of the period were commonly multi-instrumentalists, so that techniques easily passed among different instruments.

By the time the recording industry began giving its full attention to the ferment of popular styles, ragtime had already been largely displaced or infiltrated by jazz. But a good number of earlier, illustrative recordings survive, as for example the "Southern Blues" recorded by an anonymous duet of guitars in 1915. To judge by later standards the song actually has few blues characteristics, lacking blue notes and maintaining a perfectly straight (as opposed to swing) beat. Still, its rhythm part is in 2/4 boom-chick style, enlivened with occasional and seemingly improvised short bass-note runs and pattern reversals; and its solo line, marked by the characteristic glissandi of Hawaiian guitar style (created with a metal or glass slide), includes light chromatic ornamentation and plenty of syncopated offbeats.

Numerous virtuosos on banjo, guitar, and other plucked string instruments came up during the era spanning ragtime and early jazz, including Vess Ossman (1868–1923), Fred Van Eps (1878–1960), Papa Charlie Jackson (1885–1938), Cliff Edwards (1895–1972), Harry Reser (1896–1965), Blind Blake (1890s – c. 1933), Roy Smeck (1900–94), and Ikey Robinson (1904–90). Several continued working for decades, and with the revival of interest in ragtime since the 1960s, many guitarists and banjo players, including Stefan Grossman (b. 1945) and Bob Winans (b. 1940), have set about reviving and transcribing music from the era. Today rag and rag-related early jazz occupy a small but vibrant place among plucked string styles.

The ingredient paradoxically lacking in "Southern Blues" – the blues itself – contributed at least as much to jazz as did ragtime, and of course the guitar played a fundamental role in blues, as it still does today. Emerging toward the end of the nineteenth century, blues music had several deeply ingrained elements that would prove essential to jazz, including wailing blue notes (made on the guitar by string-bending or with a slide), a tendency to swing rhythm, and an emphasis on heartfelt melodic expression. The reliance of blues on a single, elemental chord progression (I–IV–I–V–I), remaining the same in thousands of different songs and performances, re-doubled this melodic emphasis, leaving a wide-open field for sheer musical invention and expression. In this way, the blues gave to jazz an enduring and venerable ideal for good and meaningful performance. It remains true today that no song type is more revealing of a jazz player's style and expressive voice than the blues.

Early jazz

Ragtime, blues, and other popular styles were heard in many places, but it was in the unique musical culture of New Orleans that the fateful style of jazz coalesced. New Orleans players smoothed out the ragtime busyness with a more 4/4-oriented rhythmic foundation, a more pronounced swing (as opposed to straight) rhythm, a free-wheeling polyphonic style, and an emotionalism that was grounded in the blues. While spreading around the country in the 1910s, notably to Chicago and the west coast, the New Orleans jazz style finally sparked a national jazz craze in 1917 when it was first recorded in New York. New Orleans jazz is most famous for its wind-band format, with the tenor or four-string banjo commonly part of the rhythm section. Like the double bass, the guitar was not well suited to the primitive acoustic recording technology of that time. In the earliest days of jazz, however, the guitar was probably a more important part of the jazz scene than the banjo: the oldest known "jazz-band" photograph, for example, showing the Buddy Bolden band c. 1895, includes a Martin-type flat-top guitar. Lonnie Johnson (1889–1970), Johnny St. Cyr (1890–1966), Bud Scott (c. 1890–1949), Buddy Christian (c. 1895 – c. 1958), and Lawrence Marrero (1900–59) were fine early New Orleans banjo and guitar players.

In the 1920s, jazz bands multiplied everywhere and its music and play-ing techniques became increasingly sophisticated. Alongside the smaller New-Orleans- and then "Chicago"-style polyphonic bands, larger groups, mainly society or dance orchestras, assimilated jazz style too. Top big bands in the mid-1920s were Fletcher Henderson's Orchestra, with Charlie Dixon (c. 1898–1940) on banjo, Duke Ellington's Orchestra, with Fred Guy (1897–1971), Paul Whiteman's orchestra, with Carl Kress (1907–65), and Jean Goldkette's Orchestra, with Howdy Quicksell (1901–53). The banjo was at this time preferred to the guitar as a rhythm instrument in big bands; but the guitar was gaining in popularity as a jazz solo and rhythm instrument, in part because of the fine playing of jazz guitar pioneers, notably Lonnie Johnson and Eddie Lang (1902–33). Lang's style was widely admired, so much so that his use of an L-5 Gibson arch-top guitar has been credited as a major factor behind the rise of Gibson as the preeminent jazz guitar maker. He had excellent rhythm and chordal abilities, and a perky melodic style that usually remains somewhat reticent; his solos tend to be light and playful. Lonnie Johnson modifies this recipe with a more powerful injection of blues, which helps to give his improvisations a more sustained, pithy flavor. At the moment when Louis Armstrong and other leading jazz players were transforming improvisation into a sustained soloist's art, Johnson (who sometimes played with Armstrong) and Lang brought this art most convincingly to the guitar.

A good example from the period is "Hot Fingers," one of a series of duets recorded in 1929 by Johnson and Lang together. It follows the straightforward seventh-inflected harmonies of its twelve-bar blues progression, rendered at an upbeat tempo and in a bright swing rhythm. (Listeners' note: the first two choruses are introductory, comprising only the last eight bars of the twelve-bar progression, beginning on a IV chord.) Lang remains in the background, punctuating his fine boom-chick or "stride" strumming/picking technique with occasional bass melodies, arpeggios, and hot shuffle-rhythm chords. Johnson's part seems almost entirely improvised, and rendered largely in a single-string or "horn-style" melody. He uses a twelve-string guitar, though the characteristic silvery sound of its doubled strings is not much apparent here. His melodic conception is solidly anchored to the individual twelve-bar episode, and is full of short riffy ideas, syncopations, and wailing blue thirds; every chorus begins with new repeated motives and ends with a repeated arrival on the tonic note. Several of the ideas are sufficiently interrelated to seem extrapolated from something like a tune. However, there is no distinct theme at the beginning and at the end the duet seems simply to stop, as if halted by the engineer's warning light (the song lasts just short of three minutes). Several of Johnson's choruses illustrate one or another specific melodic ornament, turn, or run; like the title, such virtuosic display is common in early jazz solo-instrument style, and also reflects the "novelty" performance styles popular on various instruments in the twenties (e.g., "Kitten on the Keys" on piano, by John Alden Carpenter, or "Nifty Pickin'" on banjo, by Roy Smeck). Throughout, the guitarists show superb rhythmic sensibility, tempering the two-beat bounce inherited from ragtime with the four-beat swing of jazz.

Proliferation of styles

The popularity of jazz affected all kinds of popular genres from the 1920s on. The blues, of course, followed its own path, but one that has intersected so closely with jazz that distinguishing between the two sometimes seems counterproductive; cross-influences as can be observed in recordings by such guitarists as Big Bill Broonzy (1898–1958), Tampa Red (1904–81), T-Bone Walker (1910–75), the young B. B. King (b. 1925), and Clarence Gatemouth Brown (b. 1924). A slightly more distant, but equally important example of jazz influence is found in hillbilly (later renamed "country") music. Its two-beat, boom-chick guitar style resonated with ragtime rhythm and its small-band style was affected by the jazz format of alternating solos. The guitarist who did most to bring rag-derived finger-picking style into hillbilly music was Merle Travis (1917–83); but from thirties-jazz influence emerged the western-swing style, pioneered by Milton Brown, Bob Wills, and other southwestern musicians. Combining the energy and suave sophistication of swing with the simpler melodies, harmonies, and rhythms of hillbilly music, western swing developed its own rhythm and solo guitar styles based on the innovations of players such as Eldon Shamblin (1916–98) and Leon McAuliffe (1917–88). Jazz has continued to play an important role in the development of country-related guitar styles ever since, as reflected in a multitude of players from Chet Atkins (1924–2001) to Lenny Breau (1941–84), Ray Benson (b. 1951), and Tony Rice (b. 1951).

Another seminal style, close in some respects to western swing, was forged in Paris by the Quintette du Hot Club de France in the 1930s. Fronted by violinist Stéphane Grappelli and guitarist Django Reinhardt (1910–53), the band was a pure "string" band, its rhythm section made up only of two other guitars and an acoustic bass. Their recordings exemplify accompanimental guitar style of the time: founded on a smooth but driving 4/4 rhythm, it uses both strummed comping (with a slightly emphasized backbeat) and "stride" style. Reinhardt's background was that of a French Gypsy, and the ingredients of French popular and Gypsy music are clearly evident in his playing, together with those of blues and swing jazz. His virtuosity is all the more remarkable in having been achieved despite the crippling of the two last fingers on his left hand, which were useless for any difficult fretting. A fine example of his playing, using a French Maccaferri Selmer guitar, can be found in the quintet's exhilarating 1936 recording of "Limehouse Blues." The high-powered rhythm section supports a classic Reinhardt solo, featuring lightning fast runs, double-time strumming, quick blue notes, brief ornamental turns, and even octave passages.

The big band era

The shift from early jazz to swing style in the later 1920s and earlier 1930s is strikingly audible in the instrumental techniques of the big bands, whose instrumentation and style evolved as they grew in size. "Oom-pah" tuba style gradually gave way to the "dum-dum-dum-dum" walking bass; stride piano style gave way to a lighter sound, sometimes using simple comping; drummers emphasized the steadier 4/4 beat, commonly rendered on the kick drum or high-hat cymbal; and the plink-plink sound of the four-string banjo was abandoned in favor of the smoother, richer, and more versatile comping of a guitar. This switch confirmed the status of the guitar as a major jazz instrument and the demise of the banjo in that capacity, although the players involved often remained the same. Big-band swing balanced the rich and tightly organized sound of a large ensemble, driven by a suave but potent rhythm section, against the high-flying improvisations of soloists, who were valued for their virtuosity, creative fire, and distinct musical personalities. Guitarists took on both rhythm and solo roles, and sometimes excelled at both. Important big-band rhythm players in the later 1930s included Freddie Green (1911–87; with Count Basie for many years), Eddie Durham (1906–87; also a trombonist and bandleader; with Bennie Moten, Count Basie, and others), and Allan Reuss (1915–88; with Benny Goodman). The guitar could play an important role in small groups as well; a celebrated instance is Art Tatum's piano–guitar–bass trio with Tiny Grimes on guitar (1916–89). The same format was adopted by Nat Cole with Oscar Moore (1912–81), and, later, by Oscar Peterson with Herb Ellis (b. 1921) and Red Norvo (on vibes) with Tal Farlow (1921–98), discussed below.

Charlie Christian and the development of bop

As the jazz guitar rose to prominence in the 1930s, technological innovation kept pace. Instruments such as the Gibson F-335 and the D'Angelico New Yorker appeared, whose bell-like tone has set the standard for jazz guitars ever since. More experimental designs were implemented, too, a prominent example being the seven-string jazz guitar (with added low A string) invented by George Van Eps (1913–98), which has seen a surge of interest from jazz players in recent years. (The original guitar was custom built for him by Epiphone in the later 1930s, but only in 1968 did Gretsch begin making its "Van Eps guitar," the first mass-produced seven-string guitar.) A different kind of technological experiment was the amplified electric guitar, whose heightened volume and sustain allowed it to stand out in any ensemble. In the 1920s and 1930s, pioneers such as Van Eps, Les Paul (b. 1916), and the brilliant craftsman Lloyd Loar worked with electric guitars; Rickenbacker successfully mass-produced its first electric Hawaiian lap steel guitar in 1932. But it was Gibson, with its arch-top, hollow-body ES-150 (ES standing for "Electric Spanish"), that finally created a major, world-wide market for the instrument. Early electric guitarists included Van Eps, Les Paul, T-Bone Walker, and Eddie Durham; the instrument's first true genius was Charlie Christian (1916–42), whose impact on its popularity was so great that the ES-150 itself would come to be known as the "Charlie Christian model."

Born in Texas and raised in Oklahoma, Christian was steeped in the earthy southwestern traditions of blues, jazz, and dance music but developed his own, highly original style. Discovered by impresario John Hammond in 1939 and featured by Benny Goodman, he quickly became a sensation among jazz musicians, and although he died a scant three years later, his career and recordings have left an indelible mark on jazz. Christian's electric guitar gave him a clean, round tone, but one with warmth and power. His solo style featured an almost casual smoothness, resulting from constrained dynamic variation (a quality common in jazz guitar playing, owing to the character of the instrument), from an ironing out of swing rhythm into more even notes, and from a tendency to fall slightly behind the beat. But underlying this smoothness was a potent rhythmic drive, deep bluesiness, and a searching improvisatory creativity rivaling that of any horn player.

Christian excelled in both big- and small-band contexts; a superb cross-section of his talents is on display in "Breakfast Feud," recorded with the Benny Goodman septet in 1939. In the chordal theme, Christian's guitar blends effortlessly with Benny Goodman's clarinet and George Auld's tenor saxophone, all three sounding against Cootie Williams's muted trumpet countermelody. The following improvised choruses are all blues. Christian lays out for the first two (Williams solo), but during the next two (Goodman solo), as well as Auld's solo near the end of the song, we hear Christian's accompanimental style in its purest form, as part of an extraordinary rhythm section including Count Basie (piano), Artie Bernstein (bass), and Jo Jones (drums). Christian's comping here consists only of simple beats, but the rhythm section is so tight and Christian's time so perfect that the accompaniment glows with energy. Later, following an inimitably spare solo by Basie, Christian takes two solo choruses, set off by a group riff. Guitar phrasing (like piano phrasing, but unlike common horn phrasing) is not bound by the duration of a breath, and Christian takes advantage of that fact by stringing ideas together unpredictably, sometimes drawing them out beyond one's expectation in a string of swinging eighth notes, sometimes breaking them into fragments. At the same time, influenced by Lester Young and Kansas City style, Christian also spins catchy riffs, returning figures, and repeated notes into his improvisation. His melodic style likewise blends the familiar and the adventurous. It includes numerous blue notes, made occasionally by string bending, but more often by playing minor and major thirds against each other; and it is also full of runs, leaps, and rapid arpeggios, sometimes outlining complex (e.g., diminished-seventh or eleventh) secondary chords.

Christian's style moved beyond the more extroverted, "hot" tendencies of earlier jazz and toward a new aesthetic that was only beginning to emerge at the time of his death. Pioneered by a small group of musicians, including Charlie Parker on alto saxophone, Dizzy Gillespie on trumpet, Bud Powell on piano, and Max Roach on drums – as well as Christian himself, who often jammed with them – bop radicalized elements of swing, with extraordinarily fast (or slow) tempos, offbeat rhythms, and complex harmonies and forms. On the heels of bop came the related style usually referred to as cool jazz, which drew on the same approach, but molded it to a more relaxed mood, with softer textures and more moderate tempos. The adaptability of the guitar to harmonic complexity made it a perfect candidate for bop style, while its relatively soft and even tone in that era was well suited to cool; but playing extremely fast runs in the advanced harmonic language was an especially demanding feat on the guitar. Nonetheless, leading jazz guitarists that came up in the forties and fifties, including Tal Farlow, Herb Ellis, Mary Osborne (1921–92), Johnny Smith (b. 1922), Barney Kessel (b. 1923), Wes Montgomery (1925–68), Jimmy Raney (1927–95), Joe Pass (1929–94), Jim Hall (b. 1930), Grant Green (1931–79), and Kenny Burrell (b. 1931), were associated with one or both of those styles, and almost all were indebted in one way or another to Charlie Christian.

Tal Farlow illustrates beautifully the bop style on guitar. His sound is in the amplified hollow-body Gibson tradition, full-bodied and warm, and his playing features virtuosity both of comping and of improvised melodic solos, played with his thumb rather than a flat-pick. The central elements of Christian's style, mentioned above, are all present, but they are now radicalized, at times to the verge of abstraction, and joined by dazzling technical innovations, such as the use of harmonics, sophisticated chordal improvisations, and even percussive patterns struck on the body of the guitar. A fine early example of Farlow's style is the standard, "This Can't Be Love," recorded in 1951 with the Red Norvo trio, featuring the perennial Norvo on vibraphone and the young but already great Charles Mingus on bass. The fast-paced performance opens with a straight rendition of the tune by Norvo; his almost total avoidance of syncopation is balanced by Farlow's comping, which, with its volatile, offbeat rhythm, follows the "dropping bombs" approach of bop. Norvo's very fast solo follows, introduced by a bit of dialogue between vibes and guitar, after which Farlow's background comping is as deft as before, and full of the complex harmonies of altered and interpolated chords. Here as elsewhere, Mingus's walking bass line, ironclad even at breakneck speed, anchors the notes and rhythms of the group. Farlow's own solo is so fast as to seem almost impossible to play, much less follow. At this speed, his notes are more or less even in length, but they are differentiated by loud and soft attack. Some notes are almost swallowed up in the line while others punctuate it sharply, giving it sudden, unpredictable shapes, although he often groups notes by fours, in keeping with the rhythmic meter. The incisiveness of Farlow's rhythms keeps us with him as he explores mind-bending harmonic regions extrapolated from the chord progression of the song. His improvisation is constructed mostly of long, looping arpeggiated runs, sometimes forming sequential modulations; they are spiced with chromaticism and sometimes articulated at the top or bottom by salient notes or turns that give a broader, though abstract, sense of movement to the line. In short, Christian's innovations in melodic extension and fragmentation are intensified here: Farlow approaches the edge of intelligibility, and sheer virtuosity prevents him from crossing it. Following his solo is the final chorus, based on a recomposition of the song theme, but with such an increase of harmonic and melodic abstraction that, by the end, it simply breaks off in mid-gesture, and outside of any key.

Three elements audible in the style of "This Can't Be Love" have defined what might be called "mainstream" jazz guitar playing since 1950. Its solid foundation is swing; its central language is bop; and its aspirations at times include a modernist abstraction – a quality which in jazz of the 1950s was usually called "progressive," and was seen as allied to analogous trends in classical music and art. Different players have explored very different styles within these parameters, and a generic distinction has been made between single-note style (e.g., Christian) and chordal style (e.g., George Van Eps), but many have also combined these and other techniques to achieve a distinct style of their own.

Wes Montgomery

Wes Montgomery is just such a player. Born and raised in Indianapolis, he came up, self-taught, in the 1940s and worked with Lionel Hampton before forming his own group in the mid-1950s, which included his two brothers on vibes and bass. Inspired by Christian's playing, Montgomery excelled in improvising smooth, swinging, exploratory lines, but he was a true original. His sound was characterized by a soft but determined attack, due in part to down-picking with his thumb, and he combined elements of bop, cool, and blues in an understated but richly inventive way. A good example of his style is his "West Coast Blues" of 1960. Montgomery's mid-tempo, 3/4 theme is bluesy – at moments, harmonically adventurous – and is tied together by recurring motives (notably an upward half-step slide and associated riff). His ensuing solo never sounds rushed or particularly intense because of his steady dynamics and relaxed-sounding rhythm, often coming in behind the beat and sometimes ironing out the swing beat into even eighths. And yet, when we listen more closely, an uninterrupted wealth of ideas comes across. The first chorus unfolds in long, rangy phrases with gentle but unexpected turns and pauses. The second chorus introduces a sequence of upward half-note slides and, later, a different, descending sequence. The next three choruses use fewer sequences, but drive steadily forward with wide-ranging lines, commonly using high notes as a means to climax and articulation; Montgomery's smooth approach and assured clarity of articulation belie the harmonic density of his thinking. At the sixth chorus Montgomery breaks into octave doubling, which came to be a signature feature of his style; the doubling precludes fast runs, but the ideas continue to proliferate, now relying increasingly on short repeated ideas and riffs. In the last two choruses he turns to chordal soloing, the top note of each chord providing the melody; here, the richness of his harmonic interpolations is directly and beautifully expressed, together with an unerring sense of swing. Despite his brief career, Montgomery's relaxed combination of melody, harmony, rhythm, and pure invention has few if any equals; he has often been named as the most influential of all jazz guitarists since Charlie Christian.

New sounds after 1950

By the time Montgomery made his most celebrated recordings, the arrival of rock and roll had already opened a new and different world to guitar styles. Based on rhythm and blues, rock and roll incorporated elements of western swing, hillbilly/country, and mainstream pop. The style was exemplified by Bill Haley and His Comets (originally named "Bill Haley and His Four Aces of Swing"), whose breakthrough recordings of 1954 prominently featured the burning electric guitar licks of Danny Cedrone (d. 1954). Ensuing rock and roll guitar-based genres, from rockabilly to the present, have continued to draw on elements of jazz, as heard in styles ranging from the "redneck jazz" of Danny Gatton (1945–94) to the "swing revival" of Brian Setzer (b. 1959). Contributing to the rock and roll sound was the solid-body electric guitar, first successfully marketed after World War II with the Fender Broadcaster (1951) and the Gibson Les Paul (1952). Having no resonating chamber, the strings on solid body electrics produced a relatively thin, hot, twangy sound, differing fundamentally from the rounder tone of hollow-body electrics. The lack of resonance chamber allowed cleaner and much stronger amplification, creating, in effect, a new instrument that paved the way for more radical developments to come.

In 1962 the bossa nova, or (roughly translated) "new thing," arrived on the American jazz scene. Using the nylon-string, finger-picked or -strummed Spanish guitar, a group of Brazilian musicians, including Laurindo Almeida (1917–95), Bola Sete (1928–87), João Gilberto (b. 1931), and Antonio Carlos Jobim (1927–94), blended their native musical traditions with the soft-spoken, relaxed sophistication of cool jazz in the later 1950s. The understated brilliance of their approach had a strong impact on the classically trained jazz guitarist Charlie Byrd (1925–99), who collaborated with saxophonist Stan Getz on a bossa-inspired jazz style (cf. *Jazz Samba*, 1962) that had a powerful effect on both jazz and popular music in the United States. Since that time, the classical and Spanish guitar have continued accommodating jazz to the folk, popular, and art idioms of Latin America, and Latin-influenced styles, always present in jazz, have become even more visible as one of its fundamental components.

If bossa nova seems like the apotheosis of cool, its exact opposite had been developing in jazz for some time. Hard bop, whose strong, earthy approach owed much to rhythm and blues and gospel, represented a vital alternative to cool. More revolutionary was the agglomeration of trends that have come to be known as "free jazz." Growing out of a variety of currents in the 1950s, including progressive jazz and hard bop, free jazz was strongly influenced by the social upheaval of the late 1950s and 1960s, especially the civil rights and counterculture movements. Guitarists were not as quick as horn players (Ornette Coleman, Roscoe Mitchell) or pianists (Cecil Taylor, Sun Ra, Richard Muhal Abrams) to develop its iconoclastic sounds, although Billy Bauer (b. 1915) appears on what may be the first "free" jazz recording (Lennie Tristano's "Intuition" of 1949), and Dennis Sandole (1913–2000) taught advanced theory to numerous jazz musicians including John Coltrane. Over time, however, guitarists would contribute significantly to free jazz, as exemplified in that era by the textural and free-improvisatory explorations of Derek Bailey (b. 1932) and the blues and modal inflections of Sonny Sharrock (1940–94). Free jazz opened up a seemingly limitless horizon of styles and influences to reexamination, ranging from avant-garde classical music to popular and ethnic musics of all kinds.

As epochal as free jazz was (and still is), most radical of all in its impact on the guitar in 1960s jazz was the triumph of rock music and rhythm-and-blues as the voice of a rebellious younger generation. For it led to a blurring of the boundary between jazz and pop in the eyes of audiences and musicians alike, and no instrument was more central to rock music than the solid-body electric guitar. Many leading rock musicians of the 1960s (e.g., Jimi Hendrix,

Eric Clapton, Jimmy Page) were primarily influenced by the blues; but the very idea of extended improvisation in rock, with all the artistic mastery and creative achievement that implied, was founded on the achievements of jazz. Leading players (e.g., Jerry Garcia with the Grateful Dead, Steve Howe with Yes, Frank Zappa with the Mothers of Invention, Allan Holdsworth with Soft Machine) admired jazz and were directly influenced by it to a greater or lesser degree; and there were numerous soul-influenced "jazz-rock" bands featuring both strong horns and strong guitars, including Blood Sweat and Tears, Chicago, Tower of Power, and the Sons of Champlin.

The development of fusion

The cross-fertilization of rock and jazz produced every conceivable type of mixture, which makes any simple definition of jazz guitar since that time impossible, much less any linear history of it. But a prime point of orientation, one that actually became a distinct genre, is the combination of jazz and funk called "fusion." The central fusion innovator was trumpeter Miles Davis. One of the supreme creative minds in jazz since his beginnings with Charlie Parker in the 1940s, Davis spurned free jazz in the 1960s, taking on instead an increasingly sophisticated abstraction of melody, harmony, and rhythm made possible to a significant degree by the rarefied talents of his truly extraordinary sidemen. Later in that decade, he moved gradually in the direction of amplification, rock, and funk, turning to electric instruments, modal or droning harmonies, open-ended group improvisations, increasingly simple thematic ideas, and finally the adoption of a richly textured, heavily repetitive rhythm. It was at this time that the electric guitar became an integral part of the Miles Davis sound.

This new direction would have been impossible without the prior invention of funk, thanks primarily to soul-singer James Brown. With the help of his backup band, Brown gradually developed the straight (vs. swing) beat, percussive electric bass lines, lapidary drum patterns, clipped horn riffs, rippling electric guitar comping, and endlessly repetitive, minimalistic, layered, and soulful rhythm that came to define classic funk style in opposition to almost everything that had come before it. Important about Brown's approach is that, like the jazz-rock bands mentioned above, he featured both electric guitar and bass and a full horn section. Others soon began picking up on the new funk style, spawning a soul-funk movement whose impact on American pop has been incalculably great: both disco and hip-hop are its descendants, as well as ongoing innovations in funk-related jazz.

Bitches Brew (1969) epitomizes the Miles Davis brand of fusion, which he developed and explored in one guise or another until his death in 1991. Its style was based on an exploded funk rhythm, with a spontaneous, multi-improvisatory approach in which every player had the freedom and responsibility to be individually creative. The result was a massive, complex sound, undergirded by a roiling rhythm section, driven in part by the keening chords and sinuous, open-ended improvisations of John McLaughlin (b. 1942) on electric guitar, and punctuated by the fragmented, abstract calls of Davis's amplified trumpet. In the later 1970s Davis issued no recordings, but in 1981 he returned to performing with an updated version of his fusion style, involving the lusher sound of electronically enhanced guitars and synthesizers and responding to evolving contemporary popular music. Davis's guitarists in the 1980s have gone on to become major musical forces in their own right, notably Mike Stern (b. 1954) and John Scofield (b. 1951); but none has been more influential than McLaughlin, featured on the Eastern-inspired *In a Silent Way* and the epochal *Bitches Brew*.

A devotee of Sri Chinmoy from 1970 to 1975, McLaughlin brought to his jazz interests a searching Eastern spirituality – entailing a fascination with the subtle modes, rhythms, and other aspects of Indian music – and a psychedelic 1960s taste in progressive, proto-heavy-metal rock. Before joining Davis's group, he worked in Tony Williams's seminal band Lifetime; after leaving Davis in 1970, McLaughlin founded the Mahavishnu Orchestra, whose breakthrough second album *Birds of Fire* is one of the watershed records in pop music history, bringing complex rhythms, melodies, and harmonies together with uncompromising speed, volume, and intensity. In 1976 McLaughlin went in a largely opposite direction, founding the acoustic group Shakti with brilliant young classical Indian musicians L. Shankar and Zakir Hussain. McLaughlin's style with that group, involving lightning-fast runs and a harmonic sensibility at times modal and at times highly sophisticated, has characterized much of his playing since. His improvisatory rhythms sometimes reflect a tendency to the ecstatic outburst rather than the swinging groove, but his technique and range of abilities are extraordinary. Since the late 1970s and early 1980s he has worked on and off in a smoothly integrated guitar-trio format with Paco de Lucía (b. 1947) and Al DiMeola (b. 1954), playfully exploring a Latin-tinged, acoustic-fusion style that – beneath a surface sometimes so relaxed as to evoke easy listening or new age music – conveys rich harmonies, rhythms, and textural interactions. He has also worked in a variety of other formats, notably using a midi-synthesizer-enhanced technique, by which he performs customarily dazzling guitar improvisations while accompanying himself with seamlessly interpolated, electronically sustained background comping played on the same instrument.

Styles in recent jazz

The broad variety and accomplishment of jazz guitar styles and players since 1970 has been accompanied by extensive cross-influences that blur any distinct categories one might propose; the question becomes, rather, how or whether to isolate any traditional understanding of "jazz" from the many other styles into which it melts or disappears. The following brief discussion will take account of six prominent and largely interwoven currents running through recent jazz.

Mainstream jazz guitar, grounded in swing and bop, has been preserved, thanks to the ongoing work of players mentioned above, from Herb Ellis to Jim Hall. Contributing to its survival in the dark "rock era" was the somewhat invisible, but lucrative and often sophisticated profession of session playing: at a time when established jazz styles seemed to evaporate as an object of popular consumption, some jazz players could still make a good living in Los Angeles, Nashville, and other centers of the recording, television, entertainment, and film industries. In recent years, mainstream jazz has experienced a major revival with such fine players as Pat Martino (b. 1944), Gray Sargent (b. 1953), Garrison Fewell (b. 1953), Emily Remler (1957–90), and Howard Alden (b. 1958). A related trend is the resurgence of big bands in cities around the United States: several of the more innovative groups include guitar as an integral part of their sound.

Free jazz, though never a popular best-seller, has established a kind of alternative, or anti-, mainstream, combining elements of diverse styles in which the guitar has at times played a highly visible role. Horn player Ornette Coleman has included the twangy sound of two or more electric guitars in his free-folk-funk Prime Time group since the mid-1970s; Henry Threadgill's early 1990s band, Very Very Circus, also featured two electric guitars. Spurred in part by the rock-guitar revolution of the 1960s, electric guitarists have themselves fronted bands frequently, with diverse highly individual styles – one is tempted to say, languages – in which experimental techniques and "out" playing have an important role. Among these are the scattered-funk approach of James Blood Ulmer (b. 1942), the dense, progressive-rock-tinged style of Larry Coryell (b. 1943), and the ironic, playful sound of Marc Ribot (b. 1954).

World music elements have flourished in jazz, as elsewhere in contemporary music. The Indian influence on John McLaughlin's style was noted above; many other jazz players have also incorporated ethnic traditions into their music. In the 1960s, stringed instruments such as the *kora* (Africa), sitar (India), or koto (Japan) were incorporated by Pharoah Sanders, Don Ellis, Paul Horn, the Art Ensemble of Chicago, and others. The Paul Winter Consort pioneered in what might be called "world-music fusion"; in 1970 members of that group, including percussionist/sitarist Collin Walcott (1945–84) and guitarist Ralph Towner (b. 1940), founded the seminal group Oregon, drawing on elements including classical Western and Indian music. From 1979 until his death in 1984, Walcott also played a variety of string instruments in the world-influenced trio Codona. A signal example of cross-fertilization between jazz and indigenous traditions can be found in the playing of Egberto Gismonti (b. 1947). Trained as a classical pianist and composer, Gismonti began studying the guitar in 1967 as a means to approach the traditions of his native Brazil. Since that time he has explored the music of Brazilian Indians, as well as traditional popular styles and contemporary art music. A multi-cultural, multi-instrumental artistry is already highlighted on an early breakthrough album, *Dança das cabeças* (ECM, 1977), whose raw intensity of textures and styles reveals an indigenous Brazilian musical world quite different, and more varied, than what one might infer from popular samba or bossa renditions.

Fusion-related music has continued to prosper, all the more given the popularity of disco, house music, and hip hop; but its range of styles has become seemingly as broad as popular music itself. Prominent jazz players who moved in a fusion direction in the 1970s were Herbie Hancock, with his funky Headhunters band (featuring Melvin "Wah Wah Watson" Ragin on guitar); Chick Corea, with his Latin-flavored Return to Forever band (featuring Bill Connors, and later Al DiMeola on guitar); and Weather Report, led by Joe Zawinul and Wayne Shorter – another spinoff band from Miles's first fusion group – who included Ralph Towner on their second album, *I Sing the Body Electric.* The harder end of the fusion spectrum, after being cultivated in the 1970s by Larry Coryell, John McLaughlin, Allan Holdsworth (with the Tony Williams Lifetime band), and others, has been explored by many guitarists, notably Vernon Reid (b. 1958), who effortlessly weaves together elements of rock, funk, folk, blues, and free jazz, played on a wide variety of plucked-string instruments. Reid starred in Ronald Shannon Jackson's Decoding Society in the late 1970s, thereafter forming his own group, Living Color. Trombonist Joseph Bowie founded the related hard-funk band Defunkt in 1980, featuring two electric guitars (Kelvyn Bell, Martin Aubert). More in a soul groove is Charlie Hunter (b. 1968), who plays on an eight-string guitar of his own invention in an eclectic style that has been related to the 1990s acid-jazz trend.

A smoother, pop-oriented style of fusion – the style perhaps most commonly associated with the term – has been cultivated by groups such as Spyro Gyra (with guitarist Chet Catallo and, later, Julio Fernandez) and the Yellowjackets (with Robben Ford). And the soft end of fusion, featuring lush electronic effects, a gentle wash of rhythms, and the addition of world music instruments (especially percussion), often verges on a new-age aesthetic; many guitarists have worked in this area also, including highly prominent figures such as Al DiMeola and the prodigious Pat Metheny (b. 1954).

Intertwined with fusion is what one might call jazz-influenced *pop music*, from soul and "top 40" to hip hop and grunge. Varieties of pop music have had considerable influence on some jazz musicians, although the fact is not always appreciated by others. Steely Dan, the extremely successful group of Walter Becker and Donald Fagen (notably featuring Denny Dias and Jeff "Skunk" Baxter on guitar), grounds its music in an accomplished fusion style of jazz harmonies and laid-back syncopated rhythms. Stanley Jordan (b. 1959), who developed an astonishing two-handed fretting technique in the early 1980s that allowed him to play bass lines, chords, and solo lines simultaneously, has recorded both jazz standards and pop. Earl Klugh (b. 1954) and Russell Malone (b. 1963), both trained as jazz guitarists, have recorded albums tending toward a smooth rhythm and blues style; and singer Cassandra Wilson has recorded albums with accompanying guitarists, in which jazz, rock, folk, and blues elements melt together to form an innovative style. The most famous crossover guitarist from jazz to mainstream pop music remains George Benson (b. 1943), who, after gaining acclaim as a soulful jazz artist in the 1960s, had a string of mega-pop-hits beginning in the 1970s. As to the ongoing relationship between jazz and hip hop, it would merit an independent discussion in its own right. Many have bridged the two in one way or another, notably Steve Coleman's Five Elements, featuring David Gilmore (b. 1964) on guitar.

Electronic technologies, though not in themselves a style feature, have affected the sound of almost all guitar players. From the later 1970s on guitar synthesizers began to appear, as well as electric guitars incorporating electronic circuitry (e.g., SynthAxe by Roland, Avatar by ARP; Paul Reed Smith and Steinberger guitars). Relatively extreme signal modifications were a logical result, allowing the guitar to sound like a horn, an orchestra, a bulldozer, or anything else the imagination might conceive. It should be noted that, by the same token, keyboard, wind, and other synthesizers could and did imitate the sounds of the guitar as well, leading at times to a complete blurring of auditory boundaries between instruments (and at times even a physical blurring, as for example with electric-guitar-shaped keyboard synthesizers). Many players, including John McLaughlin, Pat Metheny, John Abercrombie (b. 1944), and Ralph Towner, used electronic devices to timbral ends, and this has contributed greatly to the recent diversity of styles, with wah-wah, compression, chorus, phase shifting, feedback, and delay of all kinds available at the tap of a foot-pedal or twist of a dial.

Since the guitar, as a relatively quiet instrument, was the first to be fundamentally affected by electric amplification in the 1930s, it is no surprise that the advent of electronic technologies should have been so momentous for guitar sound and technique, more than for any other instrument with the exception of keyboard. Since the 1990s, thanks to constantly improving technology and to the passage of time, attention has returned to the virtuosity and beauty of more traditional acoustic sounds, as well as old electric sounds (whether produced electronically or through "period" technologies such as tube amplifiers with plate reverb). The sophistication of sound production and recording technology in the present era has likewise progressed to such an extent that almost any instrument or noise can be made to sound lush and vibrant. Needless to say, such digital virtuosity goes hand in hand with the radical improvement of home listening equipment: listeners have come increasingly to enjoy an exquisite sound environment for their music, which can be at the same time astonishingly "real" (as for example in a live concert recording) and "fake" (as for example in the partial re-recording and electronic enhancement of that concert on compact disc, or the digital addition of vinyl-like pops and scratches to the sound of CD recordings). This can lead to indulgent repetition, as heard in a good deal of the music nebulously labeled "new age"; but more generally it has been a stimulus to the music and musicians, whose work can be appreciated with an intimacy and fullness never before possible through recordings. Ironically, live concert or club performance still varies enormously in the quality of amplification, owing to uneven room acoustics and PA systems. Guitarists using amplification are obliged to bring along their own signal processors and amplifiers to ensure any reasonable control over the consistency, quality, and personality of their sound.

Finally, expanding horizons at the beginning of the twenty-first century have brought a new awareness of style itself as a kind of costume, and thence the infinitely mutable combination, manipulation, and juxtaposition of styles as an end in itself. This trend goes hand in hand with a maverick experimentalism that has characterized some of the most innovative guitar playing since the 1960s, playing that not only crosses stylistic boundaries but seems to render them meaningless. Bill Frisell (b. 1951) is the most visible exponent of this *post-modern* tradition as it relates to guitar. In John Zorn's "Naked Lunch" quartet, for example, Frisell switched instantaneously among lounge, heavy metal, bop, psychedelic, free, and other styles, making a crazy-quilt patchwork whose volatility was reminiscent both of recent sampling technology and of the classic, wild Warner-Brothers cartoon music of Carl Staller. In the *News for Lulu* album of 1987, made in a trio format with Zorn and George Lewis, Frisell plays a rich and subtle role of accompanist, soloist, and, one might say, "texturist"; the group style seems like a cross between hard bop, free jazz, and chamber art music. Frisell has demonstrated high proficiency in a variety of styles reaching far beyond jazz, but bringing to everything he does the sensitivity, musicianship, and accomplished technique that marks the best jazz players.

Education and identity in jazz

The eclecticism of recent jazz guitar playing leads one to reflect on the broadest trends affecting the history of jazz guitar, and one of these is certainly the proliferation of jazz schools since 1950. Professional jazz musicians coming up before that time were likely to have gained extensive experience in the "university" of the big bands, where they worked closely with older musicians and assimilated directly to a vast jazz community. With the gradual demise of the big bands beginning in the later 1940s came the demise of this training ground and the community it represented. Players coming up since 1950 have been faced with a different and increasingly fragmented (or re-formed) musical world. The triumph of rock, soul, and ensuing pop styles has both reflected that fact and compounded it, so that young musicians – guitarists especially – have had a proliferating variety of models to study or emulate. The growth of jazz music schools reflects this situation: since the later 1960s, a large number of guitarists have been taught at institutions such as the Berklee School of Music (in Boston; founded 1948) and the Guitar Institute of Technology (in Los Angeles; founded in 1975). Through study and diverse personal contacts, students become acquainted with an eclectic variety of styles that naturally becomes part of their own musical production, from classical to world music, avant-garde music, and, above all, fusion.

This sea-change in the pedagogical environment of jazz raises the question of where the music is going today. In some respects, jazz has never been healthier. From ragtime to post-modernism, all the major jazz-related styles are very much alive, thanks to older recordings and to the ongoing hard work of dedicated, inspired players. At the same time, the advent of other popular musics, notably rock, fusion, new age, world music, and hip hop, place jazz in a curious position. Should it retreat into established stylistic niches, and if not, how does it move forward? Recent history suggests that we will enjoy a wealth of jazz guitar for a long time to come, but that this depends, too, on how open-minded we are about what "jazz" can and should be.

References

Concise bibliography

Alexander, Charles, ed. *Masters of Jazz Guitar*. London, 1999.
Kernfeld, Barry, ed. *The New Grove Dictionary of Jazz*. 2nd edn. New York, 2002.
Mongan, Norman. *The History of the Guitar in Jazz*. New York, 1983.
Sallis, James, ed. *The Guitar in Jazz: An Anthology*. Lincoln, NE, 1996.
Summerfield, Maurice J. *The Jazz Guitar: Its Evolution, Players, and Personalities Since 1900*. 4th edn. Newcastle upon Tyne, 1998.

Recordings discussed

1. "Southern Blues": Unknown duet, guitar and Hawaiian guitar
   Original release: 44-Little Wonder 501 (c. 1915)
   Current release: *Too Late Too Late, vol. 4: More Newly Discovered Titles and Alternate Takes*. Document DOCD-5321 (1995)
2. "Hot Fingers": Lonnie Johnson and Eddie Lang [under pseudonym "Blind Willie Dunn"], guitar duet
   Original release: Columbia 403043-A (1929)
   Current release: *Great Blues Guitarists: String Dazzlers*. Sony/Columbia 47060 (1991)
3. "Limehouse Blues": The Quintette du Hot Club de France: Stéphane Grappelli, violin; Django Reinhardt, lead guitar; Joseph Reinhardt, Roger Chaput, rhythm guitars; Louis Vola, bass
   Original release: OLA-1062-1 (1936)
   Current release: *The Best of Django Reinhardt*. Blue Note 37138 (1996)
4. "Breakfast Feud": The Benny Goodman Septet: Benny Goodman, clarinet; Cootie Williams, trumpet; George Auld, tenor saxophone; Charlie Christian, electric guitar; Count Basie, piano; Artie Bernstein, bass; Jo Jones, drums
   Original release: Columbia 29512 (1941)
   Current release: *Charlie Christian: The Genius of the Electric Guitar*. Sony/Columbia/CBS 40846 (1990)
5. "This Can't Be Love": The Red Norvo Trio: Red Norvo, vibraharp; Tal Farlow, electric guitar; Charles Mingus, bass
   Original release: Discovery 167 (1951)
   Current release: *Move!* Savoy SV-0168 (1992); re-release of Savoy MG-12088 (1956)
6. "West Coast Blues": The Wes Montgomery Quartet: Wes Montgomery, electric guitar; Tommy Flanagan, piano; Percy Heath, bass; Albert Health, drums
   The Incredible Jazz Guitar of Wes Montgomery. Riverside RLP-12-329 (1960); re-release: Fantasy OJCCD-036-2 (1991)

7. *Jazz Samba* (album): Stan Getz, tenor saxophone; Charlie Byrd, guitar and bass; Keter Betts, bass; Buddy Deppenschmidt, drums; Bill Reischenbach, percussion
   Verve V6-8432 (1962); re-release: Verve 3145214132 (1997)

8. *Bitches Brew* (album): Miles Davis, trumpet; Wayne Shorter, Bennie Maupin, saxophones; Chick Corea, Joe Zawinul, Larry Young, keyboards; John McLaughlin, electric guitar; Dave Holland, Harvey Brooks, bass; Lenny White, Jack DeJohnette, drums; Don Alias, Jumma Santos, percussion
   Columbia GP-26 (1969); re-release Columbia C2K-065774 (1999)

9. *Birds of Fire* (album): The Mahavishnu Orchestra: John McLaughlin, electric guitars; Jerry Goodman, electric violin; Jan Hammer, keyboards; Rick Laird, bass; Billy Cobham, drums
   Columbia KC-31996 (1973): re-release Columbia Legacy CK-66081 (2000)

10. *Dança das cabeças* (album): Egberto Gismonti, eight-string guitar, piano, wood flutes, voice; Nana Vasconcelos, percussion, berimbau, corpo, voice
    ECM 1089 (1977)

11. *News for Lulu* (album): John Zorn, alto saxophone; George Lewis, trombone; Bill Frisell, electric guitar
    Hat Art CD-6005 (1987)

6 A century of blues guitar

JAS OBRECHT

The pioneers

A century ago, the first strains of blues guitar echoed across the American South. While the style's exact origins are lost in the distant traditions of field hollers and work songs, African influences, spirituals, ragtime, minstrel tunes, folk and pop fare, parlor instrumentals, and other musical forms, one thing is certain: From the beginning, the blues and the guitar have traveled side by side.

The earliest reported sighting of a blues performance occurred in 1903, when bandleader W. C. Handy was awakened in the Tutwiler, Mississippi train station by the strange sounds of a ragged black guitarist. "As he played," Handy wrote in his autobiographical *Father of the Blues*, "he pressed a knife on the strings of the guitar in a manner popularized by the Hawaiian guitarists who used steel bars. The effect was unforgettable. His song, too, struck me instantly: 'Goin' where the Southern cross the Dog.' The singer repeated the line three times, accompanying himself on the guitar with the weirdest music I had ever heard."[1] The man was singing about Moorehead, Mississippi, where the Southern Railroad crossed the Yazoo–Delta Railroad, "the Yellow Dog." Once Handy began orchestrating "Make Me a Pallet on Your Floor" and other popular black folk tunes, his bookings increased. His conclusion? "Negroes react rhythmically to everything. That's how the blues came to be."[2] Handy also described the fundamental structure of the blues which has remained a constant for almost a hundred years: "The songs consisted of simple declarations expressed usually in three lines and set to a kind of earth-born music that was familiar throughout the Southland."[3] Two identical or similar lines were typically answered by a third, and the whole verse was sung over a pattern involving one to three chords set to a straightforward or propulsive rhythm. Unlike field hollers and work songs, the blues was music of leisure; unlike ballads, it allowed complete self-expression. A bluesman could brag, nag, howl at God, diss "the man," or make passionate come-ons. He could fashion himself into a hero, victim, or savior.

Blues music quickly proliferated throughout the South. By 1905, Ma Rainey was singing blues songs with her traveling tent show, and Rev. Gary

Davis had heard "Candy Man" and "Cocaine Blues" in rural South Carolina. But nowhere was the blues more popular than along the Mississippi River, where it was spread by riverboats and medicine shows. Perry Bradford, who oversaw the recording of the world's first blues record, remembered, "The South was especially crazy about the blues, a cry of a broken heart that echoed from every levee and bayou up and down the Mississippi River."[4]

To country preachers and other churchified folk, the blues was "devil's music," fit only for "cornfield niggers," to use the common parlance of the day. Johnny Shines, who rambled with Robert Johnson during the 1930s, recalled, "When I was a kid, if a person heard you singing the blues and recognized your voice, you couldn't go down to their house, around their daughters."[5] To some, even the guitar itself was taboo: when young W. C. Handy proudly brought one home, his father forced him to swap it for a dictionary.

Many of the first-generation blues guitarists lived in an environment as dangerous and unforgiving as any modern 'hood. Few could read or write. Some were blind or missing limbs; many in the South and Texas were trapped in a crooked sharecropping system that kept them in perpetual servitude. Even the slightest infraction of the strict Jim Crow laws – using a "whites only" drinking fountain, for instance, or failing to step off the sidewalk to make way for a white woman – could lead to the chain gang, torture, and lynching. Some Southern communities greeted travelers with signs proclaiming "Nigger, don't let the sun go down on you here." Chain gangs were common sights; extreme poverty was the norm. "In Mississippi," remembered one old bluesman, "it was open season on black folk."[6]

Within many black communities, though, playing blues did have its rewards. Come Saturday night, country blues performers such as Charley Patton and Blind Lemon Jefferson were *stars* who could find moonshine, tips, and appreciative women in virtually any black community, work camp, or non-religious gathering. Most prewar blues songs were set to acoustic instruments – just about every imaginable configuration of piano, harmonica, fiddle, mandolin, banjo, bass, clarinet, saxophone, drums, washboard, and homemade instruments – but most often, especially in rural areas, by an acoustic guitar made by Stella, Gibson, Harmony, or National. As B. B. King remembered,

> Where I grew up at in the Mississippi Delta, there was no other instrument
> that was available to you besides guitar, really, but maybe a harmonica.
> And everybody didn't want to blow somebody else's harmonica. But
> everybody that thought in terms of music would have an old piece of guitar
> somewhere – usually. In my area, they couldn't afford keyboards of any
> kind. Only time I ever seen a piano or organ was when I went to church.[7]

Most Southern blues guitarists started out playing a one-string diddley bow fashioned by attaching a broom wire to a wall and using bottles or rocks as bridges. One hand plucked, while the other fretted or slid along the string with a bottle. Many outstanding guitarists – Robert Johnson, Elmore James, and B. B. King among them – began this way. Others fashioned primitive guitars by attaching a tin can or cigar box to a rough-hewn neck. Those who could save up enough money ordered guitars by catalog, which is how European-influenced parlor guitar music came to exert a profound influence upon the development of blues guitar.

During the late 1800s, parlor music was the rage in white America, and most catalog-bought guitars arrived with a tutorial pamphlet featuring rudimentary songs for the beginner. Two of the most common, "Spanish Fandango" and "Sebastopol," predated the Civil War, and both called for the strings to be tuned to open chords. "Spanish Fandango" in particular served as a starting point for countless rural players, and its harmonic content, voice-leading, and finger-picking pattern flowed directly into the blues of Robert Wilkins, Son House, Furry Lewis, and many others who mastered the song. To this day, the term "Spanish" is sometimes used to describe open G tuning (DGDGBD), while "Sebastopol" refers to open D (DADF♯AD).

While blues music was being played throughout the early twentieth century, no one recorded any samples of it until 1920, when Mamie Smith's jazzy "Crazy Blues" became a breakthrough hit that inspired studio execs to record dozens of women blues singers over the next few years. The recording of solo blues guitarists did not commence until November 23, 1923, when Sylvester Weaver of Louisville, Kentucky, recorded "Guitar Blues," an instrumental with slide melodies and sparse chords, performed lap style with a knife. In ads in *The Chicago Defender* and other black newspapers, Weaver's label, Okeh Records, proclaimed him "The Man With the Talking Guitar," who "certainly plays 'em strong on his big, mean, blue guitar." Weaver was also the first guitarist to back a blues singer on record, a feat he'd accomplished just a week earlier with Sara Martin. By January 1924, Bessie Smith and Clara Smith were recording classic blues with studio guitarists.

The first blues guitar heroes emerged in 1926, when Blind Lemon Jefferson and Blind Blake 78s were released on Paramount Records. Singing of booze, gambling, and dirty mistreating mamas, Jefferson had lived the themes that dominated his songs. He was raised in rural Texas, and had mostly played in the bordellos and streets of Dallas, where his wail could cut across the din of floozies and flivvers. Some of his lyrics were unadorned poetry – jivey and risqué, lonesome and forlorn, a stunning view of society from the perspective of someone at the bottom. Jefferson was a remarkable guitarist, too, flat-picking muscular bass lines and launching into elaborate, meter-stretching solos. "His touch is different from anybody on the guitar – still is," said lifelong fan B. B. King. "I practiced, I tried, I did everything, and still I could never come out with the sound as he did. He was majestic, and he played just a regular little 6-string guitar with a little round hole. It was unbelievable to hear him play. And the way he played with his rhythm patterns, he was way before his time."[8] When he died in 1929, Blind Lemon Jefferson was America's most famous bluesman. His influence was especially felt among white country blues performers such as Frank Hutchinson, Charlie Poole, and Riley Puckett.

Raised along the East Coast, Blind Blake was more swinging and sophisticated. Billed as "The Man With the Famous Piano-Sounding Guitar," he was a fast and facile finger-picker and the unrivalled master of ragtime syncopation. His warm, relaxed voice was a far cry from Jefferson's harsh country blues, and his songs were more urban. Some of Blake's 78s cast him as a hip-talking jazzman or hustling ladies man; others walked the long, lonely road to the gallows. During his heyday, Blake earned most of his income playing Southside Chicago house rent parties. With a piano in the living room, his apartment at 31st and Cottage Grove was the scene of many jams with Little Brother Montgomery, Charlie Spand, Roosevelt Sykes, Tampa Red, Big Bill Broonzy, and other blues notables.

Lonnie Johnson, who launched his recording career in late 1925, became by far the most influential prewar blues guitarist. His dexterity, advanced harmonic sensibility, and distinctive tone sparkled on his classic jazz sessions with Louis Armstrong and Duke Ellington, his unsurpassed jazz guitar duets with Eddie Lang, and stacks of his own blues, sentimental tunes, and ballads. Johnson became the hero of Robert Johnson, T-Bone Walker, B. B. King, and John Lee Hooker, among countless others. He could double on several instruments and knew many guitar styles, from backwoods country stomps to exhilarating solos and dazzling chord climbs. On his records in the 1920s and 1930s, he played a modified nine-string guitar (a twelve-string minus the lower octave strings), using his one-of-a-kind finger vibrato to approximate the sounds of a zither, mandolin, or bottleneck guitar. Lonnie Johnson played well into the 1960s, and was, as Ry Cooder describes, "one of the transcendental people who influenced everybody."[9]

Mississippi was the birthplace of a wide variety of prewar blues styles and performers. Bolton was home of the state's most famous string band, the Chatmon family's Mississippi Sheiks. Descendants of slaves, the Chatmons played to white and black audiences alike, drawing on minstrel tunes, hokum, ragtime, downhome blues, and whining hillbilly music. Their 1930 hit recording of "Sitting on Top of the World" was widely copied, and one of the band's guitarists, Bo Carter, found success as a solo artist as well. In Jackson, Rube Lacy fronted a string band with Son Spand; both men were adept at guitar and mandolin. While Lacy was known as "the blues king," he nodded to another local, Tommy Johnson, as the superior musician. Johnson played with a slippery, danceable swing that mixed double- and triple-meter picking and strumming patterns, and his walking bass in "Big Road Blues" became a staple of the Delta blues guitar style. Johnson sang with a warm, high-pitched voice with a very effective falsetto, and some-times recorded with guitarist Charlie McCoy, who also made records with Ishman Bracey as well as under his own name. Besides blues, the musicians played waltzes and popular tunes.

Skip James from Bentonia was another Jackson regular, but he was an aloof, enigmatic figure who mostly kept to himself. He tuned to an open E minor chord and accompanied his eerie, high-pitched falsetto with masterly finger-picking. With his "rediscovery" in the early 1960s, James became a favorite at folk and blues festivals and something of a mentor to struggling young guitarists.

Fife and drum bands were popular in the northeast Mississippi hill country, as were string bands augmented with saxophones and trumpets, kazoos (or "jazz horns"), wax-papered combs, and percussion ranging from tambourines, woodblocks, and homemade drums to tubs, crates, cans, and chairs. The most popular instrument there, however, was the guitar, as it was in northwest Mississippi, where Charley Patton emerged as the archetypal first-generation Delta bluesman. As a young man, Patton was enamored with the playing of Henry Sloan, an older musician who mostly strummed chords. Patton was among the first Delta musicians to apply intricate rhythms and open tunings to blues music. The gruff singer had moved to Dockery's plan-tation in the heart of the Delta before World War I, and for many years there-after performed at juke joints, parties, and picnics with Tommy Johnson, Willie Brown, and Son House. Patton's celebrated clowning – riding his guitar like a mule, playing behind his head – predated the showboating antics of Guitar Slim, Buddy Guy, and Jimi Hendrix.

Out in the country, most Delta musicians played picnics and Saturday-night getbacks, which were usually held in someone's shack, as Johnny Shines detailed:

> If you sell corn whiskey, on Saturday night, you're going to have a getback. You just take the bed and things down, probably throw sand on the floor, and you put a crap table in the back room, card table somewheres else, and then a dance floor and the musicians in the main room. You'd put a table or a door across something and sell fried fish.[10]

The best money was usually made working alone or in pairs. Once the cotton was planted, the better musicians traveled around from plantation to plantation. Sometimes the plantation store, already the sharecroppers' gathering point, doubled as a juke joint, with a room in back for gambling, dancing, and drinking moonshine.

In larger Mississippi towns like Jackson, Clarksdale, and West Helena, blues musicians played on well-traveled street corners. With the repeal of prohibition in 1933, a scattering of clubs opened in some of the larger river towns. "After Prohibition was broke," Johnny Shines explained, "whiskey come back. And then you could go into little taverns and play. But you went in on your own. They wasn't hiring you. There was many times when I just went in and sit down, and the guy said, 'You play?' 'Yeah.' 'Sit over there and play us a tune.' You sit there and play all night, long as people are pitchin' in nickels and dimes. Sit there and make yourself seven or eight dollars, and that was good money in those days. People work for much less than that for a week."[11] West Helena, Arkansas, scene of the ever-popular *King Biscuit Time* daily radio show and several wide-open gambling joints, was an especially alluring destination for bluesmen from Mississippi, Arkansas, and Tennessee.

Early recordings

The majority of the great prewar Delta blues recordings are directly attributable to H. C. Speir, a white music store owner in Jackson who served as a talent scout for RCA Victor and Paramount. Speir showed a prophetic taste for blues, arranging sessions for Charley Patton, Son House, Skip James, Willie Brown, Tommy Johnson, Ishman Bracey, the Mississippi Sheiks, Robert Johnson, and several others who likely would never have recorded without his intercession. By the end of the 1930s, over forty Mississippi artists had made 78s.

The Delta style is characterized by a strong rhythmic pulse, the use of a slide with open tunings, and thumbed bass notes. Unlike most of his peers, Charley Patton cradled his guitar on his lap to slide, a technique that was most likely brought to the United States mainland during the Hawaiian music craze just after the turn of the century. But another source figured prominently in the creation of bottleneck blues, especially in the rural South. "Slide come from Africa," insisted Johnny Shines. "Matter of fact, all your American music come out of slaves. See, everybody think the bottleneck is something new. The bottleneck was the first guitar playing that the black people did, because he didn't know how to chord a guitar. So he tuned a guitar to open tuning, and he used a slide to make his chords. Before Charley Patton, we only knew cross [open] tunings, and we only knew how to play with the bottleneck."[12]

A convicted murderer and failed preacher, Son House developed his ferocious slide style in the late 1920s, matching powerful bass notes with propulsive treble slides. Portions of his "My Black Mama" and other songs flowed directly into the repertoires of his followers Robert Johnson and Muddy Waters, who came to epitomize the Delta slide style. "Me and my guitar, we have a conversation and talk together," Waters explained. "That's from the Delta style."[13] Other notable Mississippi slidemen included raspy-voiced Bukka White, with his hypnotic guitar-body percussion and slashing slide, and Crying Sam Collins, who emphasized feeling over proper tuning and regular changes. Joe Holmes, who recorded as King Solomon Hill, used his bottleneck to imitate Lonnie Johnson riffs. Mississippi John Hurt, from Avalon, was another talented slider, but also played beautifully syncopated bare-fingered arrangements. Robert Wilkins of Hernando likewise played both slide and bare-fingered, often in open E tuning, while his neighbor Garfield Akers specialized in droning open-ended stomps.

While Muddy Waters would become the man most responsible for carrying Delta blues into the blues-rock mainstream, Robert Johnson deserves credit for creating its most brilliant recordings. "Robert Johnson is the greatest folk-blues guitar player that ever lived," declared Eric Clapton. "He's the greatest singer, the greatest writer."[14] Johnson mastered the Delta style as none had before, learning firsthand from men such as Willie Brown and Son House. He then expanded his music with outside influences from 78s by Lonnie Johnson, Kokomo Arnold, Leroy Carr, and many others, becoming a veritable "human jukebox," as former acquaintances remembered him. Johnson was truly standing at a musical crossroads when he recorded his twenty-nine songs in 1937 and 1938, simultaneously looking back to old-time Delta blues while foretelling the future of electric blues, R&B, and rock and roll.

The Delta blues style thrived in nearby Memphis, especially in the inevitable street renditions of "Poor Boy a Long Ways from Home" and "Roll and Tumble Blues," first recorded in 1929 by Hambone Willie Newbern. Memphis had long been a Mecca for musicians of all varieties. Along Beale Street, thumping country stompers commingled with fife-and-drum ensembles, jazz musicians, hillbillies, bluesmen, and local jug bands led by Gus Cannon and Will Shade. Guitarists Frank Stokes, Jim Jackson, Furry Lewis, and Robert Wilkins were Memphis regulars, while Hambone Willie Newbern, Sleepy John Estes, Mississippi John Hurt, and many others journeyed there to record.

One popular Memphis guitar style was based on pre-blues banjo technique, balancing thumbed bass strums with fingerpicked treble melodies. Played with a bottleneck by someone like Furry Lewis, these stark melodies could be extraordinarily moving. Some of Lewis's inspiration came from Gus Cannon, who around the turn of the century specialized in playing slide banjo while blowing through a jug tied around his neck. Over the decades, Lewis's voice became as deeply haunting as the whining slide that echoed his words or finished his lines.

Another thriving blues community was headquartered in Atlanta, Georgia. Peg Leg Howell played his primitive country blues on a six-string, while several other leading Atlanta bluesmen favored twelve-string instruments. Robert Hicks, who recorded as Barbecue Bob, played twelve-string in a fast, rhythmic style, alternating between bass runs and ringing, frantic bottleneck. He was sometimes accompanied by his brother, twelve-stringer Charley Lincoln; the sheer drive of their playing was occasionally matched by that of their pal, Curley Weaver. By 1928, the best twelve-stringer in town was Blind Willie McTell, who could do it all – slide, ragtime, gospel, blues, imitations of cackling hens and crowing roosters, pianos, and train sounds. Playing with a light touch on a big-bodied Stella twelve-string, McTell created shifting rhythms and resonant melodies that were as distinctive as his clear, somewhat nasal voice. Like Lead Belly, he recorded commercially as well as for the Library of Congress.

Georgia-bred, Mississippi-raised Kokomo Arnold recorded stacks of speedy, adventurous, and downright manic slide 78s, playing both lap style and regular with a flexible sense of time. Robert Johnson recycled portions of his records in "Sweet Home Chicago" and "I Believe I'll Dust My Broom," which, in turn, inspired Elmore James's roaring, reverb-drenched "Dust My Broom" of the 1950s. Casey Bill Weldon, who recorded in Atlanta and Chicago, freely drew from Hawaiian music and swing. Regional sounds developed elsewhere as well. In the Southeast's tobacco belt, Blind Blake's 78s were especially popular, while Blind Boy Fuller, Blind Gary Davis, William Moore, and Willie Walker blended ragtime and blues. St. Louis and East St. Louis had a thriving piano scene headed by Peetie Wheatstraw, Roosevelt Sykes, and Walter Davis, as well as their own guitar stars, such as Lonnie Johnson-influenced Charlie Jordan, and Henry Townsend, who doubled on piano and guitar.

Beaumont, Texas was the fearsome stage for Blind Willie Johnson, a street-corner evangelist with a fierce growl of a voice. On his landmark 1920s gospel and spiritual recordings, Johnson used a pocketknife slide to double his voice, finish a verse, or play a sparking solo. Many of his songs were gathered from old hymnals, and when the spirit moved him, his gruff voice shook with vibrato. His playing displays an exquisite sense of melody, timing, and tone. How fitting that a copy of his landmark instrumental "Dark Was The Night – Cold Was The Ground" (along with music by Chuck Berry and Beethoven) now travels toward the stars aboard the spacecraft *Voyager*.

Dallas's Central Tracks district, with its rows of black-owned stores, saloons, barbershops, and brothels, was the stomping ground of many fine Texas bluesmen, including Blind Lemon Jefferson, Henry Thomas, Willard

"Ramblin'" Thomas, T-Bone Walker, and singer Texas Alexander. Henry Thomas, who played as "Ragtime Texas" aboard trains making the rounds from Dallas to Houston, favored a heavy, stomping strum and occasionally used a capo high on the neck to strum his guitar like a banjo. He also blew quills, creating a sound similar to Mississippi fife music. Ramblin' Thomas, who divided his time between Dallas and Shreveport, Louisiana, tended to pluck a few bass notes or quick, partial chords, followed by a slide figure that doubled his relaxed vocals or added counterpoint. His younger brother Jesse was a more advanced guitarist, as evidenced by the long, flowing, slideless lines on his 1929 Victor sides.

From southwest Louisiana came Huddie Ledbetter, better known as Lead Belly. Lead Belly's voice was field-holler powerful, his twelve-string guitar playing forceful and nimble. He plied muscular bass lines and had an instinctual feel for time, easily changing tempos to heighten a song's drama. Like his acquaintance Blind Lemon, he excelled at speedy single-string breaks. Lead Belly's repertoire was estimated at 500 songs, and he recorded everything from cattle calls, slave songs, and spirituals to square dances, children's music, and Tin Pan Alley. "But when does your guitar talk the best?" his friend Woody Guthrie asked him on a record. "Well," Lead Belly drawled, "my guitar talk the best when I'm playin' and singin' blues."[15]

Urban blues guitarists

Up north, a smoother, more urban style of blues was taking hold. Indianapolis-based Leroy Carr, a dominating force in blues piano, and his longtime partner, talented guitarist Francis "Scrapper" Blackwell, scored a runaway hit with their June 1928 recording of "How Long – How Long Blues," which was one of the first songs learned by Robert Johnson and Muddy Waters.

In Chicago, studio musicians Georgia Tom Dorsey and slide virtuoso Hudson "Tampa Red" Whittaker teamed up in October 1928 to record the hokum classic "It's Tight Like That," which became one of the era's best-selling blues records. Their follow-up, "It's Tight Like That, No. 2," was the first release to proclaim Tampa Red "The Guitar Wizard," a title he certainly deserved. With his sweet resonant tone, good-time feeling, and perfect intonation, Tampa Red was instantly recognizable on records, and he made hundreds of good ones. His early ensembles were crucial to the development of Chicago blues bands, and several of the songs he composed or popularized – "Love Her With a Feeling," "Crying Won't Help You," "Sweet Little Angel," and "It Hurts Me Too" – have become blues standards. Tampa Red's influence stretched all the way from Mississippians Robert Nighthawk,

Muddy Waters, B. B. King, Earl Hooker, and Elmore James to western swing bands and prescient rock and rollers.

Another high wizard of hokum, Big Bill Broonzy, was also a frontrunner in the development of more urban-sounding blues. Raised in Mississippi and based in Chicago, Broonzy was a persuasive singer whose abilities covered many styles, allowing him to enjoy one of the longest careers in blues history. At his peak in the late twenties and early thirties, he excelled at stride-influenced, syncopated playing. He was extremely adept at stomps and fast jive, and the bent notes and hammer-ons of his slow blues were especially poignant. Broonzy proved exceptionally inventive when working within a twelve-bar format, drawing on a seemingly endless variety of string bends, multi-string slides, and other flashy embellishments. Unlike most bluesmen raised in the South, he played most of his works in C, the most common ragtime key. After World War II, Broonzy would play a crucial role in popularizing blues in Great Britain.

By the late 1930s, many Chicago-based blues artists – piano giants Big Maceo Merriweather and Memphis Slim, harmonica ace John Lee "Sonny Boy" Williamson, percussionist Washboard Sam, and guitarists Broonzy, Tampa Red, Memphis Minnie, Big Joe Williams, and Arthur "Big Boy" Crudup – were recording for producer and A&R man Lester Melrose. Occasionally exhilarating but often bland, Melrose's ensemble recordings of blues, jazz, and novelty numbers for Columbia and Victor's Bluebird subsidiary created a market-dominating sound that became known as the "Bluebird Beat." Before the war, these records tended to feature guitar and piano, with occasional support from clarinet, washboard, string bass, and harmonica or kazoo. By the end of World War II, drums and electric guitar had become part of the mix.

Tampa Red was among the first Chicago blues performers to acquire an electric guitar, which he featured on "Anna Lou Blues" from 1940. Two years earlier, though, studio guitarist George Barnes had used an electric guitar on his Chicago sessions with Big Bill Broonzy, Hattie Bolten, Blind John Davis, Jazz Gillum, Merline Johnson, and Washboard Sam. ("When I was young, I hung around Lonnie Johnson," Barnes recalled, "and he taught me how to play the blues. I made over a hundred records with fellows like Big Bill Broonzy, Blind John Davis, and a host of other bluesmen. I was the only white musician on these dates."[16]) By the early 1940s, Memphis Minnie, Big Bill Broonzy, and Moody Jones also had electric guitars.

Like their jazz counterparts, the initial wave of electric blues guitarists were deeply influenced by Charlie Christian, who in 1939 made his spectacular debut with Benny Goodman, leader of the era's most popular swing ensemble. On session after session, Christian had the tonal strength and improvisational ability to play long, flowing solos on a par with those of his bandmates, some of whom were the best in jazz. His impact was immediate, inspiring many acoustic guitarists to switch to amplified guitars, just as Eddie Lang had inspired a massive shift from banjo to acoustic guitar during the 1920s. "The electric guitar as Charlie Christian played it had its own sound," recalled Barney Kessel. "Charlie was the first one to play single lines like a horn. And Charlie's tone was the concept for what is being used today in jazz."[17] Soon after Christian's untimely death in 1941, the sound he pioneered would resound in a dynamic new blues style led by Aaron "T-Bone" Walker.

The postwar blues

At the outbreak of World War II, Jim Crow laws and other social abuses were prevalent throughout the South, and for field hands such as Muddy Waters, Howlin' Wolf, and B. B. King, life had become nearly intolerable. Work agents passing through Southern towns spread the word that jobs were plentiful up north, and thousands of sharecroppers and laborers heard their call and headed north, where, it was believed, people could forge their own destinies among sprawling cities of opportunity. "There was a big demand for steel-driving men and strong-backed women to come north and work in the steel mills and factories," explained New Orleans bluesman Danny Barker. "Automobile industry was begging for help, the steel mills of Detroit, Gary, Indiana, Cleveland, Ohio, Cincinnati. All said, 'Come north. We need workers.' And that's where the Southerners went, because the pay was better and it was a different environment, especially for black people. Above the Mason-Dixon line, where there was less pressure on you, you could walk tall and walk free."[18]

"There was more freedom," agreed Texas bluesman Sammy Price. "You could laugh if you wanted to. In the South, sometimes you'd laugh and the cop put you in jail, thinkin' you laughing at him. Or he put you in for any reason. But when you went to Chicago, you had places where you could actually go in, buy a drink, and drink it, and you didn't have to bow your head in order to get out of the place. It was a community feeling. People were meeting new friends. All of these things had a lot to do with the clubs in the North."[19]

Tampa Red and Big Bill Broonzy, Chicago's top guitarists in the mid 1940s, were renowned for helping struggling musicians newly arrived from the South. Tampa Red's spacious home was a haven for musicians, with its home cooking, guest rooms, and piano-equipped rehearsal room. His visitors and regulars were a veritable who's who of postwar Chicago blues: Broonzy, Blind John Davis, Memphis Slim, Big Maceo, Willie Dixon,

Jazz Gillum, Big Joe Williams, Sonny Boy Williamson I, Doc Clayton, Robert Lockwood, Jr., Arthur Crudup, Washboard Sam, Romeo Nelson, Little Walter, Elmore James, and Muddy Waters. Tampa had a particularly strong influence on another guest, Robert Lee McCollum, who as Robert Nighthawk would merge his mentor's facile slide approach with a sustaining Delta whine.

During the late 1940s into the 1950s, the music of these newcomers became the dominant sound of Chicago blues. The band-driven, "deep-bottom Mississippi blues" of Muddy Waters in particular struck a resonant chord with former Southerners who congregated in West and South Side taverns. Waters had come to town in 1943 with an acoustic Silvertone, which could scarcely cut through the din. "I was banging my hand all up," he recalled, "so I went to a thumbpick. That still wasn't loud enough, so I started playing electric. When I came to Chicago, I had to work my blues up in there. When I did get it through, boy, I bust Chicago wide open with 'em."[20] On the Library of Congress field recordings he made on a Mississippi Delta plantation in the early 1940s, Waters had sung, "I never be satisfied" and "I just can't keep from crying."[21] In Chicago, his message evolved to a roaring proclamation of freedom and sexuality: "I'm a man, spelled 'M,' 'A,' child, 'N.'"

Owing to rationing and material shortages, few blues records were made during World War II. Immediately afterwards, the widespread availability of magnetic tape allowed virtually anyone to make records, and dozens of independent labels sprang into existence. In 1947, Waters landed at Aristocrat, the forerunner of Chess Records. On his early Aristocrat 78s, such as "I Can't Be Satisfied" and "I Feel Like Going Home," Waters played lightly amplified Robert Johnson figures accompanied by stand-up bass. In clubs, though, he delivered a dense and explosive sound with harmonica genius Little Walter, co-guitarist Jimmy Rogers, and drummer Baby Face Leroy. The band was so ferociously good, people nicknamed them the "Headhunters," since they could "cut anyone's head" in local battles of the bands. In 1950, Waters finally recorded with his full lineup for Chess. Vastly different from the jumps and ballads dominating the R&B charts, Waters's surging, beat-heavy rhythms signaled the beginning of the greatest creative era of Chicago blues. Soon Chess and its Checker subsidiary were offering 78s by Little Walter, Jimmy Rogers, Howlin' Wolf, John Brim, J. B. Lenoir, Willie Dixon, Sonny Boy Williamson, Otis Spann, and Eddie Boyd. Many other Chicago blues artists recorded for the smaller independent labels, such as Vee Jay, Atomic H, Cobra, JOB, Parrot, United, Chance, and Cool.

Elmore James and Howlin' Wolf, who featured guitarists Jody Williams and Hubert Sumlin in his Chicago lineup, proved themselves as adept as Muddy Waters in framing Delta blues in a band context. Fronting the roaring

Broomdusters, James bottlenecked in open D tuning on a Kay acoustic outfitted with a soundhole pickup. His Chicago-cut sides for the Fire and Enjoy labels are nothing less than monumental, both in the guitar and the vocal stylings. "After me there will be no more,"[22] James predicted, but following in his wake came J. B. Hutto, Johnny Littlejohn, Hound Dog Taylor, and the all-time cleanest slider of them all, Earl Hooker. "Earl Hooker was a monster," says his cousin John Lee Hooker. "Nobody could beat him."

Just as Muddy Waters, Howlin' Wolf, Elmore James, and many other Mississippians had emigrated to Chicago during the war era, many outstanding bluesmen from Texas and Oklahoma had gone to the West Coast to work in the shipyards, play clubs, and improve their overall lifestyles. Los Angeles, with its community of jump blues honkers, shouters, and wailers, was the home base for Specialty, Aladdin, Modern, Imperial, and other independent labels dedicated to issuing the R&B music being ignored by the majors. One of the first blues stars to record there was T-Bone Walker, who established amplified Texas blues guitar as a fixture in posh nightclubs and concert halls. Walker fronted swinging big bands, and like Charlie Christian, excelled at horn-inspired, single-note solos. "To me," says Johnny Winter, "T-Bone Walker is pretty much the father of the electric blues style. He influenced everybody. He played syncopated, he changed the meter around, and he did things that nobody else did. He knew a lot of chords and was a much broader player than many people are aware of. He was the first guy who did it right, and he influenced everybody who came along after him. He really defined electric blues guitar."[23]

Other bluesmen were soon making their names on the West Coast. Pee Wee Crayton divided his time between Los Angeles and San Francisco. Lowell Fulson, from Texas by way of Oklahoma, moved to Oakland, California, where he hit big with "Three O'Clock Blues" and "Every Day I Have the Blues." Just across the San Francisco Bay, Louisiana-born Saunders King was swinging for the Rhythm label. T-Bone Walker disciple Clarence "Gatemouth" Brown made his first records in Los Angeles in 1947, but stayed in Texas, where he enjoyed a long association with the Houston-based Duke/Peacock label. By the mid 1950s, another generation of Texas-raised blues guitarists began its ascendancy: Johnny "Guitar" Watson relocated to Los Angeles and signed with Federal, while Albert Collins and Johnny Copeland began making singles in Houston.

But not all postwar Texas bluesmen gravitated toward jumping, band-oriented blues. Down-home traditionalists including Lightnin' Hopkins, Lil' Son Jackson, Smokey Hogg, and Frankie Lee Sims were making bristling records that were often a throwback to the prewar era. Hopkins was nearly as traditional as Blind Lemon Jefferson, whom he'd seen and greatly admired, and his cotton-field blues were as earthy as any on record.

"You know the blues come out of the field," Hopkins explained. "That's when you bend down, pickin' that cotton, and sing, 'Oh, Lord, please help me.'"[24] A natural-born storyteller, Hopkins had a genius for improvising songs, and placed a premium on originality. He made dozens of records for a variety of Houston- and Los Angeles-based labels, and by the early 1960s was a regular on the college circuit. During the 1960s, another great voice in old-time Texas country blues emerged from the Brazos country: Mance Lipscomb, a guileless songster and steady-handed finger-picker with a repertoire of nearly a thousand songs. To this day, though, most people associate Texas blues with horn sections and T-Bone-style solos. "A lot of people ask me what's the difference between Chicago blues and Texas blues," Albert Collins observed. "Well, we didn't have harp players and slide guitar players out of Texas, so most of the blues guitars had a horn section. That was the difference. The bigger the band is, the better they like it in Texas. It's hard to go down through there with just a rhythm section and get good response."[25]

During the mid-1950s commercial heyday of postwar blues, independent labels such as Chess, Peacock, and Imperial scored hit after hit with hardcore blues. Then, around the summer of 1955, sales began to dwindle. Some industry executives blamed a depressed economy and the power of television to draw listeners away from radio, the best forum for blues promotion. But just up that radio dial, the real culprit was crackling through loud and clear: rock and roll. Elvis Presley's "That's All Right," a reworked blues song by Arthur "Big Boy" Crudup, and Bill Haley's "Rock Around the Clock" started an avalanche of rock hits, with major and independent labels scrambling to record young artists. Chess signed Chuck Berry and Bo Diddley, who were both fine blues players as well as rockers, and began promoting their records, while the fortunes of older bluesmen such as Muddy Waters and Howlin' Wolf began to dwindle.

In Chicago's West Side clubs, though, a group of dedicated young guitarists was soon exploring an uninhibited new style. The major players – Otis Rush, Magic Sam Maghett, Freddie King, Buddy Guy, Joe Young, Luther Allison, Jimmy Dawkins, and Lonnie Brooks – were all born within a few years of each other, and during their teens or early twenties, they had all come north from Mississippi, Louisiana, or Texas. Their cathartic, vibrato-enriched vocals spoke of heartbreak and love gone wrong. Their story-telling solos were marked by visceral attacks with spiking tones and elastic bends. Their influences ranged from Waters and Wolf to B. B. King, T-Bone Walker, Bobby Bland, and Kenny Burrell. "The West Side sound was really a collaborative effort," described Buddy Guy. "We were the best of friends. During the '50s we used to have those Sunday afternoon guitar battles in blues clubs, where the guy would have a bottle of whiskey out there for the winner.

Luther Allison, myself, Otis Rush, Magic Sam, Earl Hooker – we was all doin' that stuff. There was just a lot of clubs back then, and we were playing them in circles too. Sam was here on Tuesday, Buddy Guy on Wednesday, Otis on Thursday. It was like that, and it was a lot of fun."[26]

Whereas Muddy Waters, Elmore James, and other middle-aged Chicago bluesmen regularly sat down onstage and played acoustics outfitted with soundhole pickups, the West Side upstarts stood tall and favored solidbodies. "Everybody bought Fender guitars," Otis Rush recalled. "This was something new came out. The first one Magic Sam had was a Telecaster, and then he bought a Stratocaster. Buddy had a Stratocaster too. We wanted something loud and powerful. The stronger the amp was, the better for us – that's why you'd hear a lot of loud music. The old Fender Bassman was a big seller and a strong amp."[27]

With powerful guitar jabs and fever-and-chills vocals, Otis Rush was the first among them to score a hit, with his 1956 cover of Willie Dixon's "I Can't Quit You, Baby," released on Cobra Records. Rush was soon moving in progressive directions. His sultry moaning and groaning in "My Love Will Never Die" foreshadowed 1960s soul ballads, while "All Your Love (I Miss Loving)" became a blues standard. The unrelentingly dark "Checking on My Baby" and "Double Trouble" epitomize what has become known as the "West Side sound." On Rush's nod, Cobra recorded Magic Sam in 1957, swamping "All Your Love" and "Everything's Gonna Be Alright" with a then-new tremolo groove. Freddie King, already a session player, released his first single that year, "Country Boy" on the El-Bee label. In 1958, Buddy Guy cut "Sit and Cry" and "Try to Quit You Baby" for Cobra, with Rush on backup guitar. Even on his first Chicago sides, Guy displayed the pleading, gospel-influenced vocals and idiosyncratic solos that remain his stylistic hallmarks. Within a decade of its creation, the "West Side sound" had influenced a generation of blues-rockers led by Mike Bloomfield, Jimi Hendrix, and especially Eric Clapton, who recorded a scorching cover of Otis Rush's "All Your Love" with John Mayall's Bluesbreakers. While some of the West Side originators have retired or passed away, Buddy Guy, Otis Rush, Lonnie Brooks, and Jimmy Dawkins are still carrying on this stylistic tradition.

Some Southern-born postwar bluesmen found success in St. Louis, where Ike Turner, Albert King, and Little Milton were active by the mid 1950s, and Detroit, where John Lee Hooker, Calvin Frazier, Eddie Burns, Bobo Jenkins, Eddie Kirkland, and Baby Boy Warren were regulars at house parties and clubs. Others continued to perform and record in the South. In New Orleans, Eddie "Guitar Slim" Jones thrilled audiences with his over-the-top showmanship, while Earl King found success there with his first Ace single, the two-chord Louisiana blues "Those Lonely, Lonely Nights."

Later in the decade, New Orleans-born Snooks Eaglin began a recording career that simultaneously straddled acoustic blues and R&B. Around Baton Rouge, Louisiana, Slim Harpo, Lightnin' Slim, Silas Hogan, Lazy Lester, and Lonesome Sundown were playing the relaxed, harmonica-and-guitar-driven "swamp blues" heard on many fine Excello releases.

Around the Mississippi Delta, many aspiring guitarists heard Robert Lockwood, Jr., Joe Willie Wilkins, and other guitarists on KFFA's popular *King Biscuit Time* radio program. In Memphis, B. B. King and Rufus Thomas hosted another vital blues radio show. During the early 1950s, producer Sam Phillips recorded B. B. King, Howlin' Wolf, Joe Hill Louis, and Jackie Brenston for his Memphis Recording Service, and then leased the masters to Chess and RPM, who gave the records widespread distribution. By 1955, Phillips's Sun Records had recorded Junior Parker, Walter Horton, Little Milton, James Cotton, Pat Hare, Earl Hooker, Joe Hill Louis, and Doctor Isaiah Ross, not to mention some earthshaking rockabilly by Elvis Presley and Carl Perkins (who aptly described rockabilly as "a country man's song with a black man's rhythm"). Down in Jackson, Mississippi, Lillian McMurry's Trumpet Records provided the pre-Chicago proving ground for Elmore James and Sonny Boy Williamson II.

While B. B. King, John Lee Hooker, Lightnin' Hopkins, and many of their contemporaries found fame as bandleaders and solo artists, other bluesmen proved nearly as influential via their roles as sidemen. Among the first and most impressive of these was Oscar Moore, who had played behind jazz legends Art Tatum and Lionel Hampton before the war and performed with the Nat "King" Cole Trio from 1937 through 1947, when he moved to Los Angeles and joined his brother, guitarist Johnny Moore, in the Three Blazers. In the early 1950s, Matt and Floyd Murphy, Willie Johnson, and Pat Hare exerted their influence in Memphis, while Lafayette Thomas and Johnny Heartsman played sessions in California. Some sidemen became known for their work with one or two artists, such as Eddie Taylor with Jimmy Reed and John Lee Hooker, Hubert Sumlin with Howlin' Wolf, Wayne Bennett and Roy Gaines with Bobby "Blue" Bland, and Jimmy Nolen with James Brown. Other full-time studio specialists included Mickey Baker in New York, Steve Cropper in Memphis, and Earl Hooker in Chicago.

As folk blues gained popularity during the late 1950s and early 1960s, several bluesmen who'd made 78s before World War II were "rediscovered" by blues aficionados and coaxed into recording again. Some, such as Bukka White, Skip James, Black Ace, Furry Lewis, and Mississippi John Hurt, had been performing all along. Son House, who had quit playing, had to be reminded of his old style. Rev. Robert Wilkins had long since forsaken blues for gospel, but his style was virtually intact. Testament, Vanguard, Arhoolie, Columbia, and Prestige/Riverside/Bluesville released new works by the old masters, while Origin Jazz Library and Yazoo Records reissued old 78s on LPs.

As elder bluesmen were being re-appreciated, some talented but previously unrecorded musicians were discovered. Robert Pete Williams was found in a Louisiana penitentiary during the late 1950s. Fred McDowell, who had lived in Memphis during the 1930s, emerged as the reigning slide king of north Mississippi's hill country, where his droning, highly rhythmic bottleneck style and eerie tones are still imitated today. He first recorded for folklorist Alan Lomax in 1959 and went on to make several influential albums of blues and gospel songs. McDowell generously shared his musical knowledge, tutoring Bonnie Raitt and many local musicians, and his song "You Got to Move" became a staple in the Rolling Stones' repertoire.

Transatlantic blues

"Now the story must be told," sang Brownie McGhee, "the blues had a baby, and they called it rock and roll." During the early 1960s, that offspring was the result of an international affair. While Muddy Waters, Howlin' Wolf, John Lee Hooker, and other bluesmen were virtually unknown to white America, they were heroes to the Beatles, Rolling Stones, Animals, Yardbirds, John Mayall's Bluesbreakers, and other British musicians who found their records just as inspirational as those of Elvis Presley, Buddy Holly, and Eddie Cochran. In an ironic yet welcome twist of fate, most white teenagers in America became aware of the great blues names via cover songs and songwriting credits on albums issued by their favorite rock bands.

Great Britain's love affair with the blues began during World War II, when the promotion of American folk blues, especially as played by Lead Belly, Josh White, and Big Bill Broonzy, became a cause célèbre for jazz critics, who spun their 78s on the BBC. By the early 1950s, Britain's trad jazz, a "lite" re-creation of Dixieland and other prewar American styles, was in full swing. One of its stars, Chris Barber, toured the US with his jazz band and arranged for Big Bill Broonzy, Josh White, and Brownie McGhee to perform traditional acoustic blues in British jazz clubs and recital halls.

These and other American bluesmen served as musical touchstones for the first important British guitar stars, Big Jim Sullivan and Hank Marvin. Idolized by young Jimmy Page, studio legend Sullivan was steeped in the records of Lead Belly and Sonny Terry and Brownie McGhee. "When I was starting the guitar," he recalled, "we used to go out on the Thames in a big riverboat with people like Sonny and Brownie and Big Bill Broonzy. They would be playing, and I'd just sit there watching them. That was kind of the highlight for me."[28] Instrumental star Hank Marvin, who formed the

Shadows with Cliff Richard in 1958, likewise cited Broonzy and Lead Belly as his main influences for taking up guitar.

Before his death in August 1958, Big Bill Broonzy recommended that Barber bring Muddy Waters over. Just back from a tour of raucous Southern clubs, Waters, accompanied by pianist Otis Spann, opened his British tour with his Fender Telecaster and amp at full concert volume, causing aghast purists to retreat from the hall and proclaim the performance a musical catastrophe. "They thought I was a Big Bill Broonzy, which I wasn't," Muddy told author James Rooney. "I had my amplifier, and Spann and I was going to do a Chicago thing. We opened up in Leeds, England. I was definitely too loud for them. The next morning we were in the headlines of the paper – 'Screaming Guitar and Howling Piano.' That was when they were into the folk thing before the Rolling Stones."[29] It would not be long, though, before "screaming guitar" would be all the rage.

During the late 1950s, Great Britain was enamored with skiffle, a folksy, bluesy, somewhat heavy-handed answer to America's folk boom. The movement got its name from Dan Burley's "Skiffle Boys," cut in 1946 with Sonny Terry and Brownie McGhee, and hit its peak with Lonnie Donegan's 1956 recording of Lead Belly's "Rock Island Line." Dozens of future British stars got their start strumming skiffle. "Lonnie Donegan set all them kids on the road," remembered George Harrison. "Everybody was in a skiffle group. You only needed two chords."[30]

By the early 1960s, aspiring British musicians were avidly seeking American blues and rock and roll records. Jimmy Page rapidly made the progression through Elvis, Ricky Nelson, and Gene Vincent to the hard-core blues of Elmore James and B. B. King. Eric Clapton formed his first band, the Roosters, to play covers of Lightnin' Slim, Fats Domino, and T-Bone Walker. Former boyhood pals Keith Richards and Mick Jagger woodshedded with Chess records from the mid 1950s, especially those of Muddy Waters and Chuck Berry.

The earliest country blues, issued on LP for the first time by Origin Jazz Library, were likewise enthusiastically received. Columbia's issuing of Robert Johnson's 78s on two albums had an especially profound impact on Clapton, who would ultimately spearhead the British blues boom. "Both of the Robert Johnson albums actually cover all of my desires musically," Clapton recalled. "Every angle of expression and every emotion is expressed on both of those albums."[31] His other early favorites were *Ray Charles Live at Newport*, *The Best of Muddy Waters*, *Howlin' Wolf*, *Freddie King Sings*, Jimmy Reed's *Rockin' with Reed*, Chuck Berry's *One Dozen Berries*, and B. B. King's *Live at the Regal*.

A magnet for aspiring musicians, London's Skiffle Centre was transformed into the London Blues and Barrelhouse Club, where Long John

Baldry and former Barber bandmates Alexis Korner and Cyril Davies held court. Mick Jagger, Brian Jones, Ginger Baker, and Jack Bruce all took turns in Korner's Blues Inc. "We'd all meet in this blues club, Alexis Korner's place," Keith Richards explains. "And Brian, he stunned us playing Elmore James stuff on slide onstage with Alexis, along with Cyril Davies, Nicky Hopkins, and Jack Bruce on bass. All of those guys were gathering together in just a few spots in London."[32] Jagger and Richards were soon sharing a flat with Jones. They named their band after Muddy Waters's "Rollin' Stone," and in the months to come their covers of Bo Diddley, Jimmy Reed, Slim Harpo, Muddy Waters, and Howlin' Wolf tunes would lead a new generation of listeners to the blues. "When we started the Rolling Stones, we were just little kids, right?" Richards reminisced. "We felt we had some of the licks down, but our aim was to turn people on to the blues. If we could turn them on to Muddy and Jimmy Reed and Howlin' Wolf and John Lee Hooker, then our job was done."[33] For black bluesmen back home in America, though, it was a new beginning.

Chess talent scout Willie Dixon, who first played in London in 1960, provided encouragement and demos of his songs to aspiring British rockers. In 1962 Dixon and Memphis Slim helped organize the first of nine annual American Folk Blues Festival tours of Europe. With front-row tickets for the London show, the Rolling Stones and other members of the British rock royalty watched John Lee Hooker, T-Bone Walker, Sonny Terry and Brownie McGhee, and Shakey Jake from just a few feet away. Used to playing Detroit dives, Hooker was floored by the reception: "When I got to England in '62, it was like God just let Jesus go over there. That's all you could hear: 'John Lee Hooker!'"[34] The real thing, amplified and cathartic, had arrived. The following season, Sonny Boy Williamson II, Muddy Waters, Lonnie Johnson, Big Joe Williams, Matt "Guitar" Murphy, Dixon, and Memphis Slim came over. The Yardbirds, with Clapton on guitar, recorded with Williamson at the Crawdaddy Club. By 1965, Buddy Guy, Lightnin' Hopkins, Big Mama Thornton, Mississippi Fred McDowell, Sleepy John Estes, J. B. Lenoir, and Howlin' Wolf had also played overseas.

John Mayall's London-based Bluesbreakers became the testing ground for many upper-echelon British blues guitarists, with Eric Clapton, Mick Taylor, and Peter Green passing through its ranks. Clapton's fire-breathing tracks on Mayall's *Blues Breakers* LP brought him "Clapton Is God" cult status. No mere mimic, Clapton used the sped-up licks of his idols Robert Johnson, Otis Rush, and Albert, B. B., and Freddie King to tap into an emotional reservoir all his own. Soon after the release of *Blues Breakers* in 1966, Clapton formed Cream, which covered Dixon, Waters, and Skip James tunes on its first album.

As the Beatles, Rolling Stones, Yardbirds, Animals, Cream, and other British bands began touring North America and selling millions of albums, the originators who inspired them finally began getting some recognition at home. "That's a funny damn thing," Muddy Waters reported. "Had to get somebody from out of another country to let my white kids over here know where we stand. They're crying for bread and got it in their backyard."[35] For a while, though, it was an uphill battle. Soon after landing in the US, the Beatles announced their desire to see Muddy Waters and Bo Diddley. "Muddy Waters," asked one reporter, "where's that?" An incredulous Paul McCartney is said to have answered, "Don't you know who your own famous people are here?"[36]

But by the time the Beatles landed in America, there were already some savvy – and soon to be highly influential – young musicians studying the blues masters. In Beaumont, Texas, Johnny Winter was playing along to the records of Son House, Robert Johnson, and Muddy Waters, just as John Hammond was doing in New York. In Seattle, Jimi Hendrix was copping licks from his dad's Muddy Waters and B. B. King 45s. In Chicago, Mike Bloomfield, Charlie Musselwhite, and other young white musicians were making pilgrimages to local clubs to jam with Waters, Wolf, Rush, Magic Sam, and other bluesmen. Bloomfield joined harmonica ace Paul Butterfield on the 1965 breakthrough album *The Paul Butterfield Blues Band*, which featured an integrated lineup playing the music of Elmore James, Little Walter, Muddy Waters, and Willie Dixon. America's blues-rock boom was on, and soon powered-up blues songs were being played to stadium crowds by Canned Heat, Blues Project, Fleetwood Mac, Cream, Johnny Winter, the Jimi Hendrix Experience, the Doors, Led Zeppelin, the Jeff Beck Group, and the Allman Brothers Band.

Modern blues

During the 1970s and 1980s, the blues continued to serve as a launch pad for rockers from Aerosmith and the Allman Brothers to Van Halen and ZZ Top. Bluesmen such as James Cotton, Buddy Guy and Junior Wells, and Albert Collins continued to tour the country and make records, while blues specialty labels like Delmark and Alligator made new recordings of venerable performers and introduced many up-and-comers, such as Lurrie Bell. By decade's end, the predominantly white Fabulous Thunderbirds, Roomful of Blues, and the Nighthawks, all of which blended blues, R&B, jump, and rock, had become trendy. Blues strains were resounding in world beat styles as well, with Donald Kinsey incorporating Albert King-approved licks into his performances with Bob Marley & The Wailers, and many west African musicians drawing inspiration from American blues.

Stevie Ray Vaughan's 1983 debut album, *Texas Flood*, gave the blues its biggest boost since the British Invasion. An unabashed admirer of Albert King, Lonnie Mack, Guitar Slim, and Jimi Hendrix, Vaughan had inescapable charisma and a white-hot sound based closely on that of his heroes, and his releases drew a massive audience to the blues. Until his tragic death seven years later, Vaughan remained America's foremost blues figure. Straddling blues and R&B, Robert Cray's 1986 Grammy Award-winning album *Strong Persuader* also hit hard on the crossover market, making it further up the Top 40 charts than any of Vaughan's releases.

Just as the British bands had helped resurrect the careers of bluesmen in the mid 1960s, the success of Vaughan and Cray brought an upswing in bookings, reissues, and new sessions for veterans such as Johnny "Clyde" Copeland, Albert King, Albert Collins, Lowell Fulson, Koko Taylor, Etta James, Gatemouth Brown, Otis Rush, Son Seals, Robert Lockwood, Jr., Lonnie Brooks, and Luther Allison. Meanwhile, traditional-minded performers such as Bowling Green John Cephas, Rory Block, and John Hammond focused on recreating – and occasionally updating – classic prewar country blues. The Kinsey Report and Joe Louis Walker successfully merged rock and funk, and a new school of soul blues (in which guitar played a lesser role) sprang up in Mississippi and other parts of the South, with Z. Z. Hill, Bobby Bland, Bobby Rush, and Little Milton at the head of the class.

The rock–blues crossover trend intensified in the late 1980s when B. B. King recorded with U2 and made it onto MTV. John Lee Hooker followed suit in the 1990s, recording hits with Carlos Santana and Bonnie Raitt before scoring his most lucrative gig ever, appearing in a televised Pepsi commercial. Eric Clapton enjoyed widespread commercial success by revisiting his country blues roots on 1992's *Unplugged*, and then playing a well-received set of electric blues covers on 1994's *From the Cradle*; he capped the decade with a two-CD retrospective called *Blues*. The Rolling Stones highlighted songs by Robert Johnson, Fred McDowell, Willie Dixon, and Muddy Waters during their celebrated tours of the 1990s. Buddy Guy, Otis Rush, and many other longtime bluesmen made tough new albums, and hundreds of CD reissues of previously recorded prewar and postwar blues songs hit the market.

By the late 1990s, blues festivals and cruises had become big summer draws, blues societies and magazines had proliferated, and the most dedicated fans were making pilgrimages to Mississippi to see bluesmen play their home turf, with favorite destinations being Big Jack Johnson and Booba Barnes in local clubs, and R. L. Burnside and Junior Kimbrough at authentic juke joints. And while most new blues releases tended to feature headliners backed by studio bands, Rooster Blues and Fat Possum specialized in capturing the primal, workaday band sounds of R. L. Burnside and sons, Junior Kimbrough, T-Model Ford, Booba Barnes, the Jelly Roll Kings, and Lonnie Shields.

The blues revival continues to this day, with B. B. King, Hubert Sumlin, Buddy Guy, and Otis Rush still headlining, and newer acts like Bernard Allison, Alvin Youngblood Hart, Corey Harris, Keb' Mo', Kenny Wayne Shepherd, Jonny Lang, and Deborah Coleman filling in the ranks. And whether they know it or not, virtually every blues guitarist is the musical descendant of that nameless man W. C. Handy saw in the Mississippi train station a century ago.

7 The turn to noise: rock guitar from the 1950s to the 1970s

STEVE WAKSMAN

Accidents will happen

Did rock and roll guitar emerge by accident? Certainly the creation of rock and roll itself was a complex phenomenon indicative of the shifting tides of race, class, and popular music in the mid-twentieth century United States. And yet, amidst the broader historical currents that one might consider in any rock and roll chronicle, there also exist the odd details and apparent accidents that can be seen to have made all the difference in the world. Take, for instance, the 1951 recording of "Rocket 88" by Jackie Brenston with Ike Turner and his Rhythm Kings. Said by many historians to have been the first bona fide rock and roll recording,[1] "Rocket 88" achieved much of its distinctive sound from an accident that happened on the way to the Memphis recording studio run by Sam Phillips. Guitarist Willie Kizart's amplifier fell from the roof of the band's car, leaving the amp with a burst speaker cone. Lacking the time and the resources to fix it, Phillips and the band began experimenting, and after a while found that the fuzzy tone produced by the broken speaker sounded good, giving Kizart's electric guitar a heavier sound that was almost more like a saxophone than a guitar, but was also thoroughly electric.[2] With this unique electric guitar sound holding down the bottom end of the song, "Rocket 88" took shape as a song with as much drive as the car about which Jackie Brenston sang, and laid some of the groundwork for the reconstruction of rhythm and blues that would subsequently become known as rock and roll.

Some years later, another guitarist, Paul Burlison, made a similar accidental discovery. One night Burlison dropped his amplifier before taking the stage with his group, the Rock 'n' Roll Trio, one of the most wildly energetic white rockabilly groups of the early rock and roll era. When the Trio began its first number Burlison and his bandmates were quickly aware that something was amiss. As Burlison recounted in a later interview, singer Johnny Burnett "looked around and kind of grinned. I gave him a look right back; I didn't know what it was with the amp . . . There wasn't enough distortion to really stop. It just sounded pleasant: like a fuzzy tone."[3] After the band was done with its set, Burlison proceeded to examine his amplifier to check for the source of the new sound: "I took the back off and checked all the tubes.

Looking from the backside, I saw the third tube over had dropped down a little bit. I pushed it up and I hit the strings, and it worked fine. When I'd pull it back down and I'd wiggle it, it sounded distorted."[4] Through such sonic detective work, Burlison was able to convert an accidental occurrence into a deliberate means of achieving added distortion with his guitar tone. Only weeks later, he would put this discovery to use during the Rock 'n' Roll Trio's classic 1956 recording of "Train Kept A-Rollin'," on which Burlison played a fuzzed-out, octave-laden solo on the first and sixth strings of his guitar that stretched the limits of contemporary sound engineering and set the stage for the later experiments in distortion by bands such as the Yardbirds, who would cover the song in 1965.

Willie Kizart and Paul Burlison may not be the first names one would expect to encounter in a history of rock and roll guitar. However, the "accidents" in which they were involved, and the sounds and songs that resulted, are paradigmatic examples of the ways in which rock and roll entailed, among other things, a new set of approaches to the electric guitar. Not that these new sounds were the exclusive domain of rock and roll musicians; Burlison himself admitted that the sound he attained on "Train Kept A-Rollin'" was one he had encountered before among the African American blues and rhythm and blues musicians playing the clubs along Beale Street in Memphis, Tennessee, where the Rock 'n' Roll Trio was formed.[5] Instead, guitarists such as Kizart and Burlison, Bo Diddley and Chuck Berry, Scotty Moore and Carl Perkins were all part of a broader wave of sonic exploration and experimentation that began during the late 1940s and extended into the 1950s, and that centered around the electric guitar.[6] This was more than a matter of fusing (black) blues and (white) country musical styles, as the development of rock and roll has so often been explained. The distorted tones issuing from the era's electric guitars were indicative of a deeper shift in the cultural disposition toward sound, a shift that was built around the musical incorporation of tones and timbres that had previously been classified as little more than noise.

French social theorist Jacques Attali has assigned a significance to noise that goes well beyond a simple pejorative usage. According to Attali, the boundary between music and noise is carefully guarded in modern societies, for it is a boundary that is fundamental to the production and maintenance of social differentiation and hierarchy. Noise is that which is defined as outside the norms of proper musical conduct, an unharmonious racket that disrupts social as well as musical order and is thus subject to derogation, or even to silencing measures. By the same token, though, noise also contains within it a certain transformative potential, a possibility of dissolving old norms and creating "new orders, unstable and changing."[7] The formation of rock and roll in the early to mid 1950s was a definitive moment in the recent history of US popular music when the balance of authority between music and noise altered considerably. That this moment also involved a significant level of interpenetration between black and white musical elements was no accident. It was African American blues musicians who in the late 1940s began the usage of the electric guitar in a manner consistent with a longer-standing "heterogeneous sound ideal" derived from African musical practices. According to historian and musicologist Samuel Floyd, this ideal was marked by a preference for "timbres that contrast rather than blend," and the resultant sound was a "heterogeneous fusion" of disparate sonoric elements.[8] The turn to noise among rock and roll guitarists, in the form of fuzz, distortion, and other effects that centered around the creative uses of amplification, was in large part an outgrowth of a two-sided process of adaptation involving, on the one hand, African American musicians who were using the electric guitar to innovate within an exisiting tradition of sonoric invention, and on the other hand, white Southern musicians who were caught up in the expressive possibilities of African American music.

The noise of the electric guitar in early rock and roll was not a thing unto itself. It interacted with the pulsing rhythms and the exuberant, at times guttural vocal styles that characterized the music to create an overall effect. By the same token, it was often supplemented by the visual flamboyance of the performers, whose movements onstage and on screen (both in the teen exploitation films that presented the music and on the relatively new mass medium of television) provided a bodily correlate to the unruly excitement conveyed by the sound. No doubt the most celebrated confluence of physical and musical "noise" came during Elvis Presley's string of 1956 television appearances, culminating in his (in)famous, hip-thrusting performance of "Hound Dog" on *The Milton Berle Show*. What remains striking in his performances on the shows of Berle, the Dorsey Brothers, and others is how Presley's movements seem at once highly conventionalized and incredibly spontaneous, how the undertaking of a solo by Scotty Moore on his electric guitar would invariably send Presley's lower torso into motion, only to rest when he had to reassume his position at the microphone (on the Berle show, freed by the absence of his acoustic guitar, Presley's physical routine was heightened almost to the point of self-parody).[9] As Gilbert Rodman has noted, Presley's widely viewed performances of physical enjoyment in seemingly direct response to Scotty Moore's electric guitar had much to do with solidifying the position of the guitar as *the* rock and roll instrument at a time when other instruments such as the piano and the saxophone had an equally high profile.[10]

Another performer who recognized the value of the electric guitar as a visual icon was Chuck Berry, arguably the definitive guitarist of the early rock and roll era. With his famous duck walk, Berry struck a pose that took full advantage of the electric guitar's unique physical qualities: bending his knees to bring his body toward the ground, pacing back and forth across the stage, his head butting forwards and back while his guitar pointed out from his body in a position that was playfully rather than aggressively phallic.[11] That Berry most commonly used the duck walk in the midst of a guitar solo only heightened the conjunction of bodily flamboyance with musical virtuosity. As with the incorporation of noise, such moves were carried into rock and roll from the blues arena, where African American performers such as T-Bone Walker and Guitar Slim converted the blues club into a space where black performers (especially male performers) could enact forms of physical assertion unavailable in their everyday lives away from the stage. Berry's ability to enact some version of these antics in the more mixed-race, or white-dominated, environments that he inhabited says much about the changing expectations of white audiences during the early years of rock and roll, and about Berry's success in tailoring an image that was acceptable to white audiences while still allowing himself a significant amount of expressive license.

The electric guitar was as central to the substance of Berry's music as it was to the style of his performance, if not more so. Almost all of his best-known recordings begin with an unaccompanied electric guitar, quickly establishing the instrument as the lead voice of his songs. Sometimes Berry merely strums a chord, as with the introduction to "Rock and Roll Music," but often the figures he used were more elaborate, as in "Roll Over Beethoven" and "Johnny B. Goode." The latter song, recorded in 1957, was Berry's foremost musical statement, not only because of the quality of the playing but because the structure of the song created a story of mythic proportions concerning the importance of the electric guitar as a medium of rock and roll expression and success.[12] Opening the song is what has certainly become the archetypal Chuck Berry guitar lick, a series of single notes and double-stops in the key of B♭ that follows the harmonic logic of the blues but with an added layer of rhythmic propulsion. Berry's lyrics recount the story of Johnny B. Goode, a "country boy" from Louisiana "who never learned to read and write so well / but he could play that guitar just like a-ringing a bell." As Berry moves into the chorus, his shouts of "Go" to Johnny ("Go! Go Johnny Go!") are met at each turn with a brief burst of guitar, a motif that sets the stage for the dramatic guitar solo that splits the song in half and allows Berry to stand in for the success of his fictive hero, Johnny. In all, "Johnny B. Goode" finds Berry investing the electric guitar with considerable symbolic value at the same time as he set a new standard for rock guitar performance that would exert considerable influence over the next generation of rock and roll guitarists.

Instrumental interlude

Unfortunately, Berry's career went into remission within only a couple years of the release of "Johnny B. Goode"; and by the accounts of many, so did rock and roll in general. However, one could well say that it was during the late 1950s and early 1960s, the ostensible moment of decline with regard to early rock and roll, that the electric guitar solidified its place at the center of the music. Specifically, these years saw the flourishing of the rock guitar instrumental, an offbeat subgenre that was patterned after the successful and influential instrumental recordings of electric guitar innovators Les Paul and Chet Atkins, among others.[13] The leader of the instrumental pack, Duane Eddy, used a Gretsch Chet Atkins signature guitar to achieve his trademark twangy tone on such hits as "Rebel Rouser" and "Peter Gunn." According to Dan Forte, Eddy's tone arose through the combination of the tremolo function of his amplifier (sending a distinctive quaver through the electronic signal), a significant amount of reverb, and the manipulation of the vibrato bar all applied to the accessible melodies that Eddy played on the bass strings of his hollowbody guitar.[14] Taking a more crude path toward sonic innovation was Link Wray, who used an old and tried method for altering the tone of his electric guitar, punching holes in the speakers of his Premier amplifier to bring out the fuzztone qualities of his setup.[15] "Rumble," recorded in 1958, set a new standard for distortion in the rock guitar lexicon. The slow, unobtrusive rhythmic backing of Shorty Horton on bass and Doug Wray on drums left a wide-open space for Link Wray to fill with his menacing power chords. Culminating in a meltdown of fuzz and exaggerated tremolo effects, "Rumble" showed Wray to be a guitarist who took unprecedented advantage of the sheer sound of the electric guitar.

During the early 1960s, the locus of guitar-based instrumental rock moved to the West Coast (leaving aside the influential British band the Shadows). The Pacific Northwest was to be a haven for a developing "garage band" aesthetic over the course of the 1960s. Leading the charge in this movement was the Ventures, a Seattle quartet whose 1960 hit recording, "Walk, Don't Run," was marked by crisp, tightly woven, and stripped-down interplay between the band's guitarists, Don Wilson and Bob Bogle (Nokie Edwards, the bassist on the track, would later assume the lead guitarist role for the band, while Bogle switched to bass). Originally written by jazz guitarist Johnny Smith and subsequently covered in characteristically proficient fashion by Chet Atkins, "Walk, Don't Run" was significantly simplified by the Ventures, a move that was key to the song's success, according to the band.[16] Over the next decade, the Ventures would score several more hits in the same instrumental vein, mutating their style just enough to fit the current popular sounds. One of the styles with which they found the most success was surf rock, another West Coast instrumental offshoot. Southern California was, unsurprisingly, the principal home of the surf rock style, and its main proponent was the self-proclaimed "King of the Surf Guitar," Dick Dale. Like Duane Eddy and Link Wray, Dale as an electric guitarist had a penchant for sonic exploration. Working closely with Leo Fender, the esteemed Southern California electric guitar designer and entrepreneur, Dale pioneered a loud, reverb-soaked musical style that was made to evoke the power of the waves crashing around the surfer's body.[17] In the words of Patrick Ganahl, "Dick's guitar style combined heavy, thick, snapping bass runs with staccato, chiming, often double-picked guitar lines. It was all played through a reverb, but it wasn't thin like Duane Eddy's sound, or slinky and full of echo like that of most other surf bands."[18] Largely through Dale's widespread local influence, surf rock became one of the defining sounds of the early 1960s, and the success of the style had much to do with the electric guitar remaining in the foreground of rock and roll's shifting tides.

Electricity

Surf music subsided considerably in popularity by the mid-1960s, but guitarists looking to expand the sonoric dimensions of rock would soon find other outlets. Perhaps the most notable occurrence in the latter half of the decade was the emergence of England as a crucible of electric guitar activity. Journalist Chris Welch's list of the "Magnificent Seven," seven guitarists of clearly superior talent in London c. 1967, was indicative of this geographic shift in the prominence of the electric guitar, as well as pointing to a new level of prestige open to rock guitarists.[19] By the dictates of contemporary guitar canonization, the list holds few surprises; the oddest inclusion is Stevie Winwood, who at the time had just left the Spencer Davis Group to form Traffic. Otherwise, the guitarists featured were Eric Clapton, in the throes of his tenure with Cream; Jimi Hendrix, fresh from his appearance at the Monterey Pop Festival; Pete Townshend, also fresh from Monterey and comfortably ensconced as leader of the Who; Jeff Beck, departed from the Yardbirds and trying to forge a solo career; Jimmy Page, then leading the last lineup of the Yardbirds; and Peter Green, who had just formed Fleetwood Mac after a tenure with John Mayall's Bluesbreakers. Together, these guitarists represented the convergence of electric guitar-based virtuosity with an affinity for African American music, and particularly the blues, in a manner that echoed some of the processes involved in the previous decade's music but with a new degree of intensity. For as the list itself indicates, the electric guitar and its practitioners had been elevated by the mid-1960s into a position of relative supremacy within the world of rock, such that the question of who was the best guitarist in rock became more than a passing concern. It was a question that cut to the very quick of the music, speaking to the directions in which it seemed to be moving.

It was moreover a question in which were embedded some of the deepest issues that had guided the recent development of rock. That adherence to some kind of blues-based aesthetic was almost a given among rock guitarists in the mid- to late 1960s, for instance, had much to do with the ways in which the electric guitar had been perceived by musicians in the US and, especially, England to be a means of entering an alternative world of social and musical values. Such notions were particularly pronounced for the white British musicians who gravitated to the electric guitar due to the doubly alien nature of blues and rock and roll as styles that were "black" and "American."[20] Thus did Eric Clapton, the figurehead of Chris Welch's "Magnificent Seven," recount in a *Rolling Stone* interview his progressive immersion in the world of black American music: "At first I played exactly like Chuck Berry for six or seven months . . . Then I got into older bluesmen. Because he was so readily available I dug Big Bill Broonzy; then I heard a lot of cats I had never heard of before: Robert Johnson and Skip James and Blind Boy Fuller. I just finally got completely overwhelmed in this brand-new world. I studied it and listened to it and went right down in it and came back up in it."[21] As Clapton came back up, his affinity for the blues became a deep-seated belief in the purity of the blues as a musical way that stood opposed to the commercial pressures of the pop industry. When he quit the British rave-up band the Yardbirds in 1964 out of frustration with their "commercial" career path, he demonstrated a commitment to a brand of blues-based authenticity within which artistic integrity was indissociable from the idealization of "real" black music; and such values, in turn, laid the groundwork for his subsequent lionization as a member of John Mayall's Bluesbreakers, during which time Clapton was famously hailed as a "God" of the electric guitar. The lone *Blues Breakers* album that Clapton recorded with Mayall captures the guitarist at the height of his immersion in the blues, using the fat tone of his Gibson guitar to achieve levels of sustain that, in turn, allowed him to stress the value of individual notes in a manner avowedly indebted to African American blues guitarists such as Otis Rush and Freddie King (the original performers of the album's two lead tracks, "All Your Love" and "Hideaway," respectively).

Other guitarists, though drawing significantly upon African American musical forms, were less steadfast than Clapton in sticking with the blues (and Clapton himself, it should be noted, departed from a purist approach to the music with his next band, Cream, formed in 1966). Jeff Beck, Clapton's successor in the Yardbirds, developed a guitar style that owed as much to the pre-rock and roll pyrotechnics of Les Paul as it did to Beck's favored rock and roll guitarist, Cliff Gallup, the former sideman with Gene Vincent. More notably, Beck showed a preference for electronic effects that outstripped his more blues-oriented peer and went hand-in-hand with the "experimental" pop ethos that the Yardbirds followed after Clapton's departure. The feedback-inflected solos that Beck played with the band arose from the poor playing conditions in the mid-1960s London clubs, where feedback was "unavoidable...All the amps were underpowered and screwed up full volume and always whistling...It would feed back, so I decided to use it rather than fight it."[22] On the 1966 Yardbirds album, *Roger the Engineer*, one can readily hear Beck's preoccupation with electronic sounds. The first cut, "Lost Woman," finds the guitarist lacing the song's midsection with a mix of distortion-laden power chords and feedback that provide a backdrop for Keith Relf's harmonica, while the jumpy blues number "The Nazz are Blue" features Beck slowing down the pace mid-song with a brief interlude during which one of his bends mutates into a note of feedback that decays just as the band picks up the tempo once again.

In this capacity, Beck was perhaps unwittingly following the methods pioneered by blues guitarists such as Buddy Guy in the clubs of Chicago's South and West Sides.[23] His efforts further paralleled those of Pete Townshend, architect of a wall-of-feedback approach as guitarist for the Who. Using the newly-developed Marshall amplifiers that had been built in response to the desire among British guitarists to play with greater volume and greater control over their distortion levels,[24] Townshend discovered that the sounds issuing from his setup, if used creatively, could enhance not only the musical possibilities of the electric guitar but the theatrical aspects of rock performance. In a 1968 interview, Townshend recalled his turn to feedback:

> I used to play at this place where I put my amp on the piano, so the speaker was right opposite my guitar. One day, I was hitting this note and I was going *ba-ba-bam* and the amplifier was going *ur-ur-ur-ur* on its own. I said to myself, "That's fun. I'll fool around with that." And I started to pretend I was an airplane. Everyone went completely crazy.
>
> I started to use it, I started to control it. I regulated the guitar so that the middle pickup was preamped on the inside with a battery and raised right onto the strings so that it would feed back as soon as I switched it on. And I could control it and go through all kinds of things.[25]

Like Paul Burlison and Willie Kizart had done in the 1950s, so in the 1960s did Pete Townshend take a sonic accident and appropriate it, expand upon it and refine it so that it became a new way of crafting sound by electronic means. Along with the new potential for extreme volume and excessive distortion contained in changing technologies of amplification, feedback became a resource for once again challenging the line between acceptable and unacceptable noise in popular music, as on the early Who single, "Anyway,

Anyhow, Anywhere," on which Townshend's sonic proclivities were most evident. It also became the perfect auditory complement for Townshend's later, and much celebrated, act of smashing his electric guitar as the cap to the Who's shows, a performative flourish that seemed at once to celebrate the power residing in the instrument and to renounce that power as something that could potentially overwhelm its users.

Drawing together deep-seated immersion in the blues with far-flung explorations in electronic sound was Jimi Hendrix, the African American guitarist who, as legend would have it, only found success upon leaving the United States for the foreign shores of England. Amidst the competitive, guitar-centered British music scene, Hendrix seemed to find a context for his creativity that had been largely absent in the States. He also stepped into a setting in which his visible and symbolic otherness as a black American musician became a key mark of distinction that heightened the aura of excitement, challenge and possibility perceived within his approach to the electric guitar. Eric Clapton and Pete Townshend were two of the guitarists who felt both defeated and inspired by their first encounters with Hendrix, an ambivalence that Townshend has voiced most evocatively: "[Watching Hendrix play] *destroyed* me . . . I mean, I was glad to be alive, but it was horrifying. Because he took back black music. He took R&B back. He came and stole it back. He made it very evident that that's what he was doing . . . And when he took his music back, he took a lot of the trimmings back, too."[26] Those trimmings included Townshend's demonstrative and destructive approach to electric guitar performance, which Hendrix reappropriated to greatest effect in his appearance at the Monterey Pop Festival in June 1967. Climaxing his set with a cover of the Troggs' "Wild Thing," Hendrix moved the rough-and-tumble pop song into a fit of unmitigated electronic noise that was accompanied by one of the most physically flamboyant outbursts to have graced a rock and roll stage. First simulating intercourse with his guitar and amplifier, Hendrix then moved to the front of the stage, where he proceeded to douse his guitar with lighter fluid and set it afire. Kneeling over the tortured instrument, Hendrix conjured the flames higher and then, standing up, smashed it to pieces and flung its scorched bits into the crowd before stomping off the stage, amplifiers still squealing with feedback.

"Wild Thing" found Hendrix breathing assaultive life into a version of idealized black manhood as a representation of uncontrolled physical expression. More generally, though, Hendrix's uses of the electric guitar gave lie to the notion that his talents lay principally in the realm of spontaneous outburst. Musically speaking, what set Hendrix apart from his peers in England and the US was the breadth of possibilities he heard, and was able to exploit, in the creation of sound by electronic means. Hendrix's former bandmate, Noel Redding, captured this quality of Hendrix's playing in his autobiography: "Jimi's sound had been a combination of impeccable playing of the Stratocaster and VOLUME. He had this inimitable ability to incorporate even the minutest sound coming from his guitar into a tune."[27] "Third Stone from the Sun," from the debut album by Hendrix and the Experience, *Are You Experienced?*, especially showed the guitarist putting sound to innovative uses. A rather obtuse piece of musical science fiction, "Third Stone" begins with some lush chord voicings atop a rather sprightly, jazz-inflected bass line. With Hendrix's vocals buried in the mix, the song proceeds toward a melody based around a set of Wes Montgomery-style octaves. About half-way through the track's six minutes, the melody disintegrates via the tremolo bar on Hendrix's Stratocaster, to be supplanted by wave after wave of atonal growls and high-pitched, sustaining feedback notes that the guitarist orchestrates into a free-form dance of sound.

Such sonic abstraction would inform much of Hendrix's later recorded work, most notably the sidelong suite of "1983 (A Merman I Should Turn to Be)" and "Moon Turn the Tides" on the 1968 double album, *Electric Ladyland*. Yet Hendrix's uses of noise were not always couched in these abstract terms. At times, they were inflected by more philosophical or political intentions, indicative of his ideas about the interconnectedness of music, sound and society. On several occasions, Hendrix voiced a belief that music had significant transformative potential, that sound could lead people toward new ways of relating to one another; and at one point he even called for a "new national anthem" to repair the divisions running through American society.[28] With his performance of the "Star-Spangled Banner" at the 1969 Woodstock festival, Hendrix gave musical shape to such pronouncements, enacting a war between music and noise in which the familiar strains of the national anthem were continually disrupted by shards of feedback and distortion-heavy layers of notes that were bent into all manner of permutations by the vibrato bar of his Fender Stratocaster. Hendrix used the electric guitar to translate the fractiousness of late-1960s American society into a musical statement that was at once a supreme act of defamiliarization and a stunning political critique.[29]

Beyond the threshold

Jimi Hendrix was by no means the only musician to have viewed the electric guitar as an agent of transformation at the end of the 1960s. Bands as different in orientation as San Francisco's Grateful Dead and Detroit's the MC5 were using amplification in ways that were expected to establish new forms of community through the shared bodily stimulation provoked by electric sound; Leni Sinclair, a key member of the MC5 entourage, went so far as to proclaim that "the turning point in the history of western civilization was reached with the invention of the electric guitar."[30] However, by the early 1970s, the progressive nature of the electric guitar, and of rock music more generally, was no longer so widely promoted even within the divided community of rock and roll fans, musicians, and critics. The 1969 Rolling Stones concert at the Altamont Speedway in California has been assigned an almost mythic importance as a moment, only months after the supposed triumph of Woodstock, when the limits and, indeed, the failures of rock's potential for community were brought into focus. Just as important, though, was the growing recognition that rock music was not as all-inclusive as had been thought, that in particular the rock and roll "community" was very much a male domain. Out of such awareness, Susan Hiwatt wrote of the preponderance of "cock rock," of music being used to uphold a sort of male bonding within which the roles ascribed to women were quite narrow, and not so far removed from conventional notions of "a woman's place." According to Hiwatt, the idealization of the male guitarist that had increasingly taken root during the 1960s was a key contributing factor to this phenomenon, such that "it blew my mind the first time I heard about a woman playing an electric guitar. Partly because of the whole idea we have that women can't understand anything about electronics . . . and also because women are supposed to be composed, gentle, play soft songs."[31]

The emergent forms of rock guitar as the 1970s began did not tend to involve playing "soft" songs. Granted, a number of musicians turned more and more to acoustic guitars to evoke a rustic, "mature" sensibility that was set in opposition to "harder" rock sounds. But the style of electric guitar playing that stressed sonic excess and flamboyant virtuosity was, if anything, revivified in the burgeoning rock style that became known as heavy metal. Leading the way in this movement was Jimmy Page, once guitarist for the Yardbirds, who throughout the 1970s led one of the decade's biggest bands, Led Zeppelin. Although Zeppelin as a band were notable for their ability to cross the divide between soft and loud sounds that structured so much of the era's music, Page as electric guitarist inhabited a role that had been carved out by figures like Hendrix, Beck, and Clapton, and was more squarely a "hard" rock phenomenon: the guitar hero. How Page occupied this role can best be observed through his famed "violin bow" segment captured in the 1976 Led Zeppelin concert documentary, *The Song Remains the Same*. In the midst of a lengthy (27-minute) rendition of "Dazed and Confused," one of the band's signature songs, Page is left to his own devices alone onstage. With violin bow in hand, the guitarist produces a series of echoing chords and unusual sonic effects organized into a free-floating structure that gives him maximum room for experimentation. In the context of the performance, the violin bow serves a two-fold purpose, both sides of which played into the guitar hero persona: on the one hand, the bow is a device that highlights Page's musical resourcefulness, his ability to create evocative sounds through technically demanding means; on the other hand, the bow, as a symbol borrowed from classical music, lends Page's performance a brand of virtuosic authority that transcends the usual rock conventions.[32]

A wealth of other guitarists assumed the trappings of guitar heroism during the 1970s, in one form or another. Ritchie Blackmore, lead guitarist for Deep Purple, perhaps most closely paralleled Page in the exhibitionism he brought to the arena rock stage. Blackmore's virtuosity was built upon extremes. On the one hand, he was responsible for some of the most simple, but also most enduring riffs in the history of rock guitar. His three-chord (plus a half-step) progression on "Smoke on the Water" became a ubiquitous garage band staple over the course of the 1970s, and the riff for "Space Truckin'," with its well-timed pauses and power-chord precision, enjoyed a similar fate. On the other hand, Blackmore's solos were marked by a significant degree of technical accomplishment. The rapidly plucked, classically oriented arpeggios of "Highway Star" in particular would come to have considerable influence upon the next generation of heavy metal guitarists, though also significant was the guitarist's extroverted use of the tremolo bar in a manner that was most evocative of Jimi Hendrix.[33]

Drawing even more heavily upon the influence of Hendrix was Robin Trower, former guitarist for Procol Harum, who forged a solo career by reinventing himself in the musical image of the deceased guitarist. Trower crafted a brand of blues-based electric guitar that earned him considerable accolades from the likes of *Guitar Player* magazine. On *Bridge of Sighs*, from 1974, he modulated between high-energy blasts, like "Day of the Eagle" and "Too Rolling Stoned," and more moody tracks such as the title song, on which the layering of different guitar tones took precedence over unleashed soloing. Duane Allman was another guitarist who often showed admirable restraint even as his band, the Allman Brothers, foregrounded the extended solo excursions of himself and his guitar partner, Dickie Betts. Together, Allman and Betts forged a dual guitar style the likes of which had rarely been heard in a rock setting, doubling each other's melodies and creating a sort of twin guitar counterpoint that enlivened such pieces as "In Memory of Elizabeth Reed" and "Mountain Jam" (from the albums *Live at the Fillmore East* and *Eat a Peach*, respectively). Meanwhile, Allman himself was most noted for his slide guitar work, through which he adapted the sounds and techniques of long-standing blues traditions to the demands of contemporary rock performance on songs like "Statesboro Blues," also from the *Fillmore East* album.

Beyond a proclivity for extended guitar solos that showed off their considerable musical technique, these guitarists represented the culmination of a process begun in the 1960s: the full-scale incorporation of the electric guitar into the center of popular music, or what rock critic Robert Duncan called "the paradigm of the counterculture into the mainstream."[34] As hard rock and heavy metal took their place in the arenas that became the primary venues for rock concerts during the 1970s, they fulfilled the potential of high-volume, technologically-enhanced music to create a new economy of scale, within which crowds of people experienced what, in the judgment of many, was only a simulacrum of the energy and passion that rock had once embodied.[35] Within this changing context, the guitar hero served a crucial ideological function, offering the appearance of individual achievement and mastery in the face of the growing crowds that occupied the spaces of rock performance. There were increasing numbers of fans and musicians, however, for whom such pleasures were no longer sufficient. As the 1970s wore on, they would mount a critique of the incorporation of rock within which the rock guitar "hero" would be deeply implicated.

8 Contesting virtuosity: rock guitar since 1976

STEVE WAKSMAN

Three chords

In late 1976, one of the first punk rock fanzines laid out a veritable philosophy of rock aesthetics in a graphic message. Three roughly drawn chord diagrams were laid across the page, showing the readers how to finger the A, E, and G chords on the fretboard of a guitar. Accompanying the chords was a simple message: "This is a chord . . . This is another . . . This is a third . . . *Now form a band.*"[1] The message was clear: rock music, and rock guitar playing in particular, did not have to be predicated upon the foregrounding of virtuosity. After all, despite the claims of such purveyors of "art rock" as Yes and Genesis, or such heroic guitar idols as Jimmy Page and Ritchie Blackmore, rock was not made to be "art" in any conventional sense of the term; not without cause did Chuck Berry tell Beethoven to roll over so many years earlier. Rock was meant to be basic, simple, unschooled, or else it risked losing touch with the elemental core of emotion that sparked the best rock and roll. Forming a punk band, then, should only require the most elementary skills. Three-chord song structures were at the heart of the rock and roll form, so three chords were all that any guitarist should need to put songs together and play in a band.

The renunciation of virtuosity among punk guitarists was not as all-encompassing as has often been portrayed. Depending on how broadly or narrowly one defines punk (or indeed, how one defines virtuosity), the moment of punk's formation in the mid- to late 1970s included such formidable guitar talents as Robert Quine, of Richard Hell and the Voidoids, and Tom Verlaine and Richard Lloyd of Television. Nevertheless, declarations of the power of simplicity such as the above pronouncement were a powerful ideological tool in the efforts among punk bands, fans, and critics to break away from the dominant currents of 1970s rock music. Even if all punk guitarists did not shun the acquisition of musical technique, most questioned the uses to which that technique had been put in recent years, when musical ability had played into the hierarchical separation between rock audiences and musicians. Over the next two decades, the relative value of guitar-based virtuosity would continue to be one of the defining issues in the continuing development of rock guitar. Great numbers of guitarists were drawn back into the virtuosic fold after the success of Edward Van Halen, perhaps the preeminent "guitar hero" of the era. Yet the revival of punk values that occurred in the early 1990s, combined with the displacement of the electric guitar in favor of sampling and other techniques of electronic performance in rap and techno, among other styles, have placed virtuosity in a new light, such that the continued musical and cultural viability of the electric guitar as a medium of expression has been called into question.

Within the punk ethos, antipathy toward virtuosity was contained within a broader disdain for many of the trappings of rock stardom. Punks desired to move away from the notion that rock musicians were stars who earned their privilege and separation from the mass of rock and roll followers. Although punk itself would in time enshrine many of its leading figures as stars within an alternative rock universe, opposition to the established hierarchies of rock nonetheless opened the way for the formation of bands that were predicated upon the sheer desire to play in a band, regardless of musical ability. Thus did Steve Jones, guitarist for definitive punk band the Sex Pistols, recall that he only really learned to play after Johnny Rotten had joined the band: "I'd wake up in the morning at our studio on Denmark Street, take a black beauty, and play along with an Iggy Pop record and the New York Dolls' first album . . . I barely got my barre chords together to play songs. I threw a little bit of Chuck Berry in the lead and that was it."[2] At the same time, though, Jones's comments regarding his former bandmate, bassist Glen Matlock, bear out the extent to which the ragged sound of the Sex Pistols stemmed as much from self-conscious resistance to proper musical technique as from sheer lack of ability: "Glen was always trying to show me these complicated chords . . . I wasn't interested in his Beatle-type chords. I couldn't play the chords he tried to show me. If we had played those chords, we would have sounded like Dr. Feelgood or one of those pub rock bands."[3]

Another influential punk guitarist, Johnny Ramone, voiced similar sentiments in criticizing the state of rock and roll during the 1970s. "There was no point listening . . . There was no more pure rock and roll; it was all this fusion. Forget that!" Ramone continued, "When you see a certain type of band, you feel like maybe *you* could do it – like the New York Dolls, the Stooges, Slade . . . They didn't look like you had to be playing 20 years and practicing all day. Maybe you could just get up there and play songs."[4] Along with Jones, Ramone carved out the most identifiably punk approach to rock guitar: heavy on distortion and volume, heavy as well on the use of barre chords to convey the song's pattern (extending the tradition of the power chord outlined in earlier years by Link Wray and Pete Townshend, among others), following rhythms that were accelerated well past the normal rock and roll comfort zone. *The Ramones*, released in 1976, and *Never Mind the Bollocks, Here's the Sex Pistols*, issued the following year, also set the pace for American and British punk, respectively, the one grounded in a sort of suburban *ennui* interrupted by fits of random aggression ("Beat on the Brat") or lustful yearning ("I Wanna Be Your Boyfriend"), the other issuing a proto-political barrage of sonic and verbal epithets directed at the legacy of the Holocaust ("Holiday in the Sun") or the Queen herself ("God Save the Queen").

Distinct as the bands' lyrical approaches were, both Johnny Ramone and Steve Jones used the noise of the electric guitar to fill in the cracks left by the relatively simple musical structures. As Ramone asserted in a 1985 interview, "I always wanted the guitar to sound like energy coming out of an amplifier . . . Not even like music or chords; I just wanted that energy coming out."[5] That this noise, once viewed as a primary means of expanding the tonal and expressive range of rock, was now viewed as a way to purify the music, to reduce it to its most basic essence, was one of the main paradoxes underlying punk. In turn, this paradox was linked to another, perhaps more fundamental point of tension: electric sound, viewed during the 1960s as a medium for establishing new modes of community, was within punk valued as much for its potential to create new bases of separation, new boundaries between the different styles of rock performance. Such logic was implicit in the rock guitar styles that had taken shape in the previous decade, but punk brought this logic out into the open through the aggressive combination of sonic excess and basic rock structures.

Shred

Edward Van Halen was another guitarist who knew the value of a good power chord. In Van Halen's music, though, the power chord was reset within a context where "power" and virtuosity were closely bound.[6] Nowhere was this more apparent than on the second track of Van Halen's first album, titled appropriately enough, "Eruption." The A power chord that opened the track set the harmonic center around which Van Halen spun single-note lines of dazzling speed and intricacy. A predominantly pentatonic opening section, marked by muted picking and an array of hammer-ons and pull-offs, was capped by a wildly altered depression of the low E string with Van Halen's vibrato bar, which led into a similarly wild vibrato-bar-driven ascent on open A. Three further power chords announced the shift of the track's harmonic center to D, a shift that also found the guitarist working the upper register of his instrument through a series of rapidly picked lines that culminated in an extended quotation from a well-known Rodolphe Kreutzer violin etude. All of which was prelude to the climactic final section in which Van Halen showcased the technique for which he would become best known, tapping the index finger of his right hand onto the fretboard in tandem with the hammer-ons and pull-offs fingered by the left to produce a rapidly shifting set of arpeggios that ascended up the fretboard and then moved back down, finally settling at a point of stasis that built toward a last burst of whammy-bar-driven distortion.[7]

Whereas punk rock was largely predicated upon the repudiation of musical technique, "Eruption" laid claim to both the resuscitation and revision of rock guitar virtuosity. That it was released in 1978, the same year that the Sex Pistols made their last gasp across the United States, was no idle historical concurrence. While Van Halen's success and influence among guitarists has often been attributed to the sheer force of his technique,[8] more careful consideration shows that the perceived "force" of Van Halen's guitar style had much to do with the fact that it emerged at a moment in the late 1970s when guitar-based virtuosity seemed an embattled phenomenon. Thus did Dan Hedges begin his pop biography of Edward Van Halen by musing on the supposed obsolescence of guitar heroes: "Not long ago, someone had written them off as an extinct species... [but] the closet *axemeisters* never really died out."[9] As the most celebrated of those closet *axemeisters*, Van Halen came to appear for Hedges, and for many other commentators, as a veritable phoenix rising from the ashes of arena rock to restore the electric guitar to its rightful place at the pinnacle of rock achievement. On a less grandiose level, Van Halen himself viewed his band's success in opposition to the punk aesthetic: "The reason I think we're happening is because we are one of the only *real* bands out there. We're not punk, we don't dress weird. We play good music... I'm not saying that all the things I come up with are genius-brand riffs, but neither is punk. Punk's like what I used to do in the garage."[10]

Anti-punk reaction may have provided one crucial context for the success of Van Halen, but Edward Van Halen's guitar style was also notable for its perceived difference from earlier manifestations of guitar heroism. In part this was a result of the techniques that Van Halen brought to bear upon electric guitar performance, techniques that emphasized a degree of speed that was unusual, if not downright inaccessible, among an earlier generation of guitarists. While "Eruption" was the most consolidated expression of Edward Van Halen's technical skill, many of the band Van Halen's albums contained tracks that similarly spotlighted the guitarist's abilities. On "Spanish Fly" from *Van Halen II*, Edward performed a flamenco-based instrumental on which he applied his methods of two-handed tapping to a nylon-string acoustic guitar. "Mean Streets," from *Fair Warning*, opened with the guitarist issuing a distinctive series of percussive, syncopated harmonics through a method of right-handed tapping that owed much to the "slapping" bass techniques of contemporary funk bassists. And on "Cathedral," from the band's fifth album, *Diver Down*, Van Halen used a combination of echo effects with left-handed dexterity and right-handed manipulation of his guitar's volume knob to create a classically informed instrumental that bore significant resemblance to a Bach organ work.

Although many of the band Van Halen's songs were based around fairly conventional blues and rock progressions, Edward Van Halen's recourse to a classical musical vocabulary in his soloing enhanced the aura of virtuosity surrounding rock guitar. As a writer for *Guitar World* magazine observed, "the classical approach [was already] a heavy metal tradition" by the early 1980s, having been used in different ways by guitarists such as Ritchie Blackmore, Jimmy Page, Leslie West, and German metal guitarists Michael Schenker and Ulrich Roth.[11] In the aftermath of Van Halen's success, however, classical music increasingly became the focus for a new style of electric guitar virtuosity that displaced the presiding blues-based vocabulary of heavy metal in favor of a much more Eurocentric notion of harmonic and melodic complexity.[12]

One guitarist who accelerated the move toward classical music was Randy Rhoads, who in 1980 took on the position as lead guitarist in Ozzy Osbourne's newly formed band. Rhoads's solos for Osbourne on such tracks as "Mr. Crowley" and "Revelation (Mother Earth)" were built around melodic lines that owed much to the harmonic structures of the Baroque era, and made use of his many years studying and teaching classical guitar at a Los Angeles music store. Perhaps the leading figure in the "neoclassical" turn, though, was Swedish-born Yngwie Malmsteen, who first achieved notoriety as guitarist for the short-lived LA metal band Steeler. By the time he embarked upon a solo career in 1984, Malmsteen had become a figure whose influence and notoriety generated both excitement and consternation in the rock guitar world. Many were awestruck at the speed and bravado of Malmsteen's solos on songs like "Kree Nakoorie" (recorded during his brief tenure with the band Alcatrazz) and "Far Beyond the Sun." Others, however, were concerned that Malmsteen represented an undesirable extreme in the foregrounding of musical technique.[13] Malmsteen, for his part, alternately reveled in and disowned the controversy surrounding his playing style. He repeatedly denied that his playing emphasized speed for its own sake, and rejected the notion that he was purposely in competition with the technical accomplishments of other guitarists. Yet he was also given to such pronouncements as "Classical is the peak of the development of music . . . Classical is the source of music; it's like a religion, almost," pronouncements that imposed a hierarchy of taste upon the playing of rock guitar within which all but a few musicians came up short.[14]

By the end of the 1980s, "classical" metal had become almost a sub-genre unto itself; Vinnie Moore, Tony Macalpine, Paul Gilbert, and a host of others released albums that were, at root, variations on the pattern established by Malmsteen's debut solo album, *Yngwie Malmsteen's Rising Force*. More generally, the speed-driven style of rock guitar earned an appellation derived from the ways in which guitarists were prone to "tear up" the fretboard: shred (as in, "Wow, that guy can really *shred*"). Not all "shredders" were as classically inspired as the above-named players; some, like Steve Vai, Joe Satriani, and Vernon Reid, allowed for a much greater range of styles and influences to show in their playing, including not only earlier guitar icons such as Jimi Hendrix but the more far-flung sounds of free jazz and experimental improvisation. Vai's first solo album, the lo-fi *Flex-Able* from 1984, was shaped by the guitarist's tenure with Frank Zappa, the influence of which was evident both in the tongue-in-cheek quality of many of the album's tracks and the often dissonant harmonic concepts that informed Vai's approach to composition. Satriani's earliest solo recordings, such as *Not of This Earth*, were also marked by an experimental approach to the layering of guitar sounds, though by 1987's *Surfing with the Alien* he had made a move toward blending high-speed, virtuosic solo guitar with a degree of melodic songcraft that was unique among shred specialists. The ballad, "Always with Me, Always with You," was a particular departure from the usual shred *modus operandi*, but even more uptempo tracks like "Ice 9" and "Lords of Karma" had well-defined melodies that gave the guitarist's exhibitionistic tendencies a sort of musical shape that was lacking in much of the guitar-based music of the era.

Moving even further into untapped musical territory was Reid, an African American guitarist whose prodigious technique has been matched over a long and varied career with a decided proclivity for musical boundary-crossing. For much of the 1980s Reid occupied a position as one of the most oft-featured guitarists in the New York experimental music scene, playing lead at different times with avant-funk ensemble Defunkt and the more jazz-based Decoding Society led by former Ornette Coleman drummer Ronald Shannon Jackson. With the formation of Living Colour in the latter part of the decade, Reid took on a more standard rock-based forum for his playing, though his solos on such tracks as "Cult of Personality" and "Desperate People" showed a preference for extreme whammy-bar mutations and an extensive use of chromaticism that would have been at home in more far-flung musical settings. In a 1988 interview, Reid spelled out his distinctive position relative to the current moment of rock guitar:

> If a young player wants to dig deeply into the classical music approach to metal guitar, that's fine – it's great music. What I question are guitarists who use technique to make themselves invincible – an "I'm going to blow you away with my chops" attitude . . . Listen to people who use space in their solos, like Wayne Shorter and Sonny Rollins, who are two of our greatest living improvisers. And after you check out their use of space, phrasing and note selection, try and capture their overall feeling and spirit. Too often the term "playing with feel" means playing without technique, but that's a misconception . . . There is a bridge between technique and emotional commitment.[15]

Announcing his own commitment to an improvisatory brand of virtuosity, Reid also makes plain the extent to which shred engendered a discourse about the state of rock guitar within which more than virtuosity was at issue. Notable here are Reid's observations about how different musical methods and traditions might be used to create new applications for musical technique; avoiding outright confrontation, he nonetheless raises questions about the ways in which classical music had been appropriated as a means of justifying a particular, fairly narrow concept of good musicianship.

Reid's final bridge-building remarks also speak to a perceived division that continued to widen as rock guitar moved into the 1990s. Technique vs. emotion became a hardened dichotomy by the 1990s, exacerbated by the resurgence of punk values that occurred under the rubric of "grunge." In many ways it was, as Reid noted, a false dichotomy, but for those tired of the excesses of shred it was also ideologically useful, much as the repudiation of virtuosity had been useful almost two decades earlier during the emergence of punk. Grunge guitarists such as Mike McCready of Pearl Jam, Kim Thayil of Soundgarden, and Steve Turner of Mudhoney did not eschew guitar solos with the same relish as had Johnny Ramone or Steve Jones, but rather sought to reclaim influences such as the Stooges and the MC5, Black Sabbath and Blue Cheer, and perhaps especially Neil Young, who were more celebrated for their ear-bending uses of noise than for their musical chops. Thayil and Turner were especially adept at developing solo styles that moved in alternative directions from the note-perfect approach of so many shred-based guitarists, building solos out of imprecise flurries of notes and atonal squalls of distortion that fell between the cracks of a song's melody. Young himself, in the midst of renewed notoriety, made some of the most pointed statements in favor of expression over technique, declaring that "it doesn't matter if you can play a scale. It doesn't matter if your technique is good.

If you have feelings that you want to get out through music, that's what matters."[16] On his 1991 album, *Ragged Glory*, Young injected many of the songs with concise melodies that would then be stretched into extensive solo passages within which the melody remained always present, but consistently mutated through Young's mix of picked harmonics, muted picking, and sheer joy in the weight of the amplified sound that surrounded himself and his longtime co-conspirators, Crazy Horse.

Among the younger breed, Thayil was particularly outspoken in his criticism of "sterile, overtrained classical stuff," suggesting that he didn't see "where the balls are in that."[17] Despite his rather unfortunate choice of words, Thayil was also among the guitarists most ready to note the gender bias inhering in the shred style of musical attack, dryly stating that "there's a full connection between fast metal guitar, *Soldier of Fortune*, and bikini girls."[18] Rock guitar had remained an insistently male domain throughout its history, owing to a complex set of structural and symbolic inequalities that kept female musicians from seizing hold of an instrument so rife with the trappings of masculine potency. Nonetheless, the growing consensus was that shred marked an intensification of this long-standing dynamic, a hyper-masculine display of prowess through the medium of musical technique. Just how rigid these gender lines had been drawn can be seen from the example of Jennifer Batten, a guitarist of exceptional ability who was the first female graduate from the prestigious Guitar Institute of Technology (GIT), a Hollywood music school at the center of the shred phenomenon. Discussing her subsequent experience touring as the lead guitarist for "King of Pop" Michael Jackson, Batten noted that "it's a shock for some people to see a woman playing the guitar. All over the world on the Michael Jackson tour, people would ask me whether I was a man or a woman. Just because I played guitar, they assumed I was a guy."[19] So hardened were the roles in rock that, as Batten's interviewer Joe Gore put it, "it was easier for [the audience] to believe that the guitar player was a man who *looked* like a woman than that she was actually female." Against such pressures, Batten has stood her ground to carve out a solo career centered around the sorts of chop-heavy guitar albums that have generally been the province of male musicians. Even today, she remains a singular presence, for guitar-based virtuosity is still largely guarded as male terrain.[20]

No future?

While virtuosity was challenged from within the world of rock guitar, more fundamental challenges have emerged from outside. In the wake of shred and grunge, the electric guitar's domination over the sonic landscape of popular music has weakened significantly. The emergence and success of non-guitar-based musical styles such as hip-hop and the various musical offshoots of electronic dance music (techno, electronica, jungle, drum 'n' bass, etc.) have displaced questions about the value of virtuosity onto a different plane where they have been conjoined with questions about the continued expressive vitality of the guitar itself. In her study of rap music, *Black Noise*, Tricia Rose describes the conflict over musical values surrounding rap, contrasting the open disdain that many rock fans and performers have for rap *as music* with the pointed comments of Hank Shocklee, member of the Bomb Squad production team that has worked with Public Enemy and Ice Cube: "We don't like musicians. We don't respect musicians . . . In dealing with rap, you have to be innocent and ignorant of music . . . A musician will go, 'No, those are the wrong keys. The tones are clashing.' We don't look at it that way."[21] Rose interprets Shocklee's remarks to indicate an antipathy not to "musicians" as such but to the standards of formal Western classical music. What she ignores, though, is the more immediate context of popular music, within which the electric guitar had for decades been cast as the primary symbol of musical expertise and virtuosity. Given the preponderance of classical influence upon rock guitar during the moment at which Shocklee made his statements (1990), it is probable that Shocklee's main target was the tendency of rock guitarists to elevate their practices above the sample-based modes of composition and performance employed by rap artists, rather than the classical tradition itself. For Shocklee, sampling involved a more fluid and open approach to sound than the practice of more conventional "musicians," and as such opened the way for demonstrating that "this thing called music is a lot broader than you think it is."[22]

The variety of electronic music styles that have recently emerged (many of which have been influenced by rap and hip hop) have also worked to broaden the base of musical judgment beyond the values associated with rock guitar. Simon Reynolds has captured some of this creative impulse in his recent history of techno, *Generation Ecstasy*. Describing what he calls "sampladelia" – a sample-based style of making music that draws upon and extends the approaches to sound first unearthed in late-1960s psychedelia – Reynolds refers to the music's "revolutionary implications: its radical break with the ideals of real-time interactive playing and natural acoustic space that still govern most music making."[23] However much the electric guitar has involved the distortion or more general manipulation of sound via technological means, it remains at root very much a hands-on instrument out of which the sounds produced bear a more or less direct relationship to the physical efforts of the musician. Sampling upsets the continuity involved in this relationship to a greater or lesser degree; music is created by selecting and programming sounds rather than playing notes in a more recogniz-able fashion. By extension, according to the logic of techno's most ardent proponents, the physicality of the musician – one of the key elements con-tributing to the aura of virtuosic prowess surrounding the electric guitar – is submerged beneath a collectivist ethos in which the dancing bodies of rave participants are the real locus of musical excitement. Even punk rock, with which the more populist-oriented dimensions of techno would seem to have parallels, comes to appear unnecessarily demonstrative in the judgment of those like Martin Price of Manchester house band 808 State: "[Techno] is about machines, punk was about arm power. Nobody wants to see a load of idiots torturing themselves onstage with guitars anymore. The muscles and sinews in dance music are when you're sweating your bollocks off on the dance floor."[24]

In this shifting musical setting, rock guitar has assumed an almost "traditionalist" aura for many audiences and musicians, encased in a nos-talgia for past forms that in previous eras was reserved for more folk-based styles of expression. One of the most widespread manifestations of this impulse is the surge in popularity of the "jam band" scene led by groups like Phish who have sought to fuse a sort of neo-hippie pastoralism with the conventions of arena rock in a way that leaves the contradictions inherent in such a project unresolved. At the same time, though, rock guitar has moved into more hybridized contexts wherein the polarity between analog and digital, electric and electronic musicianship, becomes the basis for creative fusion. One of the more successful techno bands, the Chemical Brothers, have built a sound out of digitally expanding "the same blaring midrange frequencies supplied by rock guitar."[25] Interviewed in *Guitar Player* maga-zine, one of the Brothers, Tom Rowlands, emphasized the band's reliance upon guitar-based sounds: "One of the major things we've done is use rough guitar effects. We've got quite a large collection of Electro-Harmonix pedals, which always add a bit of bite. You don't get that from your latest effects. When people were making effects back then, there was a wild edge to what they were doing. It was more experimental."[26]

That the sounds generated by decades-old guitar effects still retain an "experimental" aura says much about the continued expressive and even transformative potential of rock guitar when approached with an open imagination. It further attests to the notion that, despite the conscious and at times overbearing futurism surrounding electronic music, often the most interesting progress is made by looking back as one looks forward. Or, to put it differently, much sample-based music is "digitally produced but cannot be digitally created," in the words of Tricia Rose; analog sounds still retain a certain specificity and a significant appeal that makes them an ongoing point of reference in how sound should be (re)produced.[27] In the end, the technology matters less than how it is put to use, and on that level rock guitar retains the possibility of blending what we might call a virtuosity of sound – grounded in the sorts of sound experiments in which electric guitarists have engaged through much of the twentieth century, laying the groundwork for the subsequent digital "revolution" in music – with a virtuosity of notes grounded in more "well-tempered" approaches to musicianship.

9 The guitar in country music

GORDON ROSS

The guitar has always played a primary role in the composition, performance, and image of country music. The steel-string acoustic guitar, or "flat-top," provided the rhythmic and harmonic foundation in the original string bands and has since been included in all country music recordings and performances without exception. In North America, the acoustic guitar has become a symbol not only of country music, but of traditionalism, rural values, "down-homeness," and a folk-based ideology.

The authenticity of a country music performance depends upon stylistic variables that combine to create a personal musical experience both for the audience and for the performer. Musical elements such as vocal sound, subject, performance practice, and instrumentation merge with iconographic ones such as boots, cowboy hats, pedal steel guitar, and acoustic guitar in order to maintain this authenticity and produce the genre recognized by audiences as country music.

The traditionalism associated with the acoustic guitar lives on in the repertory of folk songs, ballads, dances, and instrumental pieces brought to North America by Anglo-Celtic immigrants during the seventeenth and eighteenth centuries. British folk culture came to all regions of English-speaking North America, and pockets of tradition still exist in such places as rural New England, Appalachia, and the Maritime provinces of Canada.[1] By the same token, country music is deeply rooted in the folklore of British broadside ballads, which were transported to the New World and gained life as "Americana." It speaks to its audience from a rural perspective and serves as a vehicle for tapping into and assessing public opinion, relating personal experience, and commenting on situations or events.[2]

The similarity between much country and folk music stems from the traditionalism inherent in both, which is inherited from the broadsides and other folk music forms.[3] The line of demarcation between country and folk music is blurred at best, with both styles crossing over from one to the other; many folk songs could be construed as country and vice versa. While the folk tradition mainly provides a conduit for comment and protest, country music, on the other hand, usually reflects personal experience and sentiment, avoiding overt protest. Its lyrics take the reflective tone of an observer, rather than the challenge of a manifesto. For both genres, country and folk, the acoustic guitar constitutes an important part of the necessary traditionalism.

Early country music performers used stringed instruments almost exclusively in their performances and on recordings. Solo performers such as Jimmie Rodgers (1897–1933) and Canadians Wilf Carter (1904–96) and Hank Snow (1914–99) played acoustic guitar and prominently featured the instrument in their promotional pictures. Posing with a guitar was not limited to these early performers. Hank Williams, Johnny Cash, and many others are rarely seen without an acoustic guitar as part of their image. The tradition of singing songs and accompanying oneself with the guitar pre-dates the rise of country music and a performer's use of the instrument recalls the intimacy of that tradition. Along with solo performance, the acoustic guitar was used in early country music ensembles. String bands of the 1920s usually consisted of acoustic guitar, mandolin, fiddle, stand-up bass, and banjo, or some combination ranging from duos to six-piece groups. Contemporary bluegrass bands that use a similar complement of instruments continue the tradition of string band instrumentation today.[4]

In a string band, the acoustic guitar is primarily relegated to the role of providing harmonic support. The melodic and improvisatory elements of the music are left to the fiddle, mandolin, and banjo, although acoustic guitar solos are not uncommon. Quite often the absence of a bass player required the guitarist to adopt a "quasi-bass" role. This is achieved by emphasizing the bass notes of the chord progression using an alternating bass-strumming rhythm and incorporating bass runs to link the chords and provide harmonic motion. In addition to the bass line, the task of providing a percussive element fell mainly on the acoustic guitar player, who would incorporate a slightly choked strumming style, not allowing the chords to ring fully. This strumming style is similar to the "sock rhythm" – the playing of closed chords, or the striking of all six strings while muting the notes in order to achieve a percussive effect – that became prominent in honky-tonk rhythm playing when country music moved into the honky-tonks or juke joints that were prevalent during the 1930s, 1940s, and 1950s.[5]

The acoustic guitar is available in both six- and twelve-string types, with the twelve-string being used more for folk music, its appearance in country music being almost non-existent.[6] Six-string acoustic guitars can be found in various sizes and models (see Plates 14–15). Some of the more popular ones include the parlor guitar, so-called because of its smaller size with the neck joining the body at the twelfth fret; the folk guitar, with a slotted peghead similar to a classical guitar; and the Dreadnought, the largest model with the neck joining the body at the fourteenth fret.[7]

If more than one acoustic guitar is present either in recording or in performance, a mechanical device known as a *capo* can be used to transpose

Plate 14 Martin 000M, Auditorium-sized (photo courtesy of the Martin Guitar Company)

first-position, open-string chord shapes to different keys, without changing fingering (see Example 9.1). The *capo* clamps across the neck at whatever fret the guitarist chooses, shortening the string length and, at the same time, raising the pitch of the chord tones to create a brighter sound when juxtaposed against a guitar playing standard chords and inversions. Another method of achieving this brightness is to use a high-strung guitar along with a standard acoustic guitar. The high-strung guitar is a regular six-string acoustic guitar with the bottom four strings tuned an octave higher. This tuning, sometimes known as "Nashville tuning," can be found in a variety of applications ranging from folk and country music to country rock songs

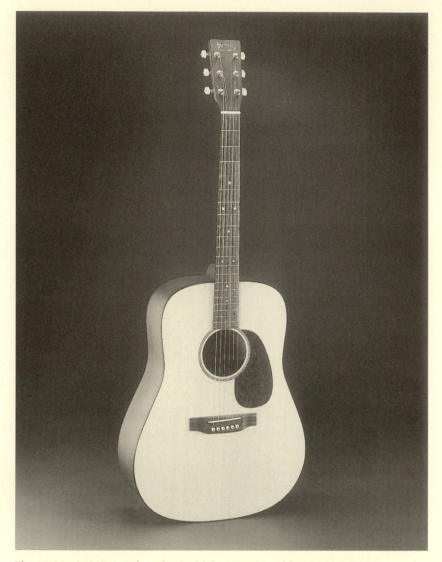

Plate 15 Martin DM, Dreadnought-sized (photo courtesy of the Martin Guitar Company)

like the Rolling Stones' 1971 recording "Wild Horses."[8] Again, a brighter sound is created when both guitars are played simultaneously.

The pick or plectrum provides a mechanical element required to produce rhythm and chords creating a louder sound than just playing with the fingers and allowing the guitarist to incorporate a strumming rhythm that suits the character of the particular song. Strumming rhythms are dependent upon the formal characteristics of the song and are bound by metrical division. A fast 2/4 rhythm would be played by picking the lowest bass note of the chord followed by a strum of the remaining chord tones resulting in a "pick/strum" rhythm. A 3/4 rhythm is played in a similar manner with two

Example 9.1 Capo and chord position

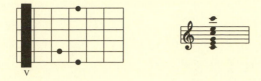

strums of the remaining chord notes creating a "pick/strum/strum" rhythm indigenous to triple meter. Using a pick/strum rhythm, the guitarist can alternate between the root and fifth of the chord on the lower strings creating harmonic movement and giving the aural illusion of a bass line (alternating bass/strum pattern). A moderate 4/4 rhythm uses a combination of down and up strokes though without the initial picking of a bass note allowing the guitarist to accent or syncopate the strum. Either a strong beat or a weak one can be emphasized in this manner, creating a seamless flow of chordal rhythm as opposed to the more choppy style of the pick/strum method (see Example 9.2).

In a country music ensemble that uses electric instruments and a drum set, the acoustic guitar is rhythmically tied to the snare drum. In other words, to emphasize forward motion, or "feel," the guitarist must accent beats two and four, or the back beats, timing the stress with the snare drum. The strum portion of a pick/strum rhythm occurs on these beats and they are slightly accented. In triple-meter songs, the opposite is true. Here, the downbeat, or beat one, is accented, with beats two and three receiving less stress. "Pushing" the beat, or playing slightly ahead of the beat creating "drive," and "pulling" the beat, or playing slightly behind to create a "laid back" feel, are usually avoided. Country music is played predominantly on the beat, making simplicity paramount, virtuosic elements and rhythmic variation being left to the solo instruments.

To play a polyrhythmic or finger-style, the guitarist must employ the thumb and one to three fingers of the picking hand, or a pick and the second and third fingers. Both methods enable the guitarist to create an independent bass line followed by arpeggiated chords or a combination of arpeggios and plucked chords interspersed with the melody. Rhythmic and harmonic flow is created by alternating the thumb or pick with each finger, making the notes of a chord "roll" out of the guitar. These methods owe much to classical guitar technique, which uses the fingers of the picking hand in a similar manner to produce the rhythmic variables required by the music. While classical guitarists avoid the use of picks, country guitarists often use either just a thumb pick or thumb and finger picks when playing finger-style. Merle Travis (1917–83) and Chet Atkins (1924–2001), two

Example 9.2 Strumming rhythms
(a) 2/4 strum
(b) 3/4 strum
(c) alternating bass
(d) moderate 4/4 strum

Example 9.3 Typical finger-style rhythms

notable country guitarists, are both credited with creating their own unique brand of finger-style guitar. Both guitarists use thumb picks only in combination with fingers. "Travis-style," as it has come to be known, uses the index finger alone along with the thumb, while Atkins employs up to three fingers more like a classical guitarist. Playing with the fingers is not limited to country music and many folk guitarists use this method as well (see Example 9.3).[9]

While the acoustic guitar is stereotypically tied to country music, the pedal steel guitar, perhaps even more so than the acoustic guitar, represents country music by virtue of its visual appearance and more importantly its sound. The characteristic "cry" of the pedal steel says "country music" and imprints that label on any song by virtue of its unique sound. "Teach Your Children," the 1970 hit for Crosby, Stills, Nash, and Young, and "Far

Away Eyes," a wonderful parody of country music on the Rolling Stones' 1978 album *Some Girls*, both incorporate the pedal steel to add a country flavor and contribute to the authenticity of the songs. Despite, however, its seemingly dominant presence in the genre, the pedal steel guitar falls in and out of favor with country artists as the quest for crossover popularity fluctuates. During the 1950s and the era of the Nashville Sound,[10] artists like Jim Reeves, Patsy Cline, Eddy Arnold, and Ray Price eschewed the hard country sounds of the steel guitar and fiddle and replaced them with softer back-up singers and string sections as they strove for a homogeneity that would appeal to a wider audience.

The steel guitar enjoyed an increase in popularity during the 1960s, when honky-tonk artists like George Jones, Merle Haggard, Loretta Lynn, and Tammy Wynette featured the instrument in a more prominent role than the Nashville Sound artists did. Additional support for the instrument came from an unlikely source. A contingent of the youth culture of the 1960s viewed country and folk as an alternative to the psychedelia and anger of the rock music of the period and incorporated folk and country traditions into their music, thereby politicizing rock and at the same time paying homage to early country and folk music pioneers. During the mid to late 1960s it was artists like Bob Dylan, Gram Parsons, the Byrds, Neil Young, and Crosby, Stills and Nash whose respect for the traditionalism of country and folk music brought rock back in touch with its country roots. Country rock and folk rock bands embraced the pedal steel and the fiddle, seeing the instruments as necessary elements to authenticate the music. Ironically, it was the California country rock group the Byrds' release of *Sweetheart of the Rodeo* in 1968 and Bob Dylan's album *Nashville Skyline* (1969) that did more to increase the profile of the pedal steel than the country music of the same period.

By 1976, the steel guitar had again fallen out of favor with country and pop artists alike because it sounded "too country." Country acts searching for a crossover hit would have nothing to do with the steel guitar. As traditional country sounds came back into vogue at the end of the twentieth century, contemporary country artists like Garth Brooks, Vince Gill, and Reba McEntire have used the pedal steel guitar to help authenticate their particular songs and performance. The steel guitar may not enjoy the same prominence in the sound of today's country artists, but it does much in identifying the music.

"Steel guitar" has become a generic term that encompasses two similar instruments, the Hawaiian steel guitar or lap steel and the pedal steel guitar. The lap steel guitar evolved from the Hawaiian guitar, which began its development around 1876.[11] The easiest definition of a Hawaiian guitar is simply an acoustic guitar with the bridge, nut, and strings elevated, laid on its back, and played on one's lap. A metal bar is slid across the strings to create the notes instead of fretting the strings in the conventional manner. A thumb pick and finger picks are often used.

As the popularity of the Hawaiian guitar grew in the land of its birth, it was introduced to the mainland around the turn of the twentieth century with the electrified version being developed during the 1930s and adopted into the big-band sound of western swing.[12] In addition to the electrified lap steel, the Hawaiian guitar spawned another offspring, the acoustic resonator guitar or Dobro.[13] The pedal steel, lap steel, Hawaiian guitar, and Dobro all use an open tuning which enables the player to strum the strings open, that is not fretted, to produce a chord. Common tunings are C, G, D, A, and E, with an added sixth, ninth, eleventh, or thirteenth:

Common tunings for acoustic steel guitar (Dobro):
lowest to highest string

Open G	C6/A7 tuning
DGDGBD	C#EGACE
Open A	C6 alternate tuning
AC#EAC#E	GCGACE
Low bass A or Hawaiian A	G9 tuning
EAEAC#E	GBDGAD
Low bass G	C13 tuning
DGDGBD	ADB♭GCE
Open E	Em or G6 tuning
EBEG#BE	EBDGBE
Open D	E13 tuning
DADF#AD	BDEG#C#E
	Cmaj9 tuning
	GCEGBD

Because of the singularity of tunings and the difficulty in re-tuning the guitar for different keys, many lap steel guitarists in western swing bands had multiple necks on their instrument to facilitate several tunings and keys. The addition of multiple necks resulted in early steel guitars resembling a table with two or more guitar necks laid across. Early swing-steelers drew influences not only from other steel guitarists, but from big-band jazz horn players as well. Western swing bands of the 1940s like Bob Wills and his Texas Playboys and Milton Brown and the Brownies were large bands usually consisting of fiddle, steel guitar, guitar, bass, drums, piano, and a vocalist. Sometimes the bands were augmented with saxophone, another fiddle, and/or a guitar player. The music drew frequently from older and diverse folk resources, but more often than not it emulated commercial music forms popular in their own day, like the swing bands of Glenn Miller and Tommy Dorsey. The rhythmic nature of western swing allowed steel guitarists to emulate horn sections and the incorporation a volume pedal enabled unusual chordal swells and "doo-wah" effects similar to a brass player's use of a derby hat or a plunger.

In 1954, Webb Pierce's hit song "Slowly" ushered in the pedal steel guitar to the normative sound of country music. Steel guitarist Bud Isaacs played a three-note pitch-bending sound for the song's introduction that seemed to move and stand still at the same time. The sound was previously unheard and steel guitarists everywhere clamored to discover the secret of Isaac's technique, which was created using the then fledgling pedal steel guitar.[14]

The pedal steel differs from its cousin the steel guitar by using mechanical means to alter ("bend") the pitch of particular strings, thereby changing the chord produced by the open strings. Pedals are attached to rods connected to a roller assembly on the bridge so that when a particular pedal is depressed the pitch of the companion string or strings is raised either a half or a whole step. Knee levers operated by both knees and connected in a similar manner to other strings perform the same task. Knee levers can either raise or lower the pitch of specific strings. Various combinations of knee levers and pedals along with the bar sliding across the strings create the pedal steel's unique sound. Pedal steel guitars typically have two ten-string necks, one tuned to an E9 chord and the other tuned to C6, with the C6 being used more for western swing songs or jazz-based chord progressions. Besides the usual open tunings, a diatonic tuning, or one involving each note of a particular major scale, typically F major, is sometimes used again predominantly for jazz-based songs. In addition, there is no standard distribution of chord tones for the tunings. Each pedal and knee lever can be tuned individually to specific notes depending on the player's preference or design of the instrument, and each pedal steel player has his "own" tuning that is similar to but subtly different from the tunings of other steelers.

Both the pedal steel and steel guitar are capable of creating sounds unique to the instrument and emulating other sounds like slide guitar, horn sections, and single-note melodies derivative of a clarinet or saxophone.[15] The pedal steel guitarist, like the steel guitarist, uses a thumb pick in conjunction with finger picks along with the bar, pedals, and knee levers. The result is rapid-fire arpeggios, double- and triple-stops with non-chord tones sliding into chord tones, and pedal notes sustained under chord changes, all delivered with precise concern for the rhythm. At the same time these techniques are being employed, the pitches of various strings are being raised or lowered, again predominantly "in time," to facilitate the chord progression of the song and allow the pedal steel guitarist to add the standard country characteristics: (1) semitone slides or portamento-type effects to chord tones from non-chord tones; (2) the bending of a string up to the third of a chord from a suspended second while maintaining the root and fifth on adjacent strings; (3) ascending and descending glissandos; (4) mild vibrato; and (5) other variations to create the characteristic pedal steel "cry."

Chording or "comping" abilities are difficult on the pedal steel and as a result, the steel guitarist will often play sporadically during verses and choruses preferring to "lay out" until the instrument is required. Usually the steel guitar is used for introductions, fills and riffs, solo sections, and ending melodies – which can sometimes end up sounding rather hackneyed.[16] Indeed, a player can garner considerable fame among his or her peers by virtue of the quality and inventiveness of their fills and riffs. It is as much technical ability as creativity that determines the success of the musician, and consequently, his or her fee for tours and recordings.

The electric guitar

In the mid-twentieth century, country music ensembles replaced the juke-boxes as the primary source of musical entertainment in many honky-tonks and juke joints, and it became necessary for the music to become more amplified. The overall noise level of these taverns and bars contributed to the technological advances that led to the amplifying of the guitar. Bands had to be louder in order to be heard over the cacophony of conversation, laughter, clinking glasses, shuffling feet of dancers, and the ubiquitous bar-fights that made up, and still make up, the atmosphere of the local drinking establishment. The steel-string acoustic guitar was simply not loud enough on its own to compete with a drum set and the general racket of the tavern. Amplification was a necessary next step in the guitar's evolution in country music.

Following the electric guitar's initial invention in the early twentieth century by Les Paul and the subsequent modifications and improvements by craftsmen like Leo Fender, the instrument is used in all forms of popular music from blues and rock to jazz and country. Two models were developed by Leo Fender that have become staples for country and blues musicians alike, the Stratocaster and the Telecaster.[17] By far the most popular guitar for country musicians is the Fender Telecaster, which is a single cut-away, dual pick-up, solid body design with an exceptionally bright tone that adapts well to country music. The "twang" so often associated with country guitar

Plate 16 Fender Telecaster (photo courtesy of Fender Musical Instruments)

playing can be directly attributed to the brightness of the bridge pick-up on a Telecaster (see Plates 16–17).

Early country guitarists used a bright tone to cut through the din created by the drums, bass, and most times the noise of the drinking establishments by using the Telecaster's bridge pick-up exclusively. This style of playing became known as "chicken-picking" because of the abundance of treble notes intermixed with muted ones resulting in a rhythmic, percussive sound.

Plate 17 Fender Stratocaster (photo courtesy of Fender Musical Instruments)

Guitarists such as Don Rich from Buck Owens's band, James Burton with Elvis Presley, Clarence White from the Byrds, and more recently Albert Lee, Marty Stuart, Vince Gill, and Ricky Skaggs use Telecasters and "chicken-picking" to define their sound and style.

As well as picking technique, contemporary electric guitarists use some form of signal processing as a defining aural element: reverb combined with a digital signal delay device which creates an echo or "slapback" effect; a compressor used to diminish the initial attack of the notes and provide a mildly percussive tone with increased sustain; some sort of a signal distortion device for a "raunchy" guitar sound; a phase shifter that sweeps continuously through the frequency spectrum adding a liquid quality to the sound; a flanger that sweeps the frequency spectrum in a similar manner as the phase shifter; and a chorus device to add a shimmer for an acoustic guitar quality to the electric guitar sound. All of these effects and many others are used either alone or in combination depending on the style of music. For a song requiring a "rockier" sound, the guitarist might employ a distortion device, compressor, reverb, and possibly some delay to add the rock element dictated by the stylistic components of the song.

For an electric guitarist, tone is of paramount importance both for in-dividual expression and to convey authenticity. Tone is dependent on the type of guitar being played, the gauge of the strings, the density of the pick, individual technique, the use of effects, and most importantly the type of amplifier. The choice of guitar amplifiers is extensive and new technological advances appear regularly.[18] Guitar amplifiers are available in an all-tube design, all solid-state, or a combination of both. Some guitarists feel the all-tube design gives a warmer tone with crisper definition in the upper frequency range and a more desirable ability to be "over-driven." Others feel an affinity for the solid-state models, preferring a cleaner, somewhat thinner sound. The distinctions between tube and solid-state are subtle at best, and choosing an appropriate amplifier becomes an aesthetic choice as much as a functional one.

In addition to constructing guitars, Leo Fender also manufactured guitar amplifiers that have since become standards and widely copied by a plethora of other manufacturers. The Fender Twin, possibly the most popular of all the guitar amps available, is a dual-speaker, all-tube design that has created the signature sound for a large number of country guitarists. Each guitarist has his or her own personal variables and expectations that are to be satisfied by the correct choice of amplifier. Many guitarists struggle for years trying different amps before they settle on the one model that most closely matches their own personal conception of tone. The late twentieth century saw new amplifier models like the Line 6 with built-in computers that are able to digitally model the tone of any amplifier or speaker the guitarist chooses. This negates the need to have a particular amplifier to get "the sound"; with modeling amps, the guitarist simply dials in the sound he or she wants and the computer does the rest. A Line 6 amplifier can successfully masquerade as a Fender Twin or any other amplifier.

The electric guitar was not always welcome in country music ensembles, and initial reactions to the amplification of the guitar were mixed. Many saw it as heresy, a gratuitous reminder of demon progress, a step toward the degradation of the tradition of country music.[19] Others saw it as a tool to be exploited, explored, and developed. Jazz musician Charlie Christian brought the electric guitar to the fore during the mid-1930s, and by the 1940s this new electrified sound was beginning to insinuate itself into the genres of jazz, country, and other popular music.[20] During the summer of 1941, Ernest Tubb (1914–84) recorded "Walking the Floor Over You" which featured solos by Fay "Smitty" Smith on an electric guitar. "Walking the Floor Over You" became Tubb's ticket to the Country Music Hall of Fame, and if the electric accompaniment bothered any of the millions of people who bought the record, they never made it known.[21]

The reaction to the electric guitar in country music would replay itself, albeit much more vehemently, with the folk audience at the 1965 Newport Folk Festival when Bob Dylan introduced the instrument to folk music. The folk audience voiced their displeasure at Dylan "electrifying" a traditionally acoustic genre by loudly booing and jeering the performances, whereas earlier, the country music audience had accepted the electric guitar much more readily. By the mid-1960s, largely thanks to California's burgeoning, rockabilly-influenced Bakersfield sound, which included artists like Buck Owens and Merle Haggard, the electric guitar played a central role on most country recordings. Dozens of country guitarists became stars in their own right during the 1950s and 1960s and cut excellent instrumental albums. Many of these guitarists such as Don Rich, James Burton, Thumbs Carlisle, and Jerry Reed became known as outstanding instrumentalists independent of their work as session guitarists.

Electric guitar technique in country music

A large part of electric guitar playing involves bending strings, a technique that is found in many guitar styles, though the methods behind the bends are not the same. When blues and rock players bend notes they can vary in range from a fraction of a tone to two or three half steps, combined with a somewhat heavy vibrato. The timing tends to be flexible, ranging from a quick grace note to a long slow rise or fall to the intended pitch. In contrast, country players bend notes in a more mechanical fashion. They tend to execute the bent notes with more exactitude, the bent and unbent notes falling directly on the beat with the bends themselves quick and to the point. Most bends are a precise half or whole step and can be a single note, or the double- and triple-stop variety. Vibrato, if present, is generally light.

The incorporation of the pick held between the thumb and forefinger *combined* with the second and third fingers facilitates a finger-style similar to that of the acoustic guitar and, like those of classical guitarists, fingernails

Example 9.4 Pentatonic scale example

Example 9.5 Lick example (B = bend)

are cultivated on the picking hand for more volume and a plectrum-like sound.[22] This also allows the second and third fingers to "snap" a string, not unlike *pizzicato* for violinists, which adds to the percussive element in the "chicken-picking" sound. Using a "pick and fingers" technique is fairly universal among country guitarists, especially for the aforementioned "chicken-picking," and as well for emulating the "cry" of the steel guitar. The electric guitar often imitates the steel guitar, especially in ensembles that do not have one, and to incorporate the authenticity required to successfully represent the music as country. In order to achieve this, string bends are fundamental and necessary.[23]

Country guitar players most often use a major pentatonic scale as the basis for the creation of licks, riffs, and solos, whereas rock and blues players predominantly play a minor pentatonic scale which more closely mirrors the modal-based chord progressions of many rock and blues songs. This is not to say that the major pentatonic scale is the only scale used by country guitarists, but it is the most common because of the diatonic chord progressions of most country songs. Blues elements are present in country music, but generally songs are folk-based tonic, subdominant, dominant progressions or progressions that incorporate "song style" elements such as I–vi–IV–V^7, or I–ii^7–V^7–I. For these types of songs, a major pentatonic scale is preferred. For the country guitarist, the major pentatonic scale falls into natural positions on the fretboard allowing speed and creative flexibility (see Example 9.4).[24]

The presence of 1, 2, and 3 on a single string enables the guitarist to bend 2 up to 3 and then resolve the bend down to 1. This lick can be found in rock music, but with the addition of 5 on the adjacent string, the lick takes on distinctive "country" flair (see Example 9.5).

Example 9.6 Lick example (B = bend)

Example 9.7 Lick example

and

A popular guitar lick that emulates the pedal steel involves bending the third of a G major triad up a half step to a C to create a suspended fourth, and then back down to the third again, with both bend and resolution occurring on the beat (see Example 9.6).

Both electric and steel guitarists use thirds and sixths in their solos and fills. One of the more common "licks" can be seen in Example 9.7. This is also found in blues and rock music, but in keeping with the "country" style, it is delivered on the beat and with little or no vibrato.

Conclusion

What separates country music from other genres is a degree of consistency that can be found in its musical rules and practices. Country music, with its identifying musical elements and performance practice, "sounds" country much the same way Vivaldi's use of sequential material and idiomatic writing "sounds" Baroque, or Schumann's lyrical, melodic quality and harmonic color "sounds" Romantic. To adequately present the music as being "country," the guitarist underscores the crucial elements that define the music as country: folk-based song forms, simple arrangements, singable melodies, "clean" sounds from the rhythm instruments, on-the-beat playing, and subject matter that the audience can identify with.

References

Books and articles

Dalton, Joe. "Get Bent!: Mastering the Art of Country Squeezin'." *Guitar Player* (March, 1995), 61–65.

Fishell, Steve. "An Artists Roundtable: The Future of Pedal Steel." *Guitar Player* (December, 1980), 30–7.

Green, Douglas. "The Guitar in Early Country Music." In *The Guitar Player Book*,
   by the editors of *Guitar Player* magazine. New York, 1978, 281–83.
Gritzner, Charles F. "Country Music: A Reflection of Popular Culture." *Journal of
   Popular Culture* 11 (1978), 857–64.
Ivey, Bill. "Commercialization and Tradition in the Nashville Sound." In *Folk Music
   and Modern Sound*, ed. William Ferris and Mary Hart. Jackson, 1982, 129–41.
Jensen, Joli. *The Nashville Sound: Authenticity, Commercialization, and Country
   Music.* Nashville and London, 1998.
Kienzle, Rich. "The Electric Guitar in Country Music: Its Evolution and
   Development." *Guitar Player* (November, 1979), 30–41.
Malone, Bill C. *Country Music U.S.A.* Revised edn. Austin, 1985.
   Southern Music American Music. Lexington, 1979.
McCloud, Barry, et al., eds. *Definitive Country: The Ultimate Encyclopedia of
   Country Music and its Performers.* New York, 1995.
Mitchell, Donald D. Kilolani and George S. Kanahele. "Hawaiian Steel Guitar:
   Origins and Development." *Guitar Player* (July, 1980), 32–45.
Scheurer, Timothy E. *Born in the U.S.A.: The Myth of America in Popular Music
   From Colonial Times to the Present.* Jackson, 1991.

Websites
Anon. "Steel Stuff." *Mister B's Bassment/Musicians Corner.* 2003.
   www.cox-internet.com/misterb/music/html#steel
Anon. "Dobro story." *Gibson Musical Instruments.* 2000.
   http://www.gibson.com/products/OAI/dobro/story.html
Kuo, Elisa. "History." *National Reso-Phonic Guitars.* 2000.
   http://www.nationalguitars.com

PART III

Baroque and classical guitar today

10 Radical innovations, social revolution, and the baroque guitar

CRAIG H. RUSSELL

Guitar chords with a flurry of strummed strings – sonorities we now regard as commonplace – revolutionized the sound of music at the end of the 1500s and opened up a new universe of musical thought in Western culture. Melody and counterpoint had reigned supreme throughout the Renaissance as the principal musical aspects of a composition, but around 1600 their role was challenged by a startling new concept – harmony. Whereas previously music consisted of horizontal melodic threads interwoven into a lush polyphonic fabric (in which harmonies arose merely as an incidental byproduct), a new school of thought in the seventeenth century held that a work could be governed from the outset by its harmony. Chords were the *starting* point of a composition, not an afterthought. The vertical alignment of sounds, as opposed to the horizontal, became paramount. No instrument better represents this radical transformation than the guitar, which was at the forefront of this aesthetic revolution from the horizontal to the vertical. This shift is born out in the guitar's early notational systems, performance techniques, musical repertoire, and functional roles in society.

Equally importantly, the guitar found itself in the center of the social turmoil and upheavals of the seventeenth and eighteenth centuries. In the 1500s, the guitar was a lowbrow instrument that was overshadowed by the more sophisticated vihuela and lute. But in the 1600s, the guitar was elevated from the culture of the street to that of the royal courts. No longer confined to such venues as neighborhood barber shops or gypsy camp fires, the guitar now found itself equally at home on the operatic stage or in the hands of kings and queens. In the 1700s, traditional European class systems were turned topsy-turvy by scientific advances, a transformed economy based on industrial technologies as opposed to agricultural production, a burgeoning middle class, and world explorations that opened the door for the ensuing interactions of continents and cultures. Once again, the mercurial guitar – always adapting to new situations – found itself at the center of this newly transformed society with its middle-class values and multifarious ethnic identities.

Nothing better illustrates the shift from the horizontal perspective to the vertical around 1600 than guitar notation and guitar treatises. The first publication dedicated to the five-course guitar, Joan Carles Amat's *Guitarra española y vandola* (1586), underscores the dominance of harmony over melody, since his treatise delves into the chord fingerings and harmonic progressions – the plucking of individual notes is never an issue.[1] Amat compares the harmonies of a piece to the colors of a painting and then makes the bold claim that anyone can play along on any piece if he or she understands the harmonic structure:

> The good and expert painter has ready at his disposal all of the colors that are necessary for painting; they are available at his whim and fancy if he wants to paint a man, or a lion, or an ox. In the same way, we have equipped ourselves with all of the chord fingerings, that are like raw material and like the painter's colors, from which one can form every kind of tonality and key by leaping from one [chord] to the next. With these fingerings one can play the *vacas, gallardas, villanos, italianas, pavanas* – and other similar ones – in all twelve keys. And that which makes one marvel (and to many will seem impossible!), is that with these chord fingerings, anybody at all can play along with any musical instrument on whatever piece one might play or might be able to play.[2]

The notation itself, too, highlights harmonic thinking. Amat indicates full chords with a single numeral. His number "1" results in E major, his "2" is A major, "3" is D major, and he continues in this manner through the circle of fifths until he ultimately reaches number "12" which completes the cycle on B major. He accommodates minor chords by adding the suffix "b" for *bemolado* (meaning "flat") to the numerals, and similarly wanders through all twelve minor harmonies; "1b" is E minor, "2b" is A minor, "3b" is D minor, etc. Thus, Amat's orthography splendidly clarifies each chord, but this notation leaves melody to fend for itself. In one stroke, Amat completely reverses the priorities of lute and vihuela tablature notation of the 1500s in which melodic points are depicted with precision, but harmonies occur only as the incidental byproduct of the melodic voice leading.

After Amat's treatise, the Italians dreamed up yet another notational system called the *alfabeto* in which alphabet letters – rather than numerals – indicate to the guitarist which chord fingerings should be depressed. Although *alfabeto* fingerings are handy shortcuts that tell the guitarist particular chord *shapes*, unfortunately these alphabet letters do not correspond to the names of the chords in a traditional music theory sense. That is, the *alfabeto* chord shape designated as "A" does not produce an A major harmony but instead results in a G chord. The ensuing match-ups are equally confusing and counterintuitive. The *alfabeto* shape designated as "B" produces a C major harmony, the letter "C" results in a D major, the letter "D" produces an A minor... and the system winds its way forward in a semi-arbitrary fashion. Its problems aside, alphabet tablature does provide sufficient information to get a novice strumming along with the rest of the

Example 10.1 Millioni and Monte, *Vero e facil modo d'imparare* (1678), p. 6, "Alfabeto straodinario nuovamente inventato"

crew. And like Amat's notation, this is harmonically driven. It is the chords, not the tune, that the guitarist is playing.

The first appearance of the Italian *alfabeto* occurs in Montesardo's *Nuova inventione d'intavolatura* of 1606.[3] Montesardo's chord shapes are explicit, but his rhythms are up for grabs; the works are only playable if one already knows the piece. Sanseverino, on the heels of Montesardo, resolves the issue of rhythmic ambiguity and he also verbally articulates what previously has been implied by Montesardo's notation system – that is, the dominant role that harmony plays in this guitar literature. He postulates that "it seems to me that the Spanish guitar ought to be played with full strokes and not otherwise . . . [since plucking] removes entirely the harmony."[4] Abatessa and Colonna subsequently explore further harmonic possibilities with "shifted chords" (what we now call "bar chords") than can be slid up and down the neck of the guitar to any location. They also compose short harmonic loops as a form of variation; Abatessa and Colonna embellish harmonies through the use of "satellite chords," brief chordal excursions that are caught in the orbit of the original chord and revolve around it as a sort of temporary harmonic center.[5] Once again, we see the conceptual shift from melody to harmony; whereas Renaissance composers had viewed embellishment as the addition of florid runs that decorate the melody, Abatessa's and Colonna's embellishments are fully chordal, where active chord changes spin around the chordal contour.

To further spice up the harmonic palette, several guitarists present chord symbols that are embedded with dissonances. Foriano Pico in his *Nuova scelta di sonate per la chitarra spagnola,* flavors his compositions with unstable, dissonant chords that he labels *lettere tagliati* – and which subsequent authors sometimes call *lettere false, alfabeto falso,* or *alfabeto disonante.*[6] Similarly, Pietro Millioni's and Lodovico Monte's new additions to the *alfabeto* system employ wildly dissonant, spunky harmonies that they identify as "newly invented, extraordinary alphabet chords" (*alfabeto straordinario nuovamente inventato*) (see Example 10.1).[7]

Even Berlioz, Wagner, or Liszt would be hard pressed to match their harmonic daring. What is particularly striking is that the harmonic dissonance is not something that arises from careful voice leading, but is instead an autonomous property of these chord shapes. They are made to be charged with dissonance; the art of preparing and resolving them seems to be of secondary importance. Stefano Pesori and Giovanni Paolo Foscarini incorporate appoggiaturas and fluid passing tones into their chord progressions – usually by moving fingers on the first and second courses – in a kind of "mixed tablature" that fuses together elements of both the newer chordal *alfabeto* system with the individual note placements made possible in the older lute tablature. These "altered alfabeto" chords are interpolated between stable triads, and as chords are slightly altered and restored, the rudimentary elements of melody begin peeking out of the texture once again.[8]

The elegant interplay between strummed and plucked styles found in Foscarini's fifth book served as a model for Francesco Corbetta's transition to the mixed style in his second publication, the *Varii capricci per la ghitarra spagnola* (Milan, 1643).[9] In the hands of Corbetta, at last the guitar was elevated from the level of an amateur's hobby to that of a virtuoso instrument. It would be hard to overemphasize the role Corbetta played in promoting the guitar as an instrument worthy of serious study and development across the European continent. He brought together and synthesized the two disparate worlds of the lute and the guitar: he maintained the strummed techniques from the early guitar's genesis (rich in their vertical harmonies) and wove into that texture the single melodic notes and momentary counterpoint from the lutenist's realm. These mixed elements, first distilled by Foscarini and Corbetta, were then perfected by subsequent masters such as Bartolotti, Roncalli, de Visée, Campion, Murcia, Le Cocq, and Sanz – and in their hands the mixed style survived up to the middle of the 1700s when the Classical aesthetic supplanted that of the Baroque.

Baroque vs. classical guitar

The baroque guitar differs dramatically from its younger sibling, the six-string "classical guitar."[10] Its body is much smaller with a reduced string length, and the curvature of the upper and lower bouts is more slender. Instead of employing the "fan bracing" developed by Antonio Torres in the nineteenth century, the baroque guitar uses a simple pair of parallel braces running on either side of the sound hole – producing a much lighter and introspective sonority (see the chapter by Stewart Pollens in this volume for detailed technical information on baroque guitar construction). The baroque guitar ideally utilizes light-tension gut strings that give a translucent sparkle to the instrument; its crystalline sonorities are further "lightened" in some tunings in which bass strings (*bordones*) are few or absent altogether. Like those of the lute, the baroque guitar's strings leave the bridge directly from holes drilled in the bridge. This system differs substantially from the modern classical guitar's where the strings, having left the bridge's drilled holes, must then immediately ascend over a small piece of ivory (or plastic) called a saddle. Although visually small, this addition gives the modern guitar an enormous boost in sound volume, for once a string is plucked, the vibrations are efficiently transmitted into the guitar's soundboard via the saddle. On the baroque guitar, however, much of a string's energy is absorbed by the bridge without directly motivating the soundboard.

Whereas the classical guitar's range spans several octaves, its six single strings extending from the bass to the soprano registers, the baroque guitar's range is more constrained; it employs five courses rather than six (a course being either a single string or a pair of strings that are grouped so closely that they comprise one performable unit). The first course is usually a single e^1 (its singing clarity earning it the name of *cantino* or *chanterelle*) with the remaining eight strings being spaced together into four pairs. On the surface, all the baroque guitar's standard tunings resemble the modern guitar's first five strings that descend in order: e^1bgda. One baroque tuning replicates the modern guitar with its uninterrupted descent from high- to low-sounding strings (see Example 10.2a). On the other hand, the baroque guitar offered other options that result in lighter textures. One popular tuning, for instance, abandons bass sonorities altogether and advocates the exclusive use of high-pitched treble strings.[11] In this tuning, beginning with the first course, the pitches descend from e^1 to b to g (like the modern guitar), but then suddenly leap *upwards* to a treble d^1 and a – thus making the g on the third course the lowest-sounding note on the instrument (see Example 10.2b). Some guitarists identify this stringing as "re-entrant" tuning, since the treble sounds initially descend but then later "re-enter" as one strums across the instrument. Another tuning splits the fourth and fifth courses into octaves with each of them having both a treble and a bass string; thus a d^1 is grouped with a d on the fourth course, and an a is coupled with an A on course 5 (see Example 10.2c). Still another tuning arose that was particularly adored by the French and other guitarists within the orbit of French influence; this solution employs the octave split on the fourth course and a pair of unison treble strings on the fifth course. For this last tuning, the lowest-sounding note is the bass d on the fourth course (see Example 10.2d). Lastly, a handful of instrumentalists employed yet another tuning in which the third course is split into octaves; the highest-sounding g^1 soars above its neighbors (see Example 10.2e).[12]

These distinctions between the modern and baroque guitars are not

Example 10.2 Baroque guitar tunings

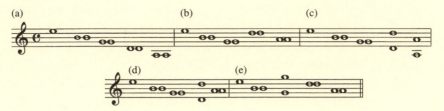

mere academic curiosities; they lie at the heart of different artistic sensibilities. The classical guitar is perfectly designed for polyphony and the interweaving of separate contrapuntal lines. The baroque guitar is designed for homophony and is ideal as a strummed chordal instrument. The bulk of classical guitar literature is for solo performance with the spotlight on the individual rather than the ensemble. In the baroque, these preferences are inverted; the sparkling tinkle of the baroque guitar was a standard element of ensemble performance (as evidenced by the nearly obligatory sections on accompanying in baroque guitar manuals). The sound qualities of the baroque guitar and classical guitar are worlds apart: the classical guitar is imposing and resonant; the baroque is introspective and delicate.

Ornamentation, strumming and other effects

It was this sparkling world of delicacy that became the core of baroque guitar literature. A perusal of baroque guitar books reveals a fascination with "flavor" or color. Even from the outset, when technique concentrated on strumming rather than plucking, guitarists already presented a myriad of different effects such as the *repicco* and *trillo*. Pietro Millioni in 1627 describes the rather complex strumming technique known as *repicco* in which the thumb and middle finger strum downwards, and then the thumb returns in an upwards direction along with the index finger which plucks the first string rather than enveloping all the courses. There is a flurry of undulating sonority followed by the index finger's single melodic note that rings out above the texture.[13] Similarly, the *trillo* (which has no relationship to the melodic trill) employed the index finger in a rapid up-and-down strum.[14] The strumming techniques or *batterie* reached new heights in Francesco Corbetta's *La Guitarre royalle dediée au Roy de la Grande Bretagne* (Paris, 1671).[15] He uses stems of various lengths to indicate which finger of the right hand strums; in his "Caprice de chacone," Corbetta fashions a torrent of cascading strums that foreshadow the energetic fervor of a modern flamenco bulerías.[16]

In later repertoire where individual notes are plucked, ornamentation abounds, and each phrase – sometimes each note – is given a different nuance or "flavor." More than any other feature, it is the variety of flavored shadings that motivated the baroque guitar aesthetics in the last half of the seventeenth century. Francisco Gueráu, for example, decorates almost every available pitch with adornments, and he verbally emphasizes the importance of ornamentation in his introductory comments to his *Poema harmónico* (1694).[17] In his "Advice to Beginners," Gueráu elucidates the rudiments of performance technique, the way to read tablature notation, and the way to play ornaments such as slurs (*extrasinos*), trills (*trinos* or *aleados*), mordents (*mordentes*), and vibrato (*temblor*). At the conclusion of his explication, he sums up the indispensable role of ornamentation by stating:

> These performance tips that I have explained – as well as ones that I will not address – are required by the guitar of anyone who might wish to play it with some skill. And although all of these points are essential for a good result, that which is the most gorgeous and causes the most harmony is the persistence of the trill, mordent, slur, and arpeggio. And although it is true that it will sound just fine if one plays good music in rhythm on an instrument that is in tune, nevertheless, by using these adornments – which are the heart and soul of music – you will see the difference between one [good] performance and the other.[18]

Other guitarists cover similar territory in their tablature books, praising the effects of ornamentation and providing detailed lists of the specific adornments or *agréments*. Francesco Corbetta's *La Guitarre royalle* maps out the proper execution of ornaments (explaining them in both Italian and French), covering the trill (*tremblement* or *tremolo*), appoggiatura (*cheute* or *abelimento*), slur (*roullement* or *strascio*), mordent (*martellement* or *rebatimento*), vibrato (*flattement* or *tremolo sforzato*), cadence figures (*cadenses* or *cadenzze*), and the sustaining of a pitch (*tenüe* or *tenute*).[19] Nearly every other prominent guitarist ventures into the same collage of sonorities, some even exploring further refinements such as the different sonority evoked by different right-hand fingerings.[20] Robert de Visée and Nicolas Derosier prescribe which right-hand finger executes any given gesture, and they clearly are attuned to multifarious and subtle distinctions caused by different-sized fingers and the different timbres produced by fingertips and fingernails.[21] A finger's downstroke emphasizes the crisp attack of the nail against the string, whereas the same finger in an upstroke elicits a warmer grouping of overtones as the broad flesh of the finger brushes by the string. The thumb's pudgy width and its strength produces a rotund and forceful sound compared to the narrower and brighter-sounding index finger whose crispness is preferred by de Visée at final cadences. Nuanced colors apply to the playing of chords as well: sometimes a chord's notes are simultaneously plucked and at other times they are rolled in a gentle arpeggio. At times a chord is enunciated by the crisp, downward stroke of the fingernail, and at other times the guitarist produces a mellower strum by the soft flesh of the thumb as it descends across the strings. In short, subtle variance of timbre is the aesthetic prize. This is in direct opposition to the Classical aesthetic where consistency of timbre was the desirable goal; for classical guitarists, the melodic line is a unified thread – much like a strand of spaghetti. For baroque guitarists, however, an elegant musical phrase should be rich in nuanced timbres, each note and each chord having its own color and articulation – rather like a salad of diverse and refreshing flavors that somehow blend and combine according to the whim of the chef.

And de Visée carefully arranges the fingerings to bring out the proper octave of a course; that is, his specific choices result in a finger striking harder the particular string of the pair that will best maintain smooth voice leading in the context of the phrase. When the bass string is to dominate, he has the index finger strike in an upward direction, bringing out the *bordón* (for it is strung closest to the floor). If he wants the treble to penetrate, he selects the thumb – which will strike the treble string initially and with greater force.

Several artists explore more adventuresome timbral options. Santiago de Murcia employs a percussive *golpe* – presumably the striking of the guitar top with the right hand – in his lively setting of the African-American *cumbé*.[22] One of the most spectacular and novel effects peculiar to the baroque guitar is *campanelas* (bell-like runs), made possible by the instrument's re-entrant tuning.[23] Since the five courses all have strings that sound in the *same* octave, the guitarist is therefore able to play ascending or descending scales in stepwise motion merely by changing strings, not by depressing notes with the left hand as is necessary on the modern guitar. Since consecutive pitches are played on different strings, they continue to ring in a bell-like effect (hence the name *campanelas*, derived from the word *campana* meaning "bell"). The glittering notes race by but continue to project in much the same way that un-stopped sounds continue to resonate in a piano when one depresses the damper pedal. The effect is stunning, and one has only to look at the splendid lines in the works of Gaspar Sanz, Bartolotti, or Santiago de Murcia to see what a breathtaking effect it can be. Sadly, *campanelas* is impossible on the modern classical guitar since the rapid shifting between strings generates all sorts of octave displacements that preclude any linear melodic movement.

Accompanying

Yet another element reinforcing the guitar's role in the revolution from polyphony to homophony around 1600 was its incessant appearance as an accompanying instrument. New styles and social contexts required *chordal* accompaniments, and few instruments were better suited than the guitar. Throughout the Baroque, the guitar thrived in both the courtly and the popular milieu – in the tavern, at the palace, or in the plaza. It was the quintessential accompanying instrument, and in that respect its role differs dramatically from that of the modern classical guitar. Whereas a modern guitarist has to scramble to find first-rate *ensemble* literature, the baroque guitar was as much a part of mainstream ensemble playing as the harpsichord or organ. Most guitarists addressed accompanying in a substantial way, and many – such as Corbetta, Granata, Matteis, Murcia, Doizi de Velasco, Campion, and Sanz – wrote perceptively on the figured bass and the art of accompanying.[24]

The critical role of accompanying in guitar literature is apparent from the first moments of the Baroque. If one peruses Italian publications of Italian homophony from the first half of the seventeenth century, one finds as nearly obligatory the presence of guitar *alfabeto* letters above the melody to facilitate chordal strumming.[25] Girolamo Montesardo – an accomplished vocalist himself and the very same individual who was first to publish a guitar book utilizing the *alfabeto* system – sent to press an impressive collection of vocal pieces, *I lieti giorni di Napoli* (1612), that included accompanying guitar chords over the bass line.[26] Similarly, Kapsberger, Falconieri, and Vitali meticulously place the *alfabeto* chords over the basso continuo lines in their vocal publications in the early decades of the seventeenth century.[27] Undoubtedly, the proper accompaniment for these delightful works should include the strummed guitar as part of the musical texture. For the aforementioned artists who were accomplished and erudite musicians, errors in guitar indications are infrequent. But the rage for accompanied vocal songs spurred lesser talents into the arena as well. Sometimes, an author's flimsy understanding of music theory results in *alfabeto* accompaniments that are rather laughable. One such fiasco occurs in Abatessa's song arrangements in the *Cespuglio di varii fiori* (1635) in which all bass notes are harmonized as if they were root position chords, and he cannot figure out the difference between major and minor chords.[28] Of course, Abatessa's ineptitude is the exception rather than the rule.

As the Baroque unfolded, several major artists continued to devote considerable attention to the guitar as the accompanying instrument for vocal music. Giovanni Casalotti's "Villanelle di più sorte," a gargantuan tome typical of these compendiums, presents almost 200 songs.[29] Similarly, Ms. 2804 in the Biblioteca Riccardiana contains 173 texted songs, here identified as *passcagli*.[30] Vocal accompaniments occur in baroque guitar books with the exquisite craftsmanship of virtuosi such as Corbetta in his *Guitarre royalle* (1671) and Henry Grenerin in his *Livre de guitarre* (1680).[31]

The baroque guitar and the theater

The stage played a role equal to song in the performing life of baroque guitarists. During the late seventeenth and eighteenth centuries, the guitar remained a mainstay of the Spanish stage and performed at most *comedias*, either during the play itself or in the small musical skits that were customarily inserted between the main acts.[32] Before the play's opening act, the players usually presented a brief *loa* (a sort of preface without any direct bearing on the drama that was to ensue); after Act I either an *entremés* (entr'acte) or a *jácaras* was mounted. An *entremés* normally involved a brief comic plot with a song or two that often were accompanied by dancing. Not infrequently, the characters mercilessly skewer prominent officials in their witty banter and riotous pranks. The *jácaras* was a specific subgenre of entr'acte in which the personages were lovable ruffians or peasants who found themselves in some predicament or humorous setting. Even if the playlet's text does not label a piece specifically as a *jácaras*, its style can be implied by the characters' names in the libretto. Escarramán, Zurdo, Zurdillo, and Clarín are stereotypical *jaques* – likeable servants, blind beggars, or low-life scoundrels in trouble with the law – and most often when their names appear, one can expect the music accompanying their antics to be a *jácaras*. Between Acts II and III, the single member of the cast or the whole troupe could present yet another short theatrical number, this time the *baile* or dance scene. As its title suggests, it could be based on any of the popular dances of the time, usually folkloric or "regular" everyday dancing as opposed to aristocratic courtly dance or ballet. It represents "popular" street culture, not pageantry. And after Act III, to conclude the evening's entertainment, the theater troupe could tack on a *mojiganga* or *fin de fiesta*. The *mojiganga* characteristically featured performers with outlandish masks, animal costumes or extravagant disguises – much like the fantastical costumes worn at Mardi Gras.

In Spain, the standard theater band for a Golden-Age play consisted of the baroque guitar coupled with either the harp or *violón* (a term which could imply violin as well as cello).[33] Several theater troupes graced the stages of the three theaters in eighteenth-century Madrid (the Teatro del Príncipe, Teatro de la Cruz, and Caños del Peral), and they habitually brought with them a small ensemble of two or three musicians, which almost always included the guitar. The theater troupe of Juan Bautista Chavarría featured a band with Chavarría on harp and Juan de Serqueira on guitar. The reputable musicians working the theaters or *coliseos* included guitarists Serqueira, Pedro de Castro, and Joseph de Salas; the star harpists were Chavarría and Manuel de Ferreyra; and the *violón* parts were deftly played by Juan de Chaves, Salvador de Navas, or Pedro de Castro. Remarkably, to this day, that baroque combination of harp and baroque guitar (now called a *jarana*) – and even much of the repertoire from its Baroque ancestry – thrives in the folk music of Veracruz, Mexico.[34] The masterly Spanish guitarist and theorist Santiago de Murcia was probably the composer for the theatrical works by Francisco de Castro, Spain's most important playwright in the opening decades of the eighteenth century.[35] His guitar teacher, the phenomenal Francisco Gueráu, also penned dramatic works: one might reasonably assume that the guitar found its way into Gueráu's accompanying ensembles.[36]

In France, too, the guitar was an indispensable part of the opera and ballet orchestra. Lully's and Campra's luxuriant stage works include guitarists repeatedly and in multiple contexts, and the guitar parts were surely played with aplomb given that Corbetta, de Visée, Grenerin, and Campion were all involved with theatrical productions. One can imagine the splendor and thrill when Corbetta himself strolled onto stage leading a group of guitarists in the première of Lully's *Ballet de la galanterie du temps* in 1656.[37] Henry Grenerin, yet another master of guitar and theorbo, played in Lully's *Ballet de Psyché* and the *Ballet royal de l'impatience* (1661).[38] De Visée, who studied under Corbetta's tutelage, ascended to unprecedented heights in his compositional subtlety and skill; he too was intimately involved with Lully's sumptuous productions, as is evidenced by the large number of Lully transcriptions in de Visée's tablature books.[39] Guitarists continued playing excerpts from French masterpieces long after the original theatrical works closed – well into the 1700s. As far away as Mexico and California, Campra and Lully comprised part of the core instrumental literature, as is illustrated by the numerous "fake books" or anthologies found in the New World that have Lully and Campra peppered throughout their pages. A list of top hits indicates that any self-respecting guitarist would have been able to launch into Campra's "Amable" from *Hésione* or the Bourée from Lully and Colasse's *Achilles* at a moment's notice.[40]

Baroque dance and the guitar

After song and stage, dance occupied a third critical area for guitar accompaniment. The Italian tablature books are chock-full of dance genres such as the balleto, brando, corrente, sarabanda, alemanda, and giga. Their binary constructions place the double bar halfway through or slightly before the midpoint. The French have corresponding cousins in the allemande, courante, sarabande, gigue, bourée, gavotte, menuet, etc. Of course, a good deal of this repertoire is dance-inspired, but not necessarily intended for dance accompaniment.[41]

That is not the case, however, with the copious settings of French *danses à deux* and contredanses, which are "practical" and utilitarian in nature. The *danse à deux* took Europe by storm in the late seventeenth and early eighteenth centuries. For people of high social station, it was all the rage, and the aristocracy expended countless hours in the time-consuming task of learning each new dance as it rolled off the press of Raoul-Auger Feuillet in Paris. Feuillet and Pierre Beauchamp solved the thorny problems of dance notation so that entire choreographies (including foot placement, hand motions, arm movement, etc.) could be realized and reconstructed solely by using abstract symbols rather than relying on verbose, meticulous textual descriptions or realistic graphic depictions of dancers. Feuillet's ingenious system, like music notation, was abstract, adaptable, and reasonably self-sufficient. In the *danse à deux*, a single couple dances at a time (unlike group dances where many couples simultaneously participate) etching out elegant, symmetrical patterns that are directed toward the "presence" – an important spectator such as the king or some other imposing royal person. Each new dance carefully joined choreography to a particular accompaniment – for every measure of music, the couple had to memorize the specific step patterns uniquely designed for that location. Thus, it did not help much to know last year's repertoire; it was irrelevant. But as soon as a new dance arrived from France, the studious dancers had to start from scratch once again to memorize each of its choreographic instructions. The task was never-ending. Feuillet's press issued four to six *danses à deux* a year, and dancing fans eagerly sought them out as fast as they rolled off the press – in a sense, the *danse à deux* was the "rock and roll" of the era.

The guitar was at the center of this fad. Countless manuscripts and publications from the early 1700s embrace *danse à deux* settings, and it is clear they were intended for actual accompaniment. No source better illustrates the utilitarian role of the guitar's accompanying function for *danses à deux* than Santiago de Murcia's *Resumen de acompañar la parte con la guitarra* (1714).[42] If one compares the "Catalogue" of Feuillet's available publications with the table of contents of Murcia's *Resumen*, one finds they progress along chronologically in an identical fashion(see Plate 18 and Table 10.1).[43] This ordering would have made perfect sense for practicing performers of the time who surely would have known the year that a particular tune had been released – in much the same way that modern pop performers who make a living playing cover versions of Billboard hits can easily tell you the year that a pop tune hit the charts. In short, Murcia's *Resumen de acompañar* is a veritable jazz "fake-book" that supplied the necessary information for guitarists who played at *danses à deux* functions.

Table 10.1 *Comparison of the contents of Feuillet's* Catalogue des Livres de Danses *with Murcia's* Resumen de acompañar la parte (1714)

Feuillet's *Catalogue*	Murcia's *Resumen* (1714)	Page	[Composer]
Scavoir			
Le Livre de la Chorégraphie	–		
Le gros Recüeil . . . de Mr Pécour			
La Bourée d'Achille	La Buree de Chil	58	Lully/Colasse
La Mariée	La Mariee (with its "Giga")	58	Lully
Le Passepied	Paspied Viejo	57	
La Contredance	Otra Giga	60	Lully
Le Rigaudon	Rigodon (with "Otro" [Rigodon])	61	
La Bourgogne	La Bourgogne	61	
La Savoye (Bourée)	La Saboyana Buree	63	
La Forlana	La ferlana	63	Campra
La Conty (Venitenne)	La Contij	64	Campra
Danses de Bal			
La Pavanne des Saisons [1700]	La Pabana des Sesons	65	Lully
Le Passe-Pié Nouveau [1700]	Paspied Nuebo	57	
l'Aimable Vainqueur [1701]	La Amable Despa[ci]o	66	Campra
l'Allemande [1702]	La Alemanda	67	Campra/Lully
Petits Recüeils Annuels			
la Païsanne (1703)	Los Paysanos	66	
les Contrefaiseur Contredanse (1703)		–	
la Saltarelle (1704)	La Saltarele	68	Campra
la Carignan (1704)	La Cariguan	68	Gillier
la Madalena (1704)	La Madalena	69	
la Babeth (1705)	La Babet	70	de la Barre
la Bretagne (1705)	La Bretaignee Paspied	70	Campra
la Triomphante (1705)	La Triumphante	(84)	Campra/Lully
la Baviere (1706)	La Babiere. Menuet	70	de la Barre
la Fanatique (1706)	La Marcha de Fanatiques	71	
le Cotillon (1706)	El Cotillon	71	
la Bacchante (1707)	La Bacante	72	La Coste
la Matelotte (1707)	La Mathalote	72	Marais
le Menuet a quatre (1707)	Le Menuet a quater	72	
la Nouvelle Bourgogne (1708)	La Nueba Bergoña Paspied	73	
la Nouvelle Mariée (1708)	La Nueba Mariee	74	Lully
la Nouvelle Gaillarde (1709)	La Nueba Gallarda	74	
le Menuet d'Alcide (1709)	El Menuet de Alcides	75	Lully/Marais
le Charmant Vainqueur (1709)	La Charmant de Vainqueur Grave	75	
la Bourbon (1710)	La Borbon	76	Campra/Lully
la petite Bourée (1710)	La Pequeña Buree	76	
la Gouastala (1710)	La Guastala	77	
la Nouvelle Forlanne (1711)	La Nueba Forlana	77	
le Passepied à quatre (1711)	El Paspied a quatro	78	
la Medicis (1711)	Rondo La Medicis	78	
la Silvie (1712)	La Silbia Grave	79	
la Dombe (1712)	La Dombe	80	
l'Asturienne (1712)	La Asturiana Rigodon	80	
la Melanie (1713)	La Melanie	81	
la Denain (1713)	La Denain	81	

The French aesthetic was not the only one that thrived in Spain in the early eighteenth century. For several centuries – beginning in the late 1500s and continuing well into the mid-1700s – the Spanish delighted in two different families of indigenous dances (*danzas* and *bailes*) that were readily

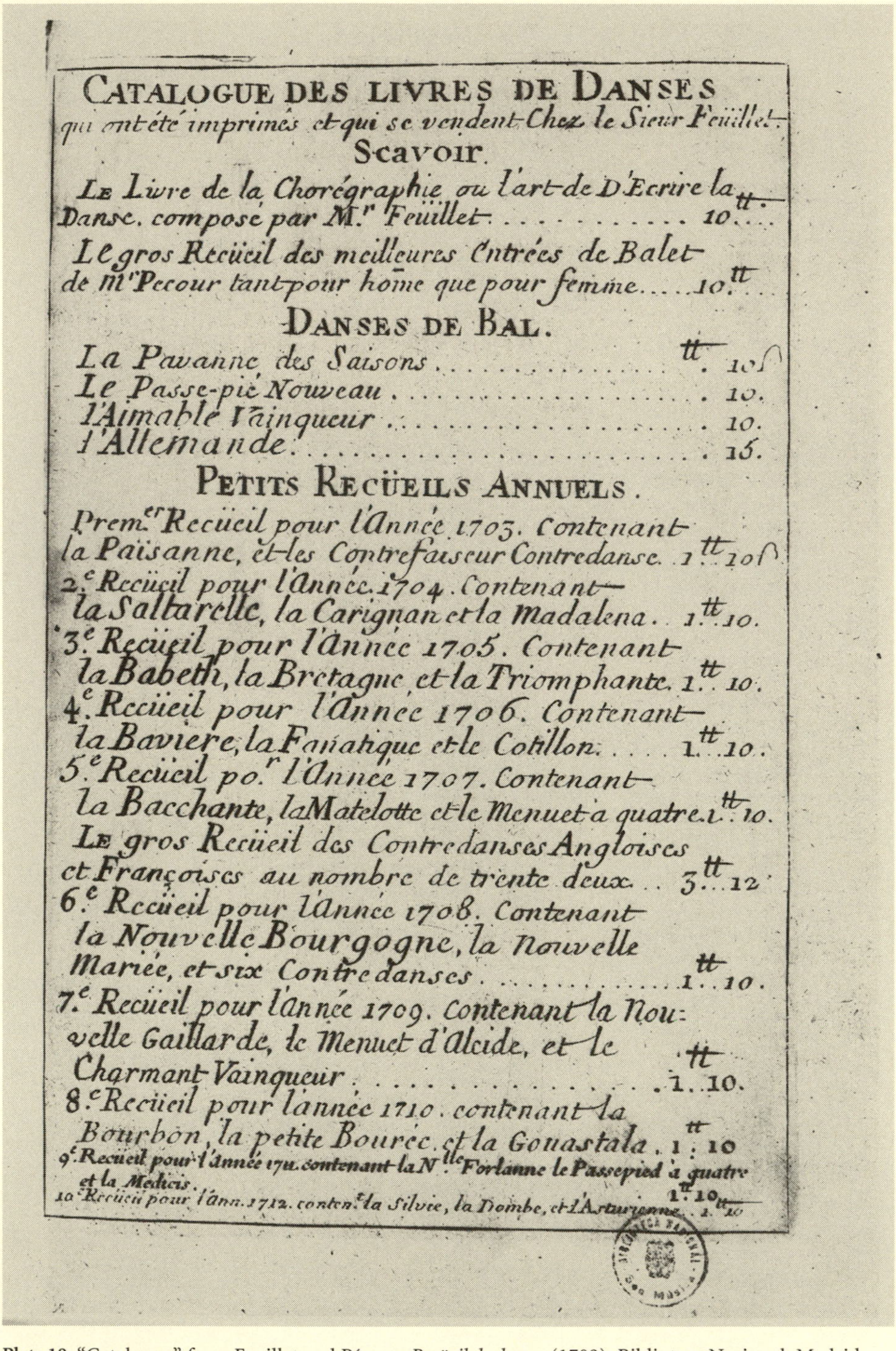

CATALOGUE DES LIVRES DE DANSES
qui ont été imprimés et qui se vendent Chez le Sieur Feüillet.
Scavoir.

Le Livre de la Chorégraphie ou l'art de D'Ecrire la Danse. composé par M.r Feüillet 10.tt

Le gros Recüeil des meilleures Entrées de Balet de M.r Pecour tant pour home que pour femme 10.tt

DANSES DE BAL.

La Pavanne des Saisons . . . . tt. 10s

Le Passe-pié Nouveau . . . . 10.

l'Aimable Vainqueur . . . . 10.

l'Allemande . . . . 15.

PETITS RECÜEILS ANNUELS.

Prem.er Recüeil pour l'Année 1703. Contenant la Païsanne, et les Contrefaiseur Contredanse. 1.tt 10s

2.e Recüeil pour l'Année 1704. Contenant la Saltarelle, la Carignan et la Madalena . . 1.tt 10.

3.e Recüeil pour l'Année 1705. Contenant la Babeth, la Bretagne, et la Triomphante. 1.tt 10.

4.e Recüeil pour l'Année 1706. Contenant la Baviere, la Fanatique et le Cotillon . . . . 1.tt 10.

5.e Recüeil po.r l'Année 1707. Contenant la Bacchante, la Matelotte et le Menuet a quatre. 1.tt 10.

Le gros Recüeil des Contredanses Angloises et Françoises au nombre de trente deux . . 3.tt 12

6.e Recüeil pour l'Année 1708. Contenant la Nouvelle Bourgogne, la Nouvelle Mariée, et six Contredanses . . . . 1.tt 10.

7.e Recüeil pour l'année 1709. Contenant la Nouvelle Gaillarde, le Menuet d'Alcide, et le Charmant Vainqueur . . . . 1.tt 10.

8.e Recüeil pour l'année 1710. contenant la Bourbon, la petite Bourée et la Gouastala . 1.tt 10

9.e Recüeil pour l'Année 1711. contenant la N.lle Forlanne le Passepied a quatre et la Medicis 1.tt 10

10.e Recüeil pour l'Ann. 1712. conten.t la Silvie, la Dombe, et l'Asturienne . . 1.tt 10

Plate 18 "Catalogue" from Feuillet and Pécour, *Recüeil de danses* (1709), Biblioteca Nacional, Madrid

2.ᵉ Recüeil de Nouvelles Contredanses Françoises
et Angloises de l'Année 1712. au nomb. de 28.. 3ᵗᵗ 12.

11.ᵉ Recüeil pour l'Année 1713, contenant la Melanie
et la Denain . . . . 1ᵗᵗ 10.

12.ᵉ Recüeil pour l'année 1714. contenant la Gavotte
de Scaux, le Rigaudon et la Chamberry. . 1ᵗᵗ 10.

13.ᵉ Recüeil pour l'année 1715. Contenant la Transilvanie
et le Menuet d'Espagne . . . . 1ᵗᵗ 10.

14.ᵉ Recüeil pour l'année 1716. Conten.ᵗ la Gavotte du Roi
la Bourée Nouvelle et le Cotillon des Fêtes de
Thalie . . . . 1ᵗᵗ 10 ſ.

Plate 18 (*cont.*)

distinguishable from each other.[44] On the one hand, *danzas* were rather subdued in nature (at least with regard to their choreography), were danced from the waist down with no upper body or hand motions, and were associated with the aristocratic upper classes. The *bailes*, in contrast, were rowdier in mood (often of a lascivious nature that could even approach the scandalous), were associated with the lower classes or even low-life scoundrels, and were performed with enticing and florid motions in the arms and hands. *Bailes* often were accompanied by the clatter of castanets, rattle of tambourines, or percussive drive of small hand drums, unlike the more restrained and demulcent *danzas* that normally precluded the use of hand percussion. The guitar books, beginning with Amat's and continuing through Murcia's, present the standard chord progressions for the plethora of *bailes* and *danzas* that were the rage in Spain and her colonies.

The performance of these Spanish dances represents the epitome of Baroque jazz – the guitarist spells out the chordal basis of the work by initially strumming through the well-known progression a few times (in much the same way that Bird Parker or Dizzy Gillespie would play the "head" of a particular composition) and then blasts off into wild flights of improvisational fancy in a series of *diferencias* (which would correspond to the "choruses" in a Parker or Gillespie jazz recording). Much of the notated repertoire in Spanish guitar books, then, consists of intabulated examples (that is, arranged for tablature) of sample variations – rather than "finished" and complete compositions.

For example, Sanz repeatedly gives a title and then provides only a phrase or two of music; they are tasty snippets but not complete meals. He would be shocked to see the modern-day performances of these musical hors d'oeuvres where the disparate dances are strung together into incongruous "suites" that change topics every twenty seconds and never elaborate or expand on a single idea. To play fifteen of these tiny segments one after another and then call it a "suite" would be rather like stringing together fifteen movie trailers into an hour-and-a-half, visual hodge-podge and then calling it a "film." Although the experience might even be pleasurable, it would not be typical or representative of modern cinematography. Similarly, a string of patched-together guitar improvisations (each improvisation based on a different harmonic progression) is not representative of the Spanish performance traditions during the Baroque.

Improvisation

Fortunately, we do have representative examples of the guitarist's improvisatory art that reveal the skills that were expected in the realization and performance of *danzas* and *bailes*. Some of the best examples of *diferencia* realization are found in an important manuscript located in Spain[45] that anthologizes works by "the best authors." With the exception of several pieces by Francesco Corbetta and a handful also set by Santiago de Murcia, the lion's share of the manuscript is devoted to Gaspar Sanz's *Instrucción de música sobre la guitarra española* (1674). Some of the selections are faithful copies of the Sanz originals, but more interesting are the numerous renditions that depart from them. Careful scrutiny of these two sources reveals that phrases are, in fact, modules that can be removed, inserted, and interchanged to create "new" pieces. The "Libro de diferentes cifras" lops off the final variations of Sanz's "Passacalle de la L."[46] Sometimes the opening strum patterns are excised (since it would have been implicit they were to be performed anyway), as in the reworked version of Sanz's "Passacalle de 3° tono."[47] Near the middle of the piece, the order of two phrases is inverted. In a subsequent example, the "Libro de diferentes cifras" excises the strummed introduction to Sanz's "Passacalles por la C" and then launches directly into the heart of the piece. The manuscript meticulously copies the following three-and-a-half phrases from Sanz, but from that point forward the two versions diverge dramatically – they become different compositions. Here, Sanz's original *diferencia* composition serves as a springboard for a totally new creation.

Particularly fascinating is the "Libro de diferentes cifras"' reworking of Sanz's "Jácaras"; it reveals the rich variety of possibilities in modular recomposition. The manipulation of phrases in this type of recomposition is not entirely arbitrary but generally follows certain patterns. One basic principle is that new modules can be generated from segments of other modules. For instance, a module can reappear several times in a work using the same beginning but spun out to a different end, as can be seen in the reworking of Sanz's Variations 2 and 5 (see Example 10.3).

Another manner of generating new phrases from old ones is to break the original into two parts and use the first as the beginning of a new module and the second as the end of another, forming a sort of musical parenthesis that creates two phrases from splitting one. Of particular interest here is the way the "Libro de diferentes cifras" draws out Variation 7 into two phrases. The *campanelas* beginning – which is the stylistic link to the *campanelas* conclusion of Variation 6 – remains unchanged, but the tail is transformed into a rapid, descending scale. The following variation uses as its conclusion the remainder of Variation 7 to lead back gracefully to the high tessitura of Variation 8 (see Example 10.4).

In this manner, all new material is inserted in such a way as to preserve the smooth transitions and essential qualities of the original.

Not only are properties of the original respected, but they are often emphasized and amplified in the reworked version. Sanz pushes to the climax

Example 10.3 Comparison of "Jácaras" phrases in Sanz and "Libro de diferentes cifras"

Sanz, *Variation 2*, mm. 5-9

"Libro de diferentes cifras," mm. 25-29

"Libro de diferentes cifras," mm. 57-61

Sanz, *Variation 5*, mm. 17-21

"Libro de diferentes cifras," mm. 5-9

"Libro de diferentes cifras," mm. 17-21

Example 10.4 Comparison of "Jácaras" phrases in Sanz and "Libro de diferentes cifras"

Sanz, mm. 25-29

"Libro de diferentes cifras," mm. 33-41

Example 10.5 Similar phrases in "Libro de diferentes cifras"

mm. 49–57

of the piece through a series of running scales (Variations 12 through 15). The "Libro de diferentes cifras" is careful not to break this drive to the climax, but even enhances the finale's strength by expanding this energetic section of fast scales from four to eight (mm. 66–96).

Only changes in vibrato and register distinguish two other variations from being identical twins (Example 10.5).

This example, and the previous ones, demonstrate decisively that a *diferencia* composition is not comprised of inviolable measures in a highly rigid order. Instead, it can be viewed as a smorgasbord of phrases that can be dropped off the menu at will – or can be supplanted with new phrases if so desired. A guitarist, then, would be expected to be fresh, original, and new; he or she would realize a particular *baile* or *danza* in different way with each performance opportunity.

The social world of the baroque guitar

The revolution in musical styles that we have already examined – the shift from a horizontal and melodic perspective to a vertical and harmonic one – occurred simultaneously with socio-political shifts in perspective that were to rock society and shake the foundations of the privileged, aristocratic system. The guitar is one of the few instruments that saw itself climb up the social ladder, from a relatively low stature in the early Baroque to acceptance in high society by the late years of that epoch. In the early 1600s, it was considered the popular instrument of amateurs or low-lifes. Luis Briçeño, in the preface to his *Método mui facilissimo*, defends his beloved instrument against its detractors who view the guitar as too lowly by stating:

> There are many, my Lady, who ridicule the guitar and its sound. But if they
> pause and think about it, they will discover that for our present era, the
> guitar is the most favorable instrument that has ever been seen! For
> nowadays, if one is trying to save out-of-pocket expenses and trouble, the

guitar is a true theatre of savings! In addition to this, it is adaptable and appropriate for singing and playing, for performing [noble] *danzas*, for accompanying leaping steps or running ones, for accompanying [low-life] *bailes*, or for accompanying [heel-clicking] tap dancing.[48]

The fad for guitar playing that swept Europe in the early 1600s was viewed with ambivalence by those who, on the one hand, enjoyed its dulcet strums, but on the other hand saw the guitar's rising popularity as a potential scourge that was displacing more "high-minded" instruments. For instance, Lope de Vega and Cervantes tip their hats in respect to Vicente Espinel for his contributions to the guitar and its popularity. But even Lope, who had praised Espinel in his *Caballero de Illescas* (1602) and *Laurel de Apolo* (1630), nevertheless expresses his melancholic regret that Espinel's guitar innovations were overwhelming and supplanting aspects of more "noble" music. In *Dorotea* (1632), Lope laments, "God forgive Vicente Espinel for bringing us this novelty and the five-course guitar with which the noble instruments are being forgotten."[49]

Musical theatre productions further clarify the social stereotypes that society held for guitarists. Typically, the cast performing *bailes* on stage to the sound of guitars are characters such as Zurdo, Zurdillo, Clarín, or Escarramán – all of whom are lovable, comical, low-class ruffians and scoundrels. And moving one step up on the social ladder, the guitar appears in the hands of menial craftsmen such as barbers. It is rare to see the guitar in the hands of the ruling aristocracy in the first decades of the seventeenth century.

But once the guitar fad began to sweep Europe, the instrument worked its way up the social ladder, rung by rung, until it was the darling of the nobility in the late 1600s. Nearly every crowned head of Europe knew a few chords and had a guitar virtuoso as a personal teacher. The real watershed in this area was Francesco Corbetta, whose private students or close acquaintances read like a "Who's Who in Seventeenth-Century Europe." Some of them include: Carlo II, the Duke of Mantua; Philip IV of Spain; Archduke Leopold Wilhelm of Austria; Duke George William of Zell at the Hanover Court; Charles II of England; James, the Duke of York; Henrietta Anne, the Duchess of Orleans; and Louis XIV of France, with whom he had a lifelong friendship.[50] The incomparable Francisco Gueráu occupied a place of importance in Carlos II's court in Madrid, and following the king's death in 1700 and the subsequent coronation of the first Bourbon king in Spain, Philip V, the guitar remained a part of daily life in the Spanish court. Gueráu's probable pupil, Santiago de Murcia, gave private instruction to the new Queen, Maria Luisa Gabriela of Savoy, and Antonio de Murcia was appointed official guitar maker for the monarchs.[51] Other European courts lavished attention

Example 10.6 Fandango rhythm

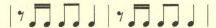

on their guitar instructors and makers. Clearly, the guitar was no longer relegated to the gutter.

Of particular interest is the way the guitar became adopted by the newest social class to rise to prominence in the late seventeenth and eighteenth centuries – the middle class. In the 1700s, the rise of egalitarian ideals in the Age of Reason and the concurrent rise of the middle class shook the foundations of the ailing aristocratic system. No instrument better illustrates those social revolutions than the guitar. The guitar was the working man's instrument. It was relatively inexpensive, highly portable, extremely popular, and easily learned with self-instruction books. Several of the guitar books flagrantly brag that they can teach an interested person how to play without their having to take lessons.[52] The painters of the time, first Watteau and later Goya, place the guitar in the hands of ordinary people (rich, poor, or middle class) in nearly every imaginable setting and venue.[53] New dance genres evolved that ruptured the barriers between *danzas* and *bailes*, and in each case, the new appeal was a common ground where the middle class, rich and poor, aristocrat and servant, could meet on equal footing. Among these social newcomers were the seguidillas, jota, sombras, and most important of all, the fandango. In each case, the preferred instrument for dancing accompaniment was the guitar. The earliest known musical settings of the fandango, jota, and seguidillas occur in Santiago de Murcia's "Códice Saldívar No. 4" for guitar. His setting of the fandango is one of the highlights of the guitar repertoire with its incessant, hypnotic alternation of D minor and A major chords, its infectious build-up in intensity, florid and virtuosic runs, and its recurring and driving rhythm. By the time fandangos were commonplace in the late eighteenth century, the genre had developed a cliché rhythm that was inextricably associated with it (Example 10.6).

The fandango became the most beloved dance in early Californian history; countless depictions from the nineteenth century show the locals dancing up a storm to the sounds of guitars and castanets, and the caption most often reads "fandango." What better dance than the fandango to represent the rugged California spirit of the *rancho* period where success depended largely on self-reliance, independence, hard work, and a solid work ethic – all values that reflect middle-class values as opposed to aristocratic ones. Not surprisingly, then, the fandango became the norm rather than the older and stuffier *danzas*.

It is significant that the guitar – and the fandango – are the musical indicators that Mozart and his librettist da Ponte select when they cook up social revolution in their subversive opera *The Marriage of Figaro* (1786). When the servant Figaro sings the memorable aria "Se vuol ballare" early in Act I, he spells out the entire thesis of the plot, and he uses the guitar as the central metaphor for lower-class supremacy over the arrogant excesses of a self-indulgent aristocracy. Figaro, who sees through the shallow attempts of the Count to bed his wife's maid and Figaro's fiancée Susanna, sings in disgust that his employer the Count will have to match wits with none other than Figaro himself, the servant. Mozart's and Da Ponte's libretto runs, "If my dear Count you want to go dancing, then *I* will play the music on *my guitar!*"[54] Social turmoil is subtly but unmistakably engendered in those lines. It is the lower-class barber Figaro – with his handy guitar – who will call the shots and play the tune, and the aristocratic Count will have to keep step to the music that the servant chooses. Brilliantly, to reinforce his point, Mozart disrupts the noble minuet rhythm that had begun the aria "Se vuol ballare" and then metaphorically trips the Count up by the sudden intrusion of a contredanse rhythm, a style associated more with the middle class than with the aristocracy. Thus the servant's contredanse literally drives out the aristocrat's minuet.

In the finale to Act III of *Figaro*, Susanna sets a trap for the unsuspecting Count by dropping a sealed note of feigned love for him to find while dancing. She supposedly will meet him in the garden for a midnight tryst, but we all know it will be his wife the Countess – not Susanna – who will be waiting for the faithless man. So, how does Mozart choose to get this clandestine note delivered? First, he opens the finale with a march that reflects the nobility and high station of the Count and Countess, which in turn is disrupted by a contredanse sung by peasant girls and the local servants. This, too, is then abruptly cut short by the strains of a fandango, and it is this universally appealing genre – one associated with the guitar – that Mozart cleverly uses as the meeting ground for Susanna and the Count. Mozart has prepared the scene by presenting the two classes as separate, non-overlapping entities. A servant girl would have been stepping above her station in an egregious way if she were to participate in the regal, majestic march that begins the scene. Similarly, the Count would never have stooped to dancing to the subsequent peasant dance. But finally, the new genre of the fandango is a meeting place where both nobles and peasants could participate; it is the great equalizer. Thus, it is during this fandango that Susanna has the opportunity to gain access to her master, the Count, and deliver the feigned confession of love that is so instrumental to the protagonists' scheming. The fandango marks the first moment in the finale where the two class structures could have interacted. Significantly, one finds the traditional and most representative rhythm of the fandango (articulated in m. 444) as the unifying rhythmic feature of Mozart's fandango as well.

Cross-cultural aspects of the baroque guitar

In addition to reflecting aspects of class and social structure, the guitar also provides a mirror for changes in the ethnic and cultural tapestry of Western civilization in the Baroque era. Before the late Renaissance, the various continents were relatively isolated from each other, but that changed forever in the 1500s and 1600s with the rapid proliferation of European claims on territory across the globe. The Portuguese, the first out of the starting blocks, explored the coast of Africa by solving the thorny problem of how to navigate in the Southern hemisphere (a frightening prospect initially since it necessitated crossing the Equator and losing sight of the Pole Star). The Spanish were soon to follow, and then the Italians. By the 1600s, nearly all of the European powers had constructed respectable navies and were staking claims to most of the Americas, Africa, Asia, and eventually Australia and the South Pacific. The great land grab was on. Once again, the guitar was carried along on naval vessels as a rule or even on overland expeditions, and it was one of the first instruments to be brought ashore in new lands. Not surprisingly, then, the guitar ended up as one of the indispensable ingredients in cultural hybrids that thrust together people and influences from various continents.

Beginning with the first voyages to the Americas, the guitar was the soldiers' and evangelists' true companion.[55] With each new territorial claim, the Spanish brought with them this highly portable instrument. According to Bernal Díaz del Castillo, who accompanied Cortez on the conquest of Mexico, as early as 1568 the Native American craftsmen were already fabricating high-quality guitars or vihuelas.[56] Bartholomé de las Casas recounts specific occasions on which guitar music resounded in the Caribbean as early as the 1530s.[57] The Incan writer Guamán Poma provides invaluable descriptions that place the guitar in a rich web of peoples, social strata, and ethnicities, and also sketches out the earliest South American drawing of the guitar.[58]

It is the guitar, or its close cousins, for which the earliest African American instrumental manuscripts are written. The musical anthology compiled by Sebastian de Aguirre around 1700 (presently in the private archive of Gabriel Saldívar y Osorio), contains the "Portorrico de los negros por 1 y 2 ras[guead]o" (fol. 20r); it is the oldest known example of African-American instrumental music.[59] The Aguirre manuscript contains a dozen other works that combine the influences of the Americas, Africa,

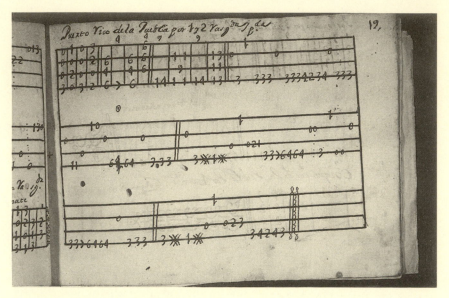

Plate 19a Aguirre Manuscript, fol. 19r

and Spain (see Plates 19 a–f). The classifications themselves reflect these exotic combinations of peoples and ethnicities. The *tocotín, corrido, guasteco*,
and *chiqueador* reflect indigenous Mexican influence.[60] The etymology of
corrido is unclear, but the term becomes associated with Mexican ballads
in the subsequent century and becomes one of the great contributions of
Mexican folklore to world culture. According to the poetess Sor Juana Inés
de la Cruz, the *tocotín* is nothing else but a *corrido*. A *guasteco* refers to a man
from that region of Mexico. The *chiqueador* is a type of jewelry or adorn-
ment worn by Mexican women during the epoch; normally they were small,
round discs carved from turtle or tortoise shells.[61] It also is an American
term that can mean "flatterer" or "pamperer" or someone who goes strutting
about.[62] Other titles in Aguirre's book imply a Caribbean connection, such
as the self-explanatory terms *panamá* and *porto rico*.[63] In addition, perhaps
"El Coquís" takes us to the Caribbean islands, since *coquí* in modern-day
Cuba and Puerto Rico refers to a small reptile whose name derives from its cry
that resembles the sound "coquí, coquí."[64] Yet another cultural group surfaces with Aguirre's title "Morisca," which literally translated means "Moorish woman"; the term *morisco* was a common ethno-social appellation for a
Moorish convert to Christianity.[65] These brief musical snapshots, combined
with the long list of traditional *bailes* and *danzas* that Aguirre inserts into
his manuscript, provide one of the richest compendiums of multicultural
influences and styles found in this (or any other) epoch.

The other gem of African American influence is Santiago de Murcia's
"Códice Saldívar No. 4" (1732), for tucked into its folios are the African

Plate 19b Aguirre Manuscript, fol. 20r

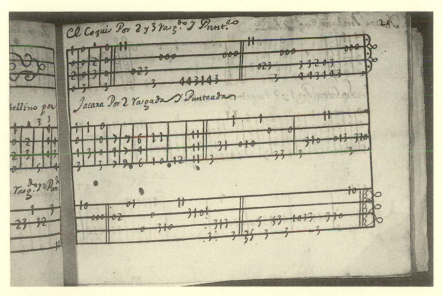

Plate 19c Aguirre Manuscript, fol. 21r

American "Cumbées" and "Zarambeques" (see Plates 20 a-b).[66] Strong evidence drawn from theatrical productions of the age suggest that the *zarambeque*, *cumbé*, and *guineo* are one and the same – they refer to a class of dances of African-American origin that generally roll along in jaunty triple meter, are full of verve and subtlety, and are chock-full of syncopation.[67] Like most

Plate 19d Aguirre Manuscript, fol. 22v

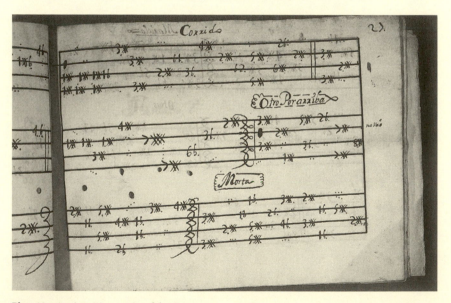

Plate 19e Aguirre Manuscript, fol. 27r

popular dance styles, the same genres and styles also entered church performance through the secular-influenced *villancico* that took music from
the street, cleaned it up slightly, and brought it into sacred church fes-
tivities, especially Matins services. Although the *guineo* (and by extension

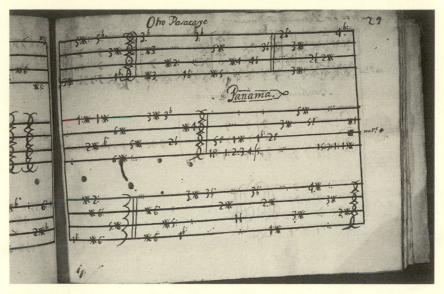

Plate 19f Aguirre Manuscript, fol. 29r

the *zarambeque*) skyrocketed to the heights of popularity as a style of African-American *villancico* during the seventeenth century, this tablature rendition by Murcia is the first purely instrumental version of the genre.

But the true treasure of Murcia's manuscript is the infectious setting of the "Cumbées," the first truly decipherable example of instrumental music in an African American style. The dance was banned repeatedly by the Inquisition, to no avail, but the condemnations open a window for us to view the delightful fun that they must have been. The Inquisition rails against the *cumbé* in 1716 with the searing complaint that its "lyrics are scandalous, obscene, and offensive to the highest degree. They are sung and accompanied by a dance no less scandalous and obscene. They are accompanied by lewd actions, lascivious displays, and indecent and provocative shaking – all to the grave ruin and scandal of the souls of the Christian community!"[68] Sounds like fun. In spite of this invective and many more, the *cumbé* enjoyed widespread popularity.

Murcia's setting of the *cumbé* begins with syncopated strums and *golpes* where the guitarist strikes the guitar top. The infectious beginning gradually gives way to the main tune and ensuing flights of fancy that are cast in ever-shifting hemiolas. The runs become increasingly frenetic and rapid, until the setting eventually concludes in a flurry of ecstatic scales and punctuating strums.

In conclusion, we see that the guitar – an instrument that in modern times is strongly associated with the social turmoil in American history of the

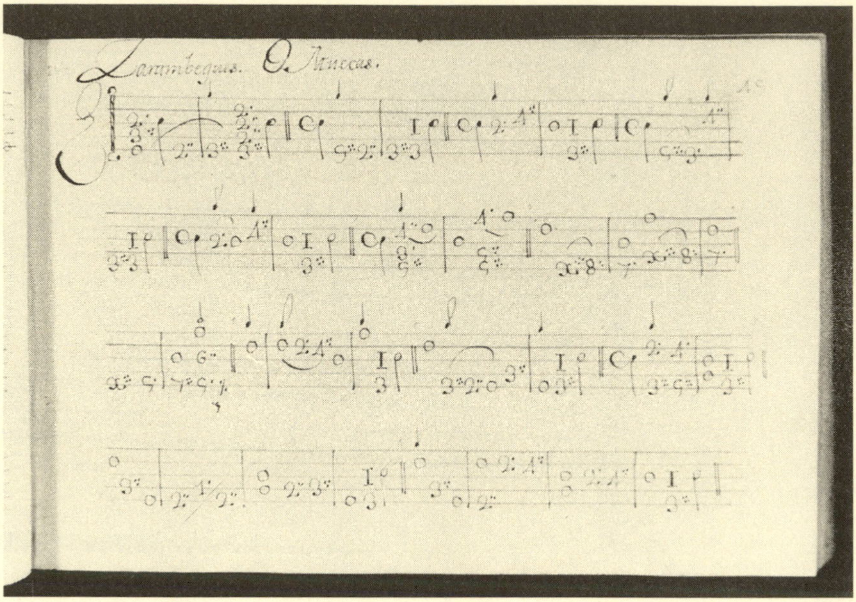

Plate 20a Códice Salvídar No. 4, fol. 45r, "Zarambeques"

Plate 20b Códice Salvídar No. 4, fol. 43r, "Cumbées"

1960s, and with the musical revolutions of jazz, blues, rock, and heavy metal in the late twentieth century – was already playing the role of revolutionary from its early history back in the 1600s and 1700s. In both eras, it was at the forefront of change. Today, we find that subversive yet noble instrument in the hands of tuxedoed classical guitarists (such as David Tanenbaum and Bill Kanengiser, playing Brouwer, Britten, and Henze), while at the same time we find it played by kids in baggy pants hunkering down to let loose a wild blues riff, rocking rhythm, or heavy-metal solo. Really, it is not as far a step from B. B. King to Murcia's "Cumbées" as we might first suspect. If we look carefully, the daring steps taken by a Hendrix or Satriani are foreshadowed in many ways by the bold and pioneering steps taken by a Montesardo or Corbetta. History has shown the guitar's ability to anticipate (or adapt to) musical and stylistic changes long before most other instruments. Rarely has the world seen an instrument more beloved, more versatile, or more attuned to the twists and turns of our ephemeral society and unpredictable history than the revolutionary, rambunctious, and radical guitar.

11 Perspectives on the classical guitar in the twentieth century

DAVID TANENBAUM

At the beginning of the twenty-first century, the classical guitar finds itself at a level of quality and popularity that was unimaginable even fifty years earlier. There are scores of degree programs in the United States alone, major and minor record labels keep increasing their catalog of guitar recordings,[1] and a growing number of international competitions are being won by young players of astounding technical facility. The ubiquitous Rodrigo *Concierto de Aranjuez* is one of the most popular concertos for any instrument of the twentieth century, new music ensembles commonly include the guitar, and virtually every major composer of our time now attempts to write for the instrument. In fact it can be argued that, for the first time, the current repertoire and performance level of the guitar rival that of any instrument. And such is the embarrassment of riches that many players are seeking out unique corners of the repertoire, becoming specialists in transcription, or nineteenth-century repertoire, or new chamber music. In short, guitarists face the daunting task of finding a voice in this crowded field, which is populated by relatively young players and teachers. But even the youngest players seem to be unfazed, as the number of students entering academic institutions to study the guitar, against all financial reasoning, appears steady.

In this chapter I will connect the major points of the guitar's extraordinary development in the twentieth century, and discuss what are, to me, some of the most promising developments for the future. Since I am foremost a performer, recording artist, and teacher of the guitar – not a musicologist – this essay reveals the thoughts of a player trying to realize his own vision of the instrument. Consequently, this is a personal, rather than an objective view.

Andrés Segovia and Francisco Tárrega

The most influential figure in the development of the classical guitar after 1900 is undoubtedly Andrés Segovia. Born in 1893, Segovia heard his calling after hearing Tárrega's *Preludes* when he was just twelve:

> I felt like crying, laughing, even like kissing the hands of a man who could draw such beautiful sounds from the guitar. My passion for music seemed to explode into flames. I was trembling. A sudden wave of disgust for the folk pieces I had been playing came over me, mixed with a delirious obsession to learn "that music" immediately... I had been captured for life by the guitar. With complete dedication, I have been totally faithful to it all my life. Faithful to only the guitar.[2]

This willpower and all-consuming passion would ultimately inspire generations of guitarists in the twentieth century. But the world he encountered during the century's first decades was very different from today. Revolutionary changes were occurring in music during Segovia's youth, but few of those developments included the guitar. Of all the important late-Romantic and early twentieth-century composers, only Mahler, Schoenberg, Webern, and Stravinsky used the guitar at all, and the repertory they produced amounts to just a few chamber pieces. In fact, the greatest ebb in the guitar's history is the late nineteenth century, since the forces required and harmonic language during this period were clearly beyond the guitar's reach. Despite some remarkable transcriptions, the late nineteenth century remains the least played period of classical music on the guitar.

What Segovia did encounter was a small but thriving guitar subculture formed around the work of Francisco Tárrega (1852–1909), the leading guitar figure of the late nineteenth century. Tárrega was by all reports a shy man who played relatively few concerts and did not travel much internationally; his days were spent entirely with the guitar in his hands, practicing and adapting music to it, as we know from his student Pujol's precious description:

> Every morning after getting dressed, Tárrega lights a cigarillo, takes his guitar and sits down on his small working chair, in a corner of the dining room. Adjusting the tuning, he stretches his fingers by caressing the strings with improvised harmonies... Breakfast interrupts the monologue, while the guitar rests on the Maestro's knees. After this, without any further preamble, to work! A matchbox on the table holds up the chromatic scales, diatonics, in thirds, sixths... Another hour of arpeggios, the same time for runs and trills and one or more hours for difficult positions or rebellious passages... Thus passes the morning. After lunch, once more the guitar, but the work is different. The complete works of Schumann for the piano are on the table... Tárrega skims through them, stops at a page, and rests it on the guitar to see if it will lend itself to transcription... Every day, toward evening, some intimate friends and aficionados come to hear him play... Then at night, after dinner, when everybody is asleep in the house, Tárrega plays for himself. This is the moment when the guitar and the artist are one. How many hours pass like this?[3]

Tárrega ended up composing more than 300 works, made countless transcriptions, and left a legacy of playing through numerous students, the most famous being Miguel Llobet and Emilio Pujol. Llobet himself composed many works in a style similar to Tárrega and played concerts internationally, while Pujol detailed the Tárrega school in the most thorough method book of the time, and also made scholarly critical editions of early vihuela, lute, and guitar music. Inevitably, perhaps, antipathy developed between Segovia and members of the Tárrega school, especially with one of Tárrega's last students, Daniel Fortea. Segovia called them the guitar's "jailers,"[4] and felt they were too insular. Llobet had indeed expressed doubts about the guitar's ability to project in large halls, in direct contradiction to Segovia's quest to place the guitar on the world's main classical stages. Although Llobet's friends included Debussy, Ravel, Fauré, Falla, and Granados, he eventually worked only with Falla on one small piece.[5] The self-taught Segovia still learned much from the Tárrega school, particularly from Llobet, with whom his interpretive style had many similarities.

But most importantly, Segovia personified the artist of great courage who would not accept the current opinion that the guitar was an "inferior" instrument.[6] As Segovia immodestly said: "I found the guitar almost at a standstill – despite the noble efforts of Sor, Tárrega, Llobet, and others – and raised it to the loftiest levels of the musical world."[7] Segovia gave his first public recital at age sixteen and his last at age ninety-four, thus completing a career that spanned almost the entire century. He felt that the key to validating the instrument was through repertoire. He was one of the first guitarists who was only casually interested in composing himself, unlike even the members of the Tárrega school, and his focus on performance led him to seek new works from other composers. He began by creating a body of work from composer friends and colleagues whose music spoke of their time and place.

The first composer he contacted was Frederico Moreno Torroba, and he followed with fellow Spaniards Joaquin Turina and Joaquin Rodrigo, the Italian Mario Castelnuovo-Tedesco, the Mexican Manuel Ponce, and the Brazilian Heitor Villa-Lobos. At the same time, Segovia was adamant in his dislike for the modernist stream of composition, resulting in a missed opportunity for guitar works from the likes of Stravinsky or Bartók. Schoenberg even offered to write for Segovia but was turned down.[8]

Ultimately more than 500 pieces were dedicated to Segovia, and he took pride in not having paid for a single one, which may partly account for the lack of great composers in his original repertoire. The many criticisms of his choice of commissions,[9] and the cavalier manner in which he changed the music composers wrote for him without ever consulting them persisted even after Segovia's death.[10] Those criticisms must be taken in perspective.

Segovia was attempting single-handedly to globalize the guitar and validate it in the classical world. His message needed to be personalized and distilled, and Segovia was playing music he believed in. At a Segovia concert, few people commented about the choice of program as they do now. His audience went for one thing, one message, even one name. His interpretations had an unbridled vigor and character, but perhaps the strongest impression he made was with his sound: a deep, beautiful tone that struck many hearts. Refusing to use amplification, even during concertos, Segovia played many concerts in his later years in oversized halls. I saw him more than once stop a concert to ask someone to refrain from coughing or rustling a program, insisting that large crowds should make the effort to hear him – and they did.

The first time I heard him was in an acoustically dry movie theater in suburban New York, and that evening that my life's work became clear to me. The last time I saw him was in San Francisco, where a young and cultish crowd had filled the hall, as they did every year. Now in his nineties, he was impossibly old to be playing a guitar concert, and his facility was understandably diminished. But his willpower remained resolute; he was going to fight in order to communicate something to his audience, and he succeeded.

It may be true that Segovia did not want to share the stage with a living equal: besides his unwillingness to work with great composers, he also never promoted or played music by a living guitarist-composer, such as Barrios, as I will discuss later. His many editions, though full of character and color, are below the level of scholarship exhibited by Pujol or Artur Schnabel. As a teacher Segovia attracted and nurtured the greatest of the next generation, but films and other evidence suggest an inflexibility concerning issues of interpretation. On a political and humanitarian level, Segovia supported Franco, and his letters to Ponce contain disturbing anti-Semitic statements – issues that now stand out when compared to the generosity and humanity exhibited by contemporaries such as Casals and Menuhin.

Still, it must be remembered that Segovia made all things possible for the classical guitarist. He transformed a landscape. In the process, he brought world fame to leading luthiers like Hermann Hauser, Jose Ramirez, and Ignacio Fleta, and he worked with Albert Augustine to introduce nylon strings for classical guitar after World War II (one of the most important developments of the century concerning the guitar). Eventually, most of the composers he worked with gained a level of world renown through their guitar works that none of their other music, to this day, has achieved. Though the music of these composers figures less in the repertoire of concert guitarists since Segovia's death in 1987, this is still a significant body of work for the guitar, which I will now examine in some more detail.

Torroba, Turina, and Tedesco

Frederico Moreno Torroba (1891–1982) was the first composer to write for Segovia, his total output for guitar comprising over 100 works that are both difficult to play and musically simple. Despite a limited harmonic vocabulary and choice of keys, his guitar pieces display a keen melodic sense and gentle nationalistic flavor that have found them a secure place in the repertoire. Torroba's Sonatina in A, with its beautiful middle movement and bright outer movements, is perhaps his most captivating piece. Joaquin Turina (1882–1949) wrote much less music for guitar, all of it solo, but he emphasized (and perhaps overused) a flamenco character. Thus, his works tend to be cast in minor keys and frequently employ *rasgueado* and other flamenco techniques. They have also found themselves a lasting place in the repertoire. His *Sevillanas* and *Fandanguillo,* well-composed pieces that capture the flavor of Spain, have achieved the status of guitar classics. Mario Castelnuovo-Tedesco (1895–1968) also wrote nearly 100 works for guitar, composed over a period of some thirty-five years. Some of these were important landmarks, including the first concerto written for Segovia in 1939. Perhaps reacting to persistent negative criticism about the quality of Castelnuovo-Tedesco's works, Segovia included them less often in his programs from the 1950s, and Castelnuovo-Tedesco in turn began dedicating his works to a wider array of guitarists. His works have found less favor from later generations, but they are a significant contribution to the repertoire.

Manuel Ponce

The second composer to respond to Segovia's call, and ultimately becoming Segovia's favorite, was the Mexican Manuel Ponce (1882–1948). Ponce met Segovia in 1923 and soon composed for him the *Canciones Mexicans* and *Sonata Mexicana,* both written in a simple harmonic language and heavily influenced by Mexican folk music. But then Ponce made a courageous decision. At forty-three years of age and already widely recognized in Mexico, he went to Paris to study with Paul Dukas between 1925 and 1933. Among his classmates there were Rodrigo and Villa-Lobos, and among his fellow Parisians was Segovia. These studies led to a new use of chromaticism and an expanded harmonic language, leading Ponce to produce the bulk of his guitar works at this time. He would go on to compose more than eighty works for guitar and would be eulogized by Segovia as having "saved the guitar."

There are two main reasons that Segovia seems to have preferred working with Ponce. First, Segovia's own compositional style was closest to Ponce's, so this music spoke to him. Second, Ponce was willing to accept Segovia's modifications with little or no objection.[11] With three recording projects of his complete guitar works currently underway,[12] Ponce's position in the repertoire seems destined to endure.

Heitor Villa-Lobos

Of the many compositions that were inspired by or dedicated to Segovia, the most enduring are by the Brazilian composer Heitor Villa-Lobos (1887–1959). An astoundingly prolific composer, Villa-Lobos learned the guitar at seven or eight, and his first guitar compositions were written five years later. Segovia and Villa-Lobos met at a party in 1924 and quarreled about Villa-Lobos's use of the fifth finger of the right hand in his guitar music. According to guitar historian Brian Hodel, that meeting might have been the "most important event in the modern history of the guitar."[13] Villa-Lobos would go on to write more than fifty guitar works spanning his creative career, works that produce a big, robust sound, ever-influenced by the *choros*, characterized by finger patterns for both hands. Segovia compared Villa-Lobos's *Douze Etudes* to the Chopin piano études in importance, saying that Villa-Lobos "knows the guitar perfectly," and they remain the only advanced studies in the general repertoire. As such, they deserve a brief discussion.

The *Etudes* were probably conceived of as a set, as there is an extended circle of fifth cycle in major keys in the first part, and a corresponding one in minor keys in the second part. Because of that, the final note (as in nos. 7 and 8) or chord (as in nos. 9 and 10) of one étude can act as a kind of dominant to the next. (Etude 5 begins with the same two notes that ended Etude 4.) But there are also marked differences between the first six and the last six. For one thing, the earlier studies use Italian expression marks, and the first four contain patterns whose purpose is mostly explained in subtitles. The first étude has become a classic arpeggio study that guitarists practice with various fingerings, and which other composers have imitated as well; the second étude is probably the hardest of the set and might be the most difficult study in the repertoire, brilliantly challenging the coordination of the hands. The études in the second half of the set, with French indications, tend to contain more than a single challenge per piece, and are more fully developed. The last four contain some wonderfully unique sounds, textures, and motivic developments: the famous eleventh étude is the best thumb study in the repertoire, and the texture in the middle of the tenth study, employing an upper line that moves eight times faster than the same material below, is unique. Recently, a 1928 manuscript of these studies has become available. It contains fascinating changes from the well-known published version, and it has already captured the imagination of guitarists, resulting in scholarly articles and recordings. Finally, Villa-Lobos's *Concerto, Preludes* and *Suite popular brasileira* are also mainstays of the repertoire.

Joaquin Rodrigo

Segovia's relationship with Rodrigo (1901–99) was more complicated. Although he dedicated numerous works to Segovia, it remains curious that the greatest and most popular of all guitar concertos was not dedicated to the pillar of twentieth-century guitar. Rodrigo wrote the *Concierto de Aranjuez* in 1939, during the same time that both Ponce and Castelnuovo-Tedesco wrote concertos for Segovia, but the concerto was dedicated to Regino Sainz de la Maza, and it was Narciso Yepes who performed the piece around the world in its early life. Later, Pepe Romero became most closely associated with the work. The *Aranjuez* was instantly popular (Victoria Rodrigo reports that after an early performance in Madrid Rodrigo was carried through the streets on the shoulders of his admirers, a scene unimaginable for a classical composer anywhere today) and has gone a long way toward bringing the guitar to the attention of symphonic audiences, providing much work for professional players. Perhaps to make amends for the dedication of the *Aranjuez*, Rodrigo dedicated his next piece for guitar and orchestra, the *Fantasia para un Gentilhombre*, to Segovia in 1954. Although Rodrigo was certainly guilty of borrowing from himself in his guitar repertoire, he left a unique and challenging body of works, of which the *Invocacion y Danza* and *Trés Piezas Españolas* are among the best.

Agustín Barrios

The most significant achievement for the guitar in the first part of the century outside of Segovia's influence is found in the life and works of Agustín Barrios Mangoré (1885–1944), regarded by many as the greatest guitarist-composer of all time. Born in Paraguay in 1885, he was a remarkable guitarist and a composer of striking originality and spirit. Barrios's frustrating career was spent mostly in Latin America and included a few trips to Europe. Desperate to achieve more recognition, he wore for a time an Indian headdress and reversed the spelling of his first name, calling himself Nitsuga, the Paganini from the jungles of Paraguay. His recordings, the first ever by a guitarist, reveal an astonishing technique and fluency, especially considering the mediocre instruments and bad metal strings he was using. He ultimately made more than thirty records and wrote over 300 pieces. His music has the earthiness and the sadness of much Latin American literature. His *Un Sueño en la Floresta*, which extends the guitar's range downward with scordatura and upward with a high C, is beginning to rival Tárrega's *Recuerdos de l'Alhambra* as the most popular tremolo piece. Roughly translating as "A Dream in the Forest," *Un Sueño en la Floresta* uses the parallel minor–major relationship of *Recuerdos de l'Alhambra,* but Barrios ingeniously stops the dream in the middle, giving relief to the tremolo effect and setting up the climactic ending section.

La Catedral, perhaps Barrios's most famous piece, brilliantly recreates his experience of hearing Bach on a church organ as he walked away down the street. The Prelude he added twenty years later was one of his last pieces. Though he never cast his music in large forms or experimented with any of the harmonic developments of his time (if he even knew they existed), Barrios's place in the guitar pantheon seems only to grow more secure with each new year. The revival of his music was started by Richard Stover, who published the first large compilation of the composer's works and wrote the first biography.[14] Barrios's reputation was solidified in the 1970s by John Williams, who was introduced to the Barrios canon and brought his works to a large public through recordings.

The Segovia–Barrios relationship is a subject of much debate. Barrios met Segovia, played for him for several times, and repeatedly gave him music. Segovia was very cordial when they first met, but less so later, leading a snubbed Barrios to say that Segovia was "deaf in the heart."[15] Legend has it that Segovia promised to help Barrios but purposely did nothing. And Barrios's continual frustration with his career was constantly coming up against the growing worldwide fame of Segovia: in 1928, for instance, Barrios scheduled three concerts in Buenos Aires but had to cancel the last two owing to a sparse crowd in the first, while at the same time across town Segovia was embarking on nine successive sold-out concerts. It is therefore ironic that although Barrios never gained great renown in his lifetime, he is more of a living presence for many young guitarists now than is Segovia.

Other early-century works

The twentieth century began with no major non-guitarist composers writing for the guitar, and it ended with almost all of them using it in one form or another. The first non-guitarist composer to accept the challenge seems to have been Manuel de Falla in 1920. Responding to a request from the periodical *La Revue Musicale* to write an article commemorating the death of Debussy, Falla chose to write the small but brilliant *Homenaje: Le Tombeau de Claude Debussy* for guitar. Working with Miguel Llobet, Falla constructed an intricate, finely detailed and colored miniature that remains one of the guitar's finest pieces. Whereas many of the Spanish composers writing for Segovia worked to evoke Spain in their music, this quintessential Spanish composer looked to France in his single effort for guitar. Perhaps not trusting that enough players would play it, Falla orchestrated his *Homenaje*. He ultimately went to Segovia's Paris debut, and in 1932 they traveled together. It is unfortunate that although Falla planned another guitar piece, he never wrote again for the instrument.

A similar fate awaited Frank Martin's *Quatre Pièces Brèves* (1933). Hearing no response from Segovia, Martin initially assumed that the piece did not work for guitar, so he made it a piano piece called *Guitare* and later orchestrated it as well. Finally published in 1953, Martin's piece was recorded by Julian Bream and now has a solid place in the repertoire. Other important, but brief, compositions for the guitar from early in the century include Poulenc's simple *Sarabande*, Darius Milhaud's *Segoviana*, Albert Roussel's *Segovia*, and Ernst Krenek's twelve-tone *Suite*.

Mid-century

By the middle of the century, Segovia was in his sixties. His career had grown steadily and he had won grudging respect for the guitar. In the 1950s, the guitar began to enter into the consciousness of a growing number of composers, and simultaneously into the masses through pop culture. Because of the decades of labor Segovia had put in up to that point, he was positioned to benefit from that trend. But it was the work of the next generation that would fully push the guitar into the mainstream classical world, by commissioning great composers, playing more chamber music, and in the case of John Williams, bringing down the barriers between the classical and pop worlds. Among the many brilliant players of this generation, mention must be made of Ida Presti – "a miracle of facility and grace," according to Pujol[16] – who dazzled audiences, but whose career was hindered by the war. Ultimately she performed in the Presti–Lagoya Duo, one of the greatest guitar duos ever, until her untimely death in 1967.

A set of ambassadors of the guitar emerged in mid-century when Spanish guitarist Celedonio Romero, who was imprisoned by Franco and later restricted from traveling and performing internationally as a guitarist, moved his family in secret to Southern California in 1957. There, with his three sons Celin, Pepe, and Angel, he formed the first guitar quartet, and for the next decades they would play all over the world as The Romeros. Pepe and Angel would eventually go on to successful solo careers, with Pepe being the most famous member of the family. He achieved widespread popular appeal and promoted the music of Spain, becoming the guitarist most closely associated with Rodrigo. A third generation of Romeros is now touring with the quartet, continuing the legacy of this remarkable family.

Bream and Williams

Two guitarists emerged from England in the late 1950s and early 1960s who would dominate the guitar field for several decades to come: the native Julian Bream and the Australian John Williams. For decades, Bream and Williams would be mentioned in the same breath, as a sort of Apollonian (Williams)–Dionysian (Bream) entity which contained the full reach of the guitar. Their careers represent an interesting dichotomy of the possibilities of the classical guitar. Bream stayed within a narrow, traditional definition of the instrument and investigated every aspect of the repertoire in great depth. He worked with the most important composers of his time and directly helped create what may be the greatest legacy of music that any guitarist has left, far more diverse and adventurous than what was written for Segovia. And John Williams, who had by all reports mastered the guitar repertoire by age twelve, quickly started to jump over the normally held bounds of the instrument, in one act foreshadowing a very popular trend and alienating Segovia. As performers with such different approaches but at the same time friends and occasional duet partners, Bream and Williams represented for many a kind of attraction of opposites that led to endless discussions, which in turn led to high record sales, concert ticket purchases, and an increased awareness of the guitar.

Julian Bream

Bream has never been the greatest technical guitar player, which he admits in his characteristically modest fashion, but his playing is full of color, originality, and imagination. He juxtaposes great contrasts in sound color – to this day many players associate extreme *ponticello* playing with "a Bream thing" – and watching his concerts one sees more right-hand playing over the fingerboard, and general right-hand wandering for color than practiced by most guitarists. These contrasts particularly make his readings of music from the classical period come alive.

In the opinion of many of today's leading lute players, Bream's Renaissance lute playing, while not considered "authentic," inspired a whole generation of "authentic" players by its pure spirit.[17] His *Music of Spain* recordings revealed a convincing take on Spanish music, but his most enduring legacy will be the many composers he inspired. One of the earliest collaborations in Bream's career was also one of the most fruitful. Bream started accompanying the British tenor Peter Pears, and soon Pears's partner Benjamin Britten contributed his *Songs from the Chinese* (1957) to their repertoire. Songs by Walton, Berkeley, Peter Maxwell Davies, and others were to follow. In 1958 Pears and Bream premiered Henze's *Kammermusik*. Finally, Bream asked Britten for a solo piece, and received the monumental *Nocturnal*, one of the finest pieces ever written for the guitar. Britten originally thought of calling the piece *Night Fancy*, and even considered writing it for Bream's lute, but the final version ended up being a set of variations on the John Dowland song *Come, Heavy Sleep*. The *Nocturnal* breached new ground by employing a sustained and unified structure lasting some eighteen minutes. Using the interval of a perfect fourth as a catalyst, the *Nocturnal* portrays a psychic experience of night, beginning with gentle musing, moving into more restless, disturbed areas, and ending in a brilliant Passacaglia, a kind of primal battle between a force of stability and wild, disturbing creativity. These distinct elements merge, and finally resolve, into Dowland's song, the work's theme, coming at the end. One of the great qualities of the *Nocturnal* is that it is not overly difficult to play; in fact, its musical difficulties are greater than its technical ones, which is a rarity in the guitar repertoire. According to guitar historian Graham Wade, "the beginning of the end of Segovia's domination over the twentieth century repertoire may be dated from the Aldeburgh première of the Nocturnal."[18] Bream included the *Nocturnal* on a ground breaking album, *20th-Century Guitar* (1967), that also included Henze's *Drei Tentos*, the Frank Martin *Quatre Pièces Brèves*, and *El Polifemo d'Oro* by Reginald Smith Brindle. After that, some of the most important contemporary composers lined up to write for Bream. They included William Walton, Richard Rodney Bennett, Michael Tippett, Peter Maxwell Davies, Henze again, Toru Takemitsu, Malcolm Arnold, and many others. They created a repertoire of striking depth and richness, and moreover it was music that avoided the ever-present influence of Spain. Each instead found a unique sound world in the guitar, exploiting the instrument's depth and dimension. While Bennett and Smith Brindle explored serialism, and Walton contributed his characteristic lighter, tonal style, perhaps the most important compositions written for Bream were by Toru Takemitsu, Hans Werner Henze, and Peter Maxwell Davies. These three composers each used the guitar as a solo and chamber instrument, and except for Maxwell Davies, wrote concertos as well.

Maxwell Davies, Takemitsu, and Henze

Peter Maxwell Davies (b. 1934), who spoke specifically of wanting to avoid Spanish influence, wrote three solo guitar works of increasing proportions in his dark, quixotic style; the most effective of those is the one recorded by Bream, *Hill Runes*. Maxwell Davies dares an amazing degree of counterpoint on the guitar, and while his works have not found a large place in the repertoire, they are brilliantly crafted and create a truly unique sound. Besides his solos and a striking work for guitar and voice, *Dark Angels*, Maxwell Davies included the guitar in many pieces created for his ensemble, The Fires of London.

The guitar works of Toru Takemitsu (1930–96) include four solos, a set of twelve song arrangements originally intended as études, three concertos, and numerous chamber works that, to various degrees, have found a niche in the repertoire of guitarists. Takemitsu was deeply interested in the guitar and its repertoire. (In 1991 I participated in a guitar festival he directed in Japan and it remains to this day the most interesting and diverse guitar festival I have ever attended.) He counted among his friends several guitarists, such as Norio Sato and Kiyoshi Shumura, and even remarked that his first piece, *Folios*, makes some caustic remarks about the guitar repertoire, reflecting his frustration with guitarist-composers who were afraid to either leave tonality or fully embrace it. He told Julian Bream that of all the instruments he wrote for, he loved the guitar the most.[19] Bream in turn has said that of all the composers he worked for, Takemitsu had both the best ear and also the most catholic tastes. Perhaps the strongest symbol of how important the guitar was to Takemitsu was the last piece he wrote, *In the Woods*. Takemitsu was ill throughout 1995, and wrote little. His last orchestral piece, *Spectrum Canticle*, for guitar, violin, and orchestra was completed earlier in the year. He finally was released from the hospital, and in November felt able to compose. With some of his last energy he then wrote *In the Woods*, his largest solo guitar work and one of our greatest pieces. The repertoire Takemitsu left us represents one of our instrument's strongest, a music that uses silence and color, particularly exploiting the darker range of the spectrum. Takemitsu uniquely blended Western and Eastern influences, and as he aged his music included more pop influences. His pioneering sense of cross-cultural fusion was ahead of its time, and in the guitar he found a perfect vehicle to express his world.

Hans Werner Henze (b. 1926) writes a social music (his first book of essays is called *Music and Politics*) that is largely affected by his young life in Nazi Germany, when he was forced to serve in the army, and the memories of his father, a Nazi officer, waving his knife while drunkenly singing songs about killing Jews. Henze finally left Germany for Italy in 1951, but those early memories were seared into him. His music is usually programmatic, and it almost always sides with the oppressed. His *Kammermusik*, for instance, is set to poetry by Hölderlin, who spent the last forty years of his life in and out of mental institutions. This work contains the solo guitar pieces *Drei Tentos*, some of the most effervescent music ever written for the instrument. After Henze declared himself a communist in the 1960s, he moved to Cuba and wrote the monumental guitar work *El Cimarrón*, in 1969–70. This work sets the story of Estabon Montejo, a runaway slave who experienced tremendous hardship as he embodied the history of Cuba for 100 years. When he finally told his story as a bitter old man of 102, it represented a perfect tale for Henze, and he set it as an evening-length drama for baritone, guitar, percussion, and flute. The guitarist in this case was Leo Brouwer, who was intricately involved in devising the unique notational system used in *El Cimarrón*, and in creating the guitar part. The piece involves much improvisation – each player is also a percussionist – but more than that, the players become *El Cimarrón*, and reflect his emotions and experiences as he tells his tale.

In the 1970s Julian Bream felt he wanted a larger, more monumental solo piece, as he had been receiving many works consisting of shorter move-ments. He approached Henze, known for his long works, and jokingly sug-gested something on the scale of Beethoven's enormous "Hammerklavier" sonata. Henze had been thinking of setting Shakespeare, and he came up with *Royal Winter Music, Sonata no. 1*, a thirty-minute extended *Sonata on Shakespearean Characters*. Five years later he completed the cycle with *Royal Winter Music, Sonata no. 2*, resulting in the longest solo guitar piece up to that time. In the introduction to the first sonata, he writes:

> The guitar is a "knowing" or "knowledgeable" instrument, with many
> limitations but also many unexplored spaces and depths within those
> limits. It possesses a richness of sound capable of embracing everything
> one might find in a gigantic contemporary orchestra; but one has to start
> from silence in order to notice this: one has to pause, and completely
> exclude noise. The *dramatis personae* of this piece enter the sound of the
> guitar as if it were a curtain. Through masks, voices and gestures, they
> speak to us of great passion, of tenderness, sadness, and comedy: strange
> events in people's lives. Into this, the whispering voices of spirits are
> mingled.[20]

The guitar indeed becomes a big, emotional instrument in this large work. The characters Henze chooses to depict are mostly not the powerful, but the wounded. The cycle begins and ends with madness and dissonance with "Gloucester" (Richard III) and "Mad Lady Macbeth," and reaches its most passive and tonal moments in the middle, with "Oberon" and "Sir Andrew Aguecheek." It is a monumental and important piece for guitar.

Henze has conceived a unique sound world in each of his major guitar pieces, he has extended the guitar beyond previously imagined limits, and he has helped reveal once again how large are the dimensions of this simple, idiosyncratic instrument.

While *El Cimarrón* brilliantly expanded the sound range of the guitar by using effects, the solo guitar music of Henze, Takemitsu, and Maxwell Davies calls for few special techniques, little scordatura, and not much unusual notation. On the other hand, Alberto Ginastera's brilliant 1976 Sonata employs several special notations to indicate indeterminate high pitches, whistling sounds, and several special tamboras derived from Argentinian folk music. Nikita Koshkin began his twenty-seven-minute long *Suite: The Prince's Toys* when he was only eighteen – it took six years to write – and he decided early that it would be an exercise in giving "effects some meaningful character." He ultimately decided upon a literary theme, and the piece tells the story using unusual effects and notations throughout. In 1967 the iconoclastic Italian composer Giacinto Scelsi (1905–88) wrote a twenty-minute, still unpublished piece called *Ko-tha* in which the guitarist lays the instrument on his or her lap and makes various percussive and string sounds. Perhaps the most extreme use of altered notation is in the monumental (but rarely performed) *Les Six Cuertas* by Alvaro Company, which employs a notation of six staves, one for each string.[21]

John Williams

I am not primarily interested in the problem which preoccupies many guitarists: the expansion of the guitar repertoire . . . The great thing that the guitar can do is to get in "with both feet" to the music that is going on in our and almost anybody else's society; and in a way that belongs to the spirit of what almost all people feel in music.[22]

John Williams has worked with composers throughout his career, the most significant being the Australian Peter Sculthorpe and Takemitsu, but his most enduring legacy is the standard of technical excellence he has maintained with such remarkable consistency through more than forty years of high-level concerts. At the beginning of the twenty-first century, Williams is undoubtedly at the top of the classical guitar field, commanding a higher fee and enjoying more popularity, by far, than any other player. And he has always seemed remarkably unfazed by it all.

What makes Williams's career so ground-breaking is his ability to exist both inside and outside the traditional boundaries of the classical guitar. After establishing himself as the dominant young guitar player of his time, he decisively stepped away, shocking many and alienating Segovia, who had virtually anointed Williams as his successor. In the 1980s he toured with his own rock band, Sky, and since then he has kept at least one foot in the pop world. Was it boredom? Foresight? Simple musical desire? Probably some of each. In the guitar world now, the boundaries between styles are thankfully disappearing. Groups like the Los Angeles Guitar Quartet and the Assad Duo have considerably broadened their audience base; they are marketed as groups that belong as much to the formerly defined pop world as they do to the classical one. Perhaps the strongest vision in this direction came from the Kronos Quartet, which forever changed the landscape of the string quartet, but Williams had anticipated all of this, doing what he wanted and crossing over stylistic borders freely. And of course, he played the perfect crossover instrument. The guitar, now played by more peoples of the world than any other instrument, belongs happily to different stylistic and cultural worlds. The nylon-string guitar certainly has a tradition of crossover players, such as Charlie Byrd and Laurindo Almeida, but they did not have as powerful an effect as did Williams, who was already at the top of the classical guitar field.

As to the classical guitar repertoire, Williams played and recorded the Segovia repertoire, focused heavily on Albeniz, recorded all the Bach lute suites, and then found the music of Barrios, which had a profound effect on him. His playing is characterized by rhythmic drive and propulsion, clarity, and flawlessness. It is not burdened by an overly nuanced "classical" approach or much affect. Given his wide musical influences, it is curious that his own transcriptions and editions reflect more conservative musical tastes than, say, Bream. Williams tends to play fewer notes and reduce effects to their essence; but what he does play is so powerful that he is known, justifiably, as the greatest guitar player of our time.

Even with all that Bream and Williams have done for the guitar, they have not been immune to criticism, as expressed by Eliot Fisk:

> My rebellion in truth is against Bream and Williams. Because I have to confess I'm a bit disappointed in both of them. From time immemorial, it has been the practice of one generation to pass on to the next what it learned. But my generation has almost no guitar fathers. Ghiglia and Diaz teach and are accessible, but Bream and Williams are not . . . I was very saddened by their inaccessibility. I feel that my generation lost a lot because of that.[23]

As always, there is another side. Bream once told me that what he felt he brought to the table was freshness, which comes from his ability to actually pull away from the guitar from time to time and recharge his batteries. I think that the same can be said of Williams, who has been careful not to let himself become overexposed. For many years, even at the height of his career as a Columbia artist, he chose to appear only rarely in the United States, largely because of his political convictions. But his reputation through recordings only seemed to grow in America during that time, and consequently each rare performance became magnified. I do not wish to defend inaccessibility, but in the case of Bream and Williams what was disappointing to guitarists may also have made them, paradoxically, better artists.

Leo Brouwer

The Cuban Leo Brouwer, who worked with both Williams and Bream, and won great respect from Takemitsu and Henze, is certainly the most popular and performed guitarist-composer of our time. Born in 1939, Brouwer began writing in 1955, and his compositions from age seventeen are still performed today. His only composition studies took place in the United States in 1960–61, sending him into an avant-garde, atonal direction that influenced his music throughout the 1960s. Many guitarists regard works from this period such as *Canticum, Elogio de la Danza,* and *Eternal Espiral* as his strongest. During the 1970s Brouwer wrote less and performed more, but near the end of the decade he sustained a hand injury that effectively ended his performing career. In the early 1980s he began a prolific period of new writing in a more tonal, popular style. This reflected the general tendency in classical music, which, led by the American minimalists, was veering back toward tonality and a steady pulse. Brouwer's second set of *Estudios Sencillos* and *El Decameron Negro* embody this new style, which he calls his New Simplicity. Brouwer has continued in this vain for the past twenty years, writing a remarkable amount of music, including numerous concertos, solos that are performed frequently, and much more. It seems that whatever style he employs appeals to audiences. Part of the secret to Brouwer's success is how playable his music is; the music works so well on the instrument, that, contrary to most of the repertoire, Brouwer's music sounds harder than it is.

The 1960s and 1970s

My life's ambitions are fulfilled. A whole new generation of classical guitarists have been born to carry on my work, and they will have their hands full. The classical guitar is just beginning. SEGOVIA[24]

The 1960s were a phenomenal time for the guitar. As rock became a global musical language, Segovia benefited from its guitar-oriented approach and reached the height of his popularity. The virtuoso twosome of Bream and Williams occupied a place of distinction as highly successful and creative recording artists. The first generation of Segovia students was emerging with Christopher Parkening in America, Oscar Ghiglia in Italy, Carlos Barbosa-Lima from Brazil, the Venezuelan Alirio Diaz was dazzling audiences, and Leo Brouwer was already a cult figure in Cuba. Many classical guitarists began initially with rock and roll, but eventually looked for something else, and discovered the classical guitar through one of these inspiring presences, usually Segovia.[25]

Thus a new and large generation of classical guitarists was bred, now middle-aged, that began to make its mark in the 1970s. They are now teaching in virtually every guitar department in the world, recording and touring, and resembling a small army that finds good composers and seduces them to write for guitar. The generation is so big and the field has become so crowded that guitarists have begun to explore many new repertoires and practices, breaking new stylistic ground in the process.

Scholarship

Besides continuing the Tárrega tradition of transcribing Albeniz and Granados for the guitar, Segovia also elevated the guitar through his transcriptions of the music of other great composers, particularly Bach. In fact, it was the ubiquitous presence of Bach on his programs that separated Segovia from his contemporaries. However, while Emilio Pujol was producing scholarly, critical editions of the vihuelists, Segovia's editions were highly personalized transcriptions, with the Bach Chaconne (from the D minor Violin Partita) in 1935 being perhaps his landmark achievement. Guitarists of the time generally followed his directions, often customizing editions with slight changes. But in the next years, good critical editions of Sor and Giuliani began to appear, and as the years passed, this scholarly trend turned into a deluge, to the point where now one can obtain the complete works of almost all the major and minor nineteenth-century guitar figures. The new high level of guitar scholarship and research led to some wonderful discoveries, such as a strong Sonata by the Spanish composer Antonio José. While the old editions of Segovia and others are valuable in revealing the aesthetics of great artists, guitarists are no longer enslaved to those editions, and often find their own interpretations by starting with what the composers actually wrote. From our perspective, the editions of Segovia reveal a kind of living performance practice that has significant historical value. Though few guitarists now use the Segovia version of, say, the Prelude and Fugue BWV 998 of Bach, in a comparison of the unedited Ponce Preludes with Segovia's vast and colorful changes, to these ears the Segovia edition is far more vivid.[26]

A strong trend emerged, promoted and perhaps begun by John Williams, to reduce and even omit the fingerings offered in guitar editions. Though this is by no means universal, Williams has expressed his reasons:

> I don't think guitar editions should be published solely for their fingering... If you want to play a note on the second string, play it on the second string. There's no great musical reason why you should play it on the first or third string. I think guitarists generally read badly and in an unmusical way in part because they tend to read fingering.[27]

Lutherie

In the early part of the century, virtually all classical guitarists played instruments built by Spanish luthiers, and most of the best luthiers came from the workshop of Manuel Ramirez. Then, following the guitar acquisitions of Segovia, a few major figures dominated the landscape – Hauser, Fleta, and then Ramirez. In the 1960s Ramirez was the guitar of choice, but soon new luthiers could be found in practically every corner of the world. As guitar audiences grew, luthiers tried to make louder instruments, perhaps culminating in the revolutionary design of Greg Smallman, the Australian luthier made world famous by John Williams. Later, after the death of Segovia in 1987 and with the advent of better technologies, guitarists began to use amplification, even in solo recitals. That is another trend pioneered by John Williams, who very successfully enhances his solo recitals in large halls. Though Pepe Romero and Manuel Barrueco continue to play the Rodrigo concerto as he preferred it, unamplified, many soloists and groups, such as the Los Angeles Guitar Quartet, now amplify, even in medium-sized halls. (The quartet members feel that their popularity increased dramatically when they started to amplify.) And while volume is still a goal of luthiers, the increase in guitarists using amplification has meant that luthiers do not have to sacrifice refinement and subtlety in their instruments for this ever elusive loud guitar. Additionally, there have been experiments with adding strings and changing the basic design of the guitar during the century, but few of these attempts resulted in widespread adoption. Narciso Yepes played a ten-string guitar, and received some brilliant music for it by Maurice Ohana, but the instrument is virtually unplayed today. The Swedish guitarist Goran Sollscher has long played the eleven-string Alt-Guitar, but while he has a few imitators, no widespread movement exists there either. There are several eight-string guitars, including a very inventive instrument played by Paul Galbraith, which has one higher and one lower string than normal, and an end-pin that fits into a resonating box on the floor. The one invention that seems to have taken hold is the Millennium design of Thomas Humphrey. Inspired by some nineteenth-century guitar designs, the Millennium features a slanted guitar face which facilitates access to the upper positions. Millenniums are played by many top performers, the design has been adapted to various degrees by numerous luthiers, and Martin Millenniums are now being mass produced.

Education

The year 1964 saw the first degree program for the guitar in the United States at the San Francisco Conservatory of Music. When I was looking for college guitar programs ten years later, there were still only a handful, but a decade after that there were dozens, and now virtually every major music school has a guitar program. This has led to a more educated generation of guitarists, one that more easily can enter the mainstream classical world through chamber music and by commissioning the best-known composers. Through discussion and interchange, technical ideas have become standardized for the first time in the history of the guitar. For instance, almost all players now position the right hand with a straight wrist. Teachers and players are also working to ease the strain of guitar playing on the body; many guitarists are demanding 65 cm string length guitars or smaller, though the standard size was 66 cm or more twenty years ago. Also, devices to replace the footstool are being invented constantly, and more and more players are using them. Another encouraging trend for pedagogy is that a body of interesting repertoire has emerged at easier playing levels, making it more enticing to learn and teach the beginning levels of guitar. Guitar faculties at conservatories and universities have evolved into two different and successful patterns: perhaps the most common has a primary professor aided by other teachers, assistants, or graduate students who primarily teach the professor's way. Another model has several peers, usually directed by a chairperson, who teach in quite different ways from each other, so that students contact diverse approaches. Among many outstanding teachers around the world, Aaron Shearer of the United States, Abel Carlevaro of Uruguay, and Isaias Savio of Brazil must be cited for producing numerous high-level professionals.

New works

The force and conviction of this generation has been so great that for the first time, every major composer of our time has written for the instrument, with a few exceptions such as György Ligeti, Arvo Pärt, and Philip Glass. Certain guitarists have been highly focused in this area, and it seems that every country has at least one major player who specializes in and is committed to playing new music. The German guitarist Reinbert Evers has worked with many composers and has particularly supported younger composers. In Sweden, Magnus Anderson has done similar work. In France there is Rafael Andia, in Japan Norio Sato, in Denmark Erling Møldrup, and in Italy Angelo Gilardino. In the US David Starobin has a remarkable record of working with major composers, and formed his own record company, Bridge, to help promote these pieces. Although Starobin has commissioned a steady stream of works for decades, with the particular help of Rose Augustine and the Albert Augustine Company, it was Elliott Carter's work *Changes* from 1983 that unleashed a stream of American works for Starobin. Still in his forties, Starobin has had more than 300 pieces written for him and he has received many awards for this work, including the first ever Avery Fisher Career Prize for a guitarist. In the middle of all these activities, he developed an interest in the nineteenth-century repertoire for the guitar on original instruments. I have done similar kinds of work with composers, and some of the results have been a concerto from Henze, *Ode an Eine Äolsharfe*, three works from Pulitzer Prize winner Aaron Jay Kernis (including one for guitar with string quartet, *100 Greatest Dance Hits*, that seems to be entering the repertoire), and a projected series of twenty-six pieces from Terry Riley. Sharon Isbin proudly proclaims that she has had more concertos written for her than any other guitarist. She has performed the concerto *Troubadours* by John Corigliano some thirty times. Luciano Berio wrote his *Sequenza XI* and *Chemins V* for Eliot Fisk (who has also worked with Robert Beaser, Nicholas Maw, and George Rochberg), Alberto Ginastera wrote his Sonata for Carlos Barbosa-Lima, and Astor Piazzolla wrote *Cinco Piezas* for Roberto Aussel and *Tango Suite* for the Assads, to name a few of the most celebrated pieces.

As part of this generation, there exist a number of guitarist-composers who are very popular, in the tradition of Sor, Giuliani, Barrios, and Brouwer. Mostly European, they include Roland Dyens, Nikita Koshkin, Carlo Domeniconi, Dusan Bogdanovic, Stepan Rak, Francis Klenyans, and Andrew York. All play programs featuring their own music. Most of these composers have a "hit single," a particular piece that is performed much more than their other works. Their music is very idiomatic and enjoyable to play, which attracts performers and audiences. Certain composers have had particular champions: Vladimir Mikulka catapulted to guitar fame by introducing the works of Rak and Koshkin, and David Russell brought Klenyans and Domeniconi to wide attention by touring their works. The guitarist-composer trend is growing, as many young players are composing as well, and much of this music blurs the formerly held lines of classical and pop.

With all due respect to these composers, my personal interest has been more in working with non-guitarist composers for the very reason that their music is not as idiomatic. I enjoy collaborating with composers who do not play the instrument because they often have to reach further to imagine sound on the guitar, and also because I become much more involved in the creation of the music and its realization on the instrument.

Latin America; chamber music

The greatest integration of classical technique and style with more popular styles comes from the long guitar tradition of Brazil.[28]

While many Brazilian guitarists use classical right-hand techniques on either electric or nylon-string guitars, and many folk guitarists there study classical methods, a style of composition has emerged that interweaves European classical guitar tradition with jazz and native styles. Thus, an earlier generation led by Baden Powell, Dino Setecordas, and Antonio Carlos Jobim bred a younger generation including Egberto Gismonti Amim Nader Yussef Bon Nader (better known by his first two names), Luis Bonfá, Sergio Assad, and Paulo Bellinati. In Argentina a similar blended music was heavily influenced by the national tango, as the non-guitarist Astor Piazzolla achieved widespread prominence in the guitar literature through a few original compositions and many transcriptions. Argentinian guitarist-composers Eduardo Falu and Jorge Morel were followed by Jorge Cardosa and Maximo Diego Pujol.[29]

In Venezuela the work of Vincente Emilio Sojo bred that of Antonio Lauro. Uruguay has had a fertile guitar scene which Segovia helped seed by his residence in Montevideo during the war, and which ultimately led to the prominence of guitarist-composer Abel Carlevaro. Often this music sounds more traditional than classical, but it finds a natural home on the nylon-string guitar, and it is performed internationally by classical guitarists. In fact, this repertoire has filled a gap, providing an audience-satisfying alternative to the Segovia repertoire or the more modern compositions written for Bream, a music that speaks more of place than does the music of the guitarist-composers mentioned above. And it has found its particular champions, such as Alirio Diaz playing Lauro, or the Assad brothers duo playing Brazilian music.

Chamber music groups like the Los Angeles Guitar Quartet and the Assad duo are playing at high levels of precision and cohesion, and have developed large popular followings. Guitar orchestras have proliferated, especially in Japan, and transcriptions abound for these groups at varying levels. Steve Reich wrote his *Electric Counterpoint* for guitar soloist with fourteen prerecorded guitars on tape, but that is now routinely done by fifteen live guitarists. A significant repertoire has been developed for flute and guitar, featuring excellent pieces by Astor Piazzolla, Takemitsu, and Robert Beaser. In fact, one can now find interesting duo repertoire for guitar with any conceivable instrument, as well as, of course, for two, three, four, and more guitars. And the larger ensemble repertoire continues to grow, with certain combinations, such as guitar and string quartet, really flourishing.

Early music

There has been a corresponding explosion of lute playing, with a brilliant generation achieving world fame, led by Paul O'Dette, Nigel North, Hopkinson Smith, Konrad Junghänel, and Jakob Lindberg. In fact, much early music seems to have been ceded to lute players, and the Renaissance period is one that may be less frequently performed on guitar now than a few decades ago. As for Baroque music on classical guitar, all of the Bach solo works for lute, violin, and cello have become common fare. But not content with that, and hungry for more Bach, guitarists have pushed the boundaries back. Recently a recording of Bach's Goldberg Variations by Kurt Rodamer, using anywhere from two to four guitars, became a popular recording on Sony, and that was topped by a recording and publication of the entire Goldberg Variations on one guitar played by József Eötvös. Two trends have evolved in the playing of Bach on the guitar, both of which directly contradict the lute technique of Bach's time. The first is an attempt to articulate trills more clearly by playing them on two strings, a so-called cross-string trill. (Interestingly, there is apparently only one such cross-string trill in the voluminous works of Bach's contemporary, the great lutenist Sylvius Leopold Weiss.) The second, probably started by Leo Brouwer in the 1970s, is to reduce or even omit all left-hand slurs as a way of avoiding unintended accents or groupings. However, the tablature of Weiss and his colleagues clearly shows a plethora of slurs as well as scale passages notated across strings that create a campanella effect. In fact, successive notes fingered on the same string (as many current Bach guitar editions call for) produce a sound that Weiss went out of his way to avoid.

The nineteenth century and transcriptions

Nineteenth-century works have been played frequently by guitarists, sometimes on earlier instruments, and when guitarists finally looked beyond Sor and Giuliani, composers such as Legnani, Mertz, Regondi, and Coste saw the light of day. One of the great discoveries was made by the indefatigable scholar (and retired airline pilot) Matanya Ophee, who unearthed *10 Etudes* by Giulio Regondi, which is arguably the finest nineteenth-century guitar work. Still not fully content, and still searching – perhaps both for musical reasons and to come up with a unique career niche – guitarists transcribed anything and everything. Manuel Barrueco opened up many ears with his ground-breaking recording of Albeniz and Granados in the late 1970s, which led to a career that has kept Barrueco near the top of the field for years. In 1981 a young Japanese guitarist named Kazuhito Yamashita exploded onto the scene with a previously inconceivable transcription of Musorgsky's *Pictures at an Exhibition*. Utilizing new techniques and sounds as if it was a new composition, the transcription garnered world attention for Yamashita and seemed to smash the boundaries of what was possible. Yamashita went on to transcribe Dvořák's *New World* Symphony, Beethoven's Violin Concerto, and many other works.

The 1980s

One theory has it that the classical guitar reached a peak of popularity in the 1980s and has gradually lost its audience since then. The problem with this argument is that it is hard to define exactly what is the "classical" guitar anymore. In the 1980s New Age music, played mostly on steel-string guitar, became immensely popular and satisfied some listeners' needs for an intimate, unplugged repertoire. Some classical guitarists like Andrew York and Benjamin Verdery have even moved in that direction, finding a niche writing and playing music that is indistinguishable from some New Age guitarists. Other players, from Barrueco and Sollscher to Ichiro Suzuki, have released Beatles records, and collaborations between classical and pop guitarists are more common. So just as listeners may have moved to the popular side of the guitar, classical guitarists seem to be going there also.

Another factor that has affected the guitar's popularity is the decline of solo recitals over the last quarter century. Consequently, guitarists now rely more than ever on guitar societies for solo recitals, and while these societies are healthy and thriving in many places, they do little toward moving the guitar into the mainstream of classical music or generating large audiences. In short, as some classical guitarists seek a specific niche for themselves, others – for both musical and professional reasons – are trying to inhabit as many musical worlds as possible. Collaborating with pop artists, playing chamber music, working with composers, and playing solo recitals for guitar societies all serve to broaden a guitarist's musical horizons, and they can provide enough work to combine into a full schedule.

The 1990s and the challenges of the new generation

A new generation is now emerging that is more numerous, more educated, and technically at an even higher standard than the previous one – and this is a healthy development. Naturally, there are the same praises and criticisms about this new generation as there are about other young instrumentalists: that while they are so technically good and facile, they are also not readily distinguishable from each other. Certainly it is a very different world from that of the early and mid twentieth century, when all instruments were dominated by a few distinct personalities. One could always recognize Segovia on the radio, or Casals, or Rubinstein – or Bream, for that matter. Composers may even be happier now, as younger artists impose less artistic personality on their works. Nevertheless, there are big challenges for younger guitarists today. One of the main ones is the scarcity of teaching positions. The relatively young age of the majority of guitar professors in colleges and conservatories suggests that they will still be teaching in their jobs for at least another twenty years. That fact, along with the decrease in the allure of solo recitals and the larger number of aspiring guitarists, makes existing in the field a daunting task. Indomitable will, risk-taking, luck, and above all, great music making are necessary ingredients.

The classical guitar itself also faces challenges. This is an instrument that is experiencing an erosion in the popularity of the traditional Segovia repertoire. There is the sense for some that, since "anything goes" and all styles seem to be merging, there are no moorings, no anchors. Certainly there are no great Beethoven sonatas to define us. And there is the tendency to define ourselves by remaining in the same insular world that we have always lived in. Thus, one can attend guitar festivals that consist largely of solo recitals consisting of music by guitarist-composers for other guitarists, a throwback to the small pre-Segovia world of Tárrega and some of his followers. We still do not take enough chances, we still do not have enough women guitarists, and there can be a dulling sameness to our efforts.

Conclusion

Accepting an honorary doctorate at Florida State University in 1969, Segovia listed "five purposes aiming at the redemption of the guitar":

> My prime effort was to extract the guitar from the noise and disreputable folkloric amusements. This was the second of my purposes: to create a wonderful repertoire for my instrument. My third purpose was to make the guitar known to the philharmonic public all over the world. Another and fourth purpose has been to provide a unifying medium for those

interested in the development of the instrument. This I did through my support of the now well-known international musicological journal, the *Guitar Review*, developed by Vladimir Bobri. I am still working on my fifth and maybe the last purpose, which is to place the guitar in the most important conservatories for teaching the young lovers of it, and thus securing its future.[30]

If we step back and scan the past hundred years, it is an amazing view. Not even the visionary Segovia could have foreseen the landscape of today. And he would certainly not like all that he saw. But all of his life's missions have been met, and the guitar is already speaking to the people of yet another century.

12 Antonio Stradivari and baroque guitar making

STEWART POLLENS

Antonio Stradivari (b. 1644; d. Cremona, 1737) is the most celebrated violin maker in history, yet it is not generally known that he also made a variety of lutes, mandolas, mandolins, guitars, and harps. Compared to the approximately 600 of Stradivari's violins, violas, and cellos that have survived, only a few mandolins and guitars and one harp are extant. Of the guitars, probably the best-known example, dated 1688,[1] is in the Hill collection at the Ashmolean Museum in Oxford (see Plates 21 a–d). Other examples include the "Sabionari" (1679), in a private collection in Italy; the "Giustiniani" (1681), also in a private collection in Italy; and the "Rawlins" (1700), in the Shrine to Music Museum in Vermillion, South Dakota. Doubts have been cast on two others: the "Canobio-Pagliari," apparently by another maker though bearing a label "Revisto e coretto da me Antonio Stradivari in Cremona l'anno 1681" ("Revised and corrected by me, Antonio Stradivari in Cremona in the year 1681"), whereabouts unknown; and the "Vuillaume" (1711), in the Musée de la Musique in Paris.[2] A guitar neck inscribed "ANT:ˢSTRADIVARIVS/CREMONEN:ˢF.1675" is privately owned in the United Kingdom.

To better understand Stradivari's contribution to the craft of guitar making, it is helpful to trace the development of the baroque guitar and to examine early writings that describe the guitar's design from a theoretical standpoint. Only two pre-baroque guitars and three early vihuelas are extant. One guitar, in the Royal College of Music (London), is labeled in Portuguese "Belchior Dias made (by) me / Lisbon month of December 1581"[3] and also inscribed "BCHIOR DIAS LXA [Belchior Dias Lisbon]"; a similar, though slightly larger and unsigned instrument (formerly in the Robert Spencer collection) is now in a private collection in the United States. Though the term *vihuela* is imprecise (during this period it referred to both bowed and plucked instruments of various sizes and shapes), three instruments of the plucked, guitar-shaped form of the vihuela have been identified: one from the sixteenth century (or earlier) in the Musée Jacquemart André (Paris) is inscribed GVADALVPE; an anonymous example, possibly from the early seventeenth century, is preserved as a relic in a shrine to S. Mariana de Jesús (1619–45) at the Iglesia de la Compañía de Jesús in Quito, Ecuador;[4] and another anonymous, undated example is in the collection of the Musée de la Musique in Paris.[5] Though the earliest non-Hispanic guitars were made in

Plate 21a–d The "Hill" Stradivari guitar, 1688 (Ashmolean Museum, Oxford)

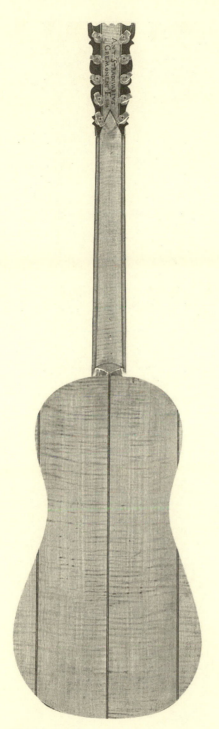

Plate 21 (*cont.*)

Plate 21 (*cont.*)

Plate 21 *(cont.)*

the fifteenth century, the oldest surviving ones date from the early seventeenth century and include examples by Christopho Cocho and Giorgio Sellas of Venice, Giovanni Smit of Milan, Giovanni Tessler of Ancona, and René Voboam of Paris.

Since technical descriptions and measurements of the three vihuelas and two sixteenth-century guitars have appeared in recent studies, only a few general comments on their construction will be made here.[6] The three vihuelas and the Belchior Dias guitar in the Royal College of Music exhibit certain structural elements, such as the one-piece neck and neck block with slots for the ribs (otherwise known as the "Spanish foot," or "slipper foot"), that are still employed in classical Spanish guitar construction. While some early seventeenth-century non-Hispanic guitars, such as those made in Paris by René Voboam, also have the integral neck and top block, others, such as those made by the Sellas family in Venice, employ an independent top block glued inside the ribs, with the neck (mitered to the neck foot) secured to the block by a long iron nail driven from the inside of the instrument. This form of construction (involving the use of an inner block and nail to secure the neck) was a feature shared with the lute as well as with Cremonese violins made through the mid-eighteenth century. The guitar's mitered heel provides an elongated gluing surface not unlike that of the lute's angled inner block. The inner block and nail is the form of construction found in Stradivari's guitars. Italian makers such as Gennaro Fabricatore of Naples continued to use the nailed-on neck into the nineteenth century.

The six-course vihuela in the Musée Jacquemart-André exhibits the most unconventional construction of the three surviving examples. The body is uncharacteristically large (length 581 mm), and the back and top are heavily built (4–5 mm and 2–3 mm thick, respectively). Because of the neck's unusual scarfed and butted construction, it is impossible to establish whether the neck and string lengths are original. Furthermore, there are two bridge positions indicated on the top, and it is unclear which is the earlier one. The string length is presently 790 mm, but if the neck is the original length and the lower bridge position is earlier, the string length may have been as long as 840 mm. As presently configured, the first and last strings would lie off the edge of the fretboard, and this, combined with the lack of evidence of wear from playing and impressions from tied frets, suggests that the instrument may not be authentic.

The six-course instrument identified as a vihuela in the shrine to S. Mariana de Jesús in Quito has a body length of 505 mm and a string length of 727 mm. The thin-walled construction of the body is more conventional than that of the vihuela in the Musée Jacquemart-André – were it not for its six-course disposition, it might pass as a seventeenth- or eighteenth-century guitar. Many instruments made in Central and South America do, in fact, exhibit archaic qualities that lead to improper dating, and some experts have questioned the early seventeenth-century date and whether this instrument is a true vihuela.[7]

The smaller six-course vihuela in the Musée de la Musique has a body length of 435 mm and a string length of approximately 645 mm.[8] Like the five-course 1581 Belchior Dias guitar in the Royal College of Music (body length 366 mm; string length 553 mm), the Musée de la Musique's vihuela has an arched back composed of seven deeply fluted ribs.

The ex-Spencer guitar (body length 454 mm) was converted to a *chitarra battente*, which involved cutting down the ribs, installing a cranked top, and reducing the neck length. It was subsequently restored as a conventional five-course guitar by building up the ribs, installing a new top (the rose is thought to be original) and bridge, and extending the neck. The Dias guitar (body length 366 mm; string length 553 mm) is also fitted with a later top and bridge.

In his *Declaración de instrumentos musicales* (Osuna, 1555), Juan Bermudo (b. Ecija, c. 1510; d. Andalusia, c. 1565) makes a distinction between the vihuela and the guitar. He gives tuning systems for vihuelas of six and seven courses, and though he indicates that the guitar was smaller in size and commonly equipped with four or five courses, he describes a "vihuela nueva pequéna" (new small vihuela) that was the size of "a large guitar strung with six courses."[9] He suggests that a vihuela could be converted into a guitar by removing the top and bottom strings.[10] Bermudo specifies that both instruments can be fitted with ten frets and provides various systems for positioning them, though he adds that "small instruments, or those that play simple music, use only five or six."[11] The number of frets specified in early descriptions of the vihuela and guitar may not be an indicator of the length of the neck, as the neck may have extended beyond the number of frets that were fitted to it.

Bartolomeo Lieto's *Dialogo quarto* of 1559 provides instructions for intabulating music for the *viola a mano* or lute. In describing the proportions of the body of the instrument (Lieto does not specify whether he is referring to the *viola a mano* or lute), the author indicates that

> you will make it according to a ternary proportion . . . decide first the length of the instrument following your desire, not including the neck, and then divide this length and make three parts, two for the width and one for the height. Make the neck as long as there is from the bridge where the strings are tied to the end of the body, excluding the small [peg head] where they are wound onto the pegs.[12]

Lieto indicates that the neck is half the string length, and thus long enough to support twelve frets. The body proportions are perhaps more suggestive of the lute than the vihuela.

Pablo Nassarre (b. Aragon, c. 1650; d. Zaragoza, c. 1730) basically reiterates Bermudo's description of the vihuela and the guitar:

> *Vihuelas* are of seven, six, or five courses (the last are called Spanish guitars); there is no distinction in material, form, or in the proportions that should be maintained in the body, nor in the material of the strings. All of these instruments are played with strings, like the harp, and are only distinguished by two things, one is that the *vihuelas* of six and seven courses have a body of greater size than those of five. The second thing is in the outline [*concavo*], because there are different types, but since there is no difference in the fabrication of the three instruments, what I say for one should be understood to apply to all.[13]

Nassarre goes on to provide detailed information about the structure and proportions of the vihuela and the guitar.[14]

Michael Praetorius indicates in his *Syntagma Musicum II: De Organographia* (1619) that "the guitar, or *chiterna*, is a four-course instrument tuned like the original lute. Its back is not round, however, but completely flat, rather like that of the pandora; the sides are at most two or three fingers-breadth in depth." He adds that "Some guitars have five courses of strings; in Italy, the *Ziarlatini* and *Salt'in banco* [clowns and mountebanks] use them for simple strummed accompaniments to their *villanelle* and other vulgar, clownish songs."[15]

Marin Mersenne (b. La Soultière, 1588; d. Paris, 1648) provides additional information on the geometry of the guitar in his *Harmonie Universelle* (1636–7):

> The first guitars, the invention of which seem to have been in Spain, had only four courses of strings, of which the first is single, and called the treble string like the first of the other instruments, because it serves for the part of the soprano and often sings the melody ... the neck is divided into eight frets, so that each string can be raised up by a minor hexachord.[16]

Mersenne's diagrams show a guitar with five pairs of double strings (though some, he says, use only a single treble course) and a fingerboard with eight frets like the preceding one. He concludes that the back of the instrument is "sometimes as flat as a table and other times a little convex. This is not of much importance, and whatever the style one gives it, its sounds are related to the kettle and always seem to whine."

We learn a little more about the proportional scheme of the guitar from Giovanni Battista Granata's introduction to his *Nuovi soavi concenti . . . opera sesta* (1680). Granata states that the neck of his guitar had eleven tied frets

Table 12.1 *Guitar and vihuela proportions (with decimal equivalents) in theoretical writings*

Author	Body length/ lower bout width	Body length/ center bout width	Body length/ neck length	Lower bout width/upper bout width	Top of body to center of rose/center of rose to bottom of body	Bout width/ rib height	Body length/ rib height	Number of frets
Bermudo 1555								10
								5–6
Lieto 1559	3:2 (1.5)					2:1 (2.0)	3:1 (3.0)	12
Mersenne 1636–37			3:2 (1.5)		1:2 (0.5)			8
Granata 1680								11
Nassarre 1724	2:1 (2.0)	3:1 (3.0)		5:4 (1.25)		5:2 (2.5)		6–8

and three of ebony glued to the soundboard. It is interesting that his earlier *Soavi Concenti di Sonate Musicali per la Chitara Spagnuola* (1659) includes an engraving of the author holding a five-course guitar having a neck that was only long enough to accommodate eight tied frets. Thus, the proportional inflexibility between neck length and body length that one finds in the violin, for example, appears to be absent in the guitar. As composers for the guitar wrote in increasingly higher ranges, the instrument's proportions were evidently adapted to provide players with more frets on the neck to make playing easier. Table 12.1 provides a summary of the proportions indicated in the theoretical works cited above.

Stradivari's guitars

Unfortunately, the Stradivari guitars that have survived are not in a pristine state. The 1679 "Sabionari" has a shortened neck, non-original fixed frets, new peg head, new bridge, as well as new blocks and internal bracing. The "Giustiniani" also has a shortened neck, non-original fixed frets, and a peg head that has been redrilled and refaced to support six double courses, which is a modification of the original five-double-course disposition. In addition to having lost its original soundboard rose, the "Giustiniani" guitar has a new bridge, reinforced internal construction, and soundboard barring in apparently non-original position. The "Rawlins" guitar also has a cut-down or, more likely, non-original neck that has been fitted with inaccurately placed fixed frets (there is no evidence that the present neck ever had tied frets). Neither the bridge nor the rose is original. The "Rawlins" guitar has some uncharacteristic features: transverse braces running across the back (the other Stradivari guitars do not have back bracing); a markedly shorter length (which may indicate that the body was cut down); a sound hole that is not positioned according to the same proportional scheme as the "Hill," "Giustiniani," and "Sabionari" guitars; a simplified ebony ornament at the bottom of the soundboard (consisting of a shallow, elongated bracket rather than the shorter bracket and inverted heart used in the "Hill," "Giustiniani," and "Sabionari" guitars); and a peg-head profile that does not match the "Hill" and "Giustiniani" guitars or any of the surviving templates in Cremona (Plate 22). The aberrant profile is highly disturbing, as the maker's name is located on the peg head. The neck and heel design and neck decoration are also unlike the "Hill" and "Giustiniani" guitars. The inlaid frets are again inaccurately positioned.

Regarding the "Hill" guitar, the original decorative projections of the bridge (the "baffo" or "moustache") have been removed. Traces of these decorative elements indicate that the present bridge is properly positioned relative to them. The bridge itself has atypical triangular openings for the strings. Though the triangular openings allow the player to adjust the string spacing (without reducing the gluing surface between the bridge and top), original bridges for mandolas, mandolins, and lutes preserved in the Museo Stradivariano in Cremona indicate that Stradivari used drilled holes 1.06–1.12 mm in diameter, rather than triangular cutouts, to position and mount the strings. Thus, it is likely that the "Hill" bridge is not original. The neck of the "Hill" guitar, though apparently the only one with its original length intact, is veneered over a core of lime or poplar wood. Frets have been fitted at a later date, and as in the "Rawlins" guitar, these are not positioned in strict accordance with the current bridge position (the twelfth fret, for example, falls considerably short of half the distance to the bridge).[17] The frets were likely fitted by someone unacquainted with the finer details of guitar construction, perhaps the Hills. The rose of this guitar has also been called into question as it is very similar in design to that of the "Canobio-Pagliardi" guitar, which is not believed to be authentic.[18] A similar rose can also be found in an anonymous guitar in the Museo degli Strumenti Musicali in Rome.[19] It is also clear that the "Hill" rose was intended for a larger opening, as all of the ornaments around the perimeter are partially occluded by the beveled orifice of the sound hole. Most guitars of this period had sunken roses; the flat rose of the "Hill" guitar resembles those employed in Italian harpsichords, its probable source.

Though the "Sabionari," "Giustiniani," and "Hill" have similar body dimensions, their outlines, and that of the "Rawlins," do not match any original

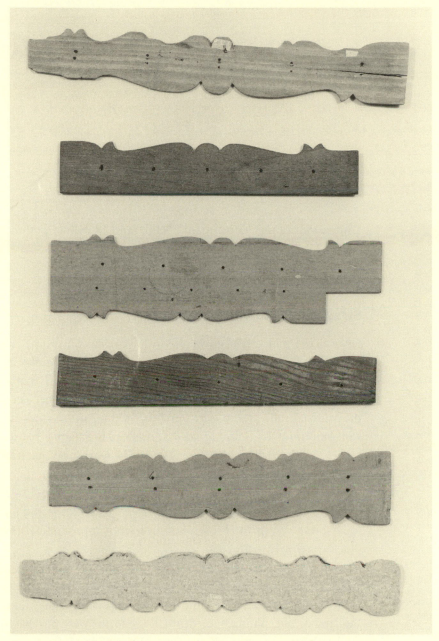

Plate 22 Stradivari peg-head templates (Cremona, Museo Stradivariano, MS 376–381)

Stradivari paper body pattern or wood form preserved in the Museo Stradivariano in Cremona and Musée de la Musique in Paris. This observation is not made to cast doubt on the authenticity of these guitars, as it is possible that some of Stradivari's patterns, forms, and templates may have been lost.

Table 12.2 *Dimensions of Stradivari's guitars*

	Body length	Upper bout width	Center bout width	Lower bout width	Rib height: top; bottom	Rose diameter	Top of body to center of rose	Neck length	Neck width: top; bottom	String length
"Giustiniani" 1681	473	211	175	269	97 105	85		294[a]	47[a] 53	649[a]
"Hill" 1688	471	214	178	270	95 105	82	161	363	46 54	742[a]
"Rawlins" 1700	439	211	170	267	78.5 89	78		249[a]	37[a] 44	640[a]

[a] Non-original dimensions due to reduction in neck length and/or non-original bridge placement

Dimensions of the "Giustiniani," "Hill," and "Rawlins" guitars are given in Table 12.2.[20]

Stradivari's workshop materials

Since all of Stradivari's known guitars have been compromised to some extent, perhaps a clearer understanding of the Stradivari guitar design can be achieved from studying the surviving templates and forms that are preserved in the Museo Stradivariano and the Musée de la Musique. The materials in the Museo Stradivariano were purchased from Antonio Stradivari's grandson, Antonio II, by Count Ignazio Alessandro di Salabue (b. Casale Monferrato, 1755; d. Salabue, 1840) in 1776.[21] The workshop materials remained in the possession of the Count's family until 1920, when the violin maker Giuseppe Fiorini purchased them. He donated these artifacts to the city of Cremona in 1930.[22] Of the approximately 700 patterns and forms that are today preserved in the Museo Stradivariano, approximately fifty were for plucked string instruments.

At the end of the eighteenth century, several of Stradivari's forms became separated from the bulk of his workshop materials. Three of these were wood forms for guitars that later came into the possession of the violin maker J. B. Vuillaume. After Vuillaume's death, these forms were purchased at auction by the museum of the Conservatoire National de Musique, and are now in the Musée de la Musique in Paris.[23] The wood forms served as a temporary platform for mounting the top and bottom blocks and ribs during the construction of the guitar body. Stradivari's paper patterns and wood forms are invaluable for the study of his instruments since they not only provide uncorrupted outlines of the body but also have positioning marks for the bridge and rose, scribed arcs indicating the tapered height of the ribs, and outlines of the fingerboard (see Plates 23 and 24). Dimensions of the three

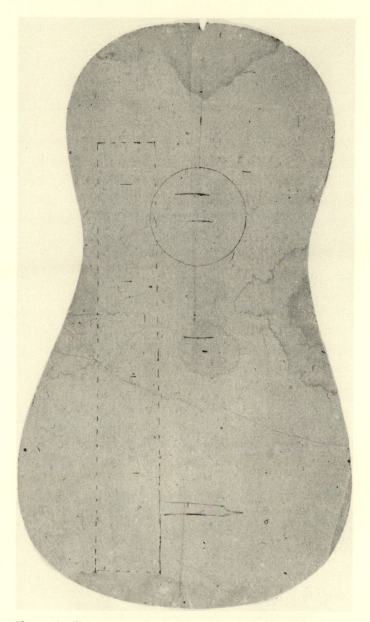

Plate 23 Stradivari paper pattern for guitar (Cremona, Museo Stradivariano, MS 374)

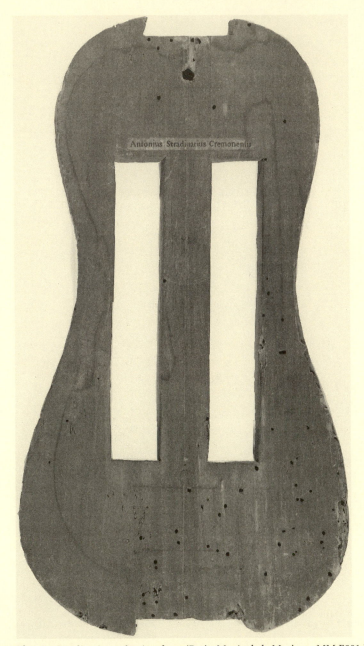

Plate 24 Stradivari wood guitar form (Paris, Musée de la Musique, MM E901d)

wood guitar forms in Paris and the four paper patterns for guitar outlines in Cremona are given in Table 12.3.

Dimensions of the paper patterns MS 719, MS 721, and MS 750 are also given in Table 12.3. These patterns are not listed in the original inventory and catalog of the Museo Stradivariano, and their provenance is unclear.[24] The proportions of the body outlines of these three patterns are consistent with those of the other Stradivari paper patterns and wood forms, and they appear to be seventeenth- or early eighteenth-century designs. Unlike the other patterns and forms, they do not include indications of fingerboard dimensions, bridge position, rib heights, or sound-hole diameters and positions. Their outer dimensions are included in Table 12.3 for comparative purposes. Proportional relationships derived from measurements of Stradivari's guitars, wood forms, and paper patterns can be found in Table 12.4. From the data presented in Tables 12.1 and 12.4, the following points are evident:

(1) There is considerable variation in the proportions given in the theoretical writings. Most notable is the discrepancy between the number of frets on the neck, which may imply different ratios of neck length to body length. Also differing are the ratios of body length to lower bout width and bout width to rib height.

(2) There is very little concordance between the proportions given in any of the theoretical writings and those found in Stradivari's patterns, forms, and extant instruments.

(3) There is a marked discrepancy between the body-length to lower-bout-width ratios of the three surviving Stradivari guitars and those of Stradivari's wood forms and paper patterns. This ratio in the "Hill" and "Giustiniani" guitars hovers around 5 : 11 (2.2), whereas the forms and patterns exhibit a ratio of about 5 : 9 (1.8). When rib thicknesses (approximately 1.2 mm) are added to the form dimensions, this significant proportional discrepancy persists.

(4) There is considerable similarity between the proportions of the "Hill" and "Giustiniani" bodies. The dissimilarities between the bout widths of these two guitars and the "Rawlins" suggest that the "Rawlins" may have been cut down in length. This might also explain why the shape of the inlaid ebony ornament on the lower edge of the "Rawlins" soundboard differs from that found on the "Hill" and "Giustiniani" soundboards.

String lengths, string diameters, and pitch

From the surviving instruments, wood forms, and paper templates, we know that Stradivari made guitars with a wide range of body and string lengths, as seen in Table 12.5.

Two seventeenth-century composers provided three or four different tuning ranges for different sizes of guitars. In 1640 Giovanni Paolo Foscarini

Table 12.3 *Dimensions of Stradivari's guitar forms and patterns*

Form or Pattern	Body length	Upper bout width	Center bout width	Lower bout width	Top to rose center	Rose diameter	Top to bridge	Neck length	Neck width: top; bottom	Rib height: top; bottom
MM E901d	382	165.5	139	207	137	56.8	321	246	43.5 69	77 82
MM E901e	338[a]	163[a]	125[a]	201[a]	86[a]	54	267[a]	283	20.4 49	75.7 82
MM E901f	220	92.5	80	117	79.3	41	181	145.5	41 44	54 61.5
MS 374	496	231	195	287	[165]	[83.5]	[407]	363	48 55	99 122
MS 719	459	195	160	255	–	–	–	–	–	–
MS 721	495	219	185	280	–	–	–	–	–	–
MS 750	412	191	157	236	–	–	–	–	–	–

[a] Altered dimensions (MM E901e was converted by Stradivari from a guitar form to a viola d'amore form; its length was considerably shortened and the waist lowered)
[ ] = Not measured directly but derived from other measurements

Table 12.4 *Proportions (decimal) found in Stradivari's guitars, patterns, and forms*

Guitar, form, or pattern	Body length/ lower bout width	Body length/ center bout width	Body length/ neck length	Lower bout width/upper bout width	Top of body to center of rose/center of rose to bottom of body	Bout width/ rib height: top; bottom
"Giustiniani" guitar	2.24	2.70	1.61[a]	1.27		2.18 2.56
"Hill" guitar	2.20	2.65	1.30	1.26	0.52	2.25 2.57
"Rawlins" guitar	2.08	2.58	1.76[a]	1.27		2.69 3.00
MM E901d wood form	1.85	2.75	1.55	1.24	0.56	2.15 2.52
MM E901e wood form	1.68[a]	2.70[a]	1.19[a]	1.23[a]	0.34[a]	2.15[a] 2.45[a]
MM E901f wood form	1.88	2.75	1.51	1.26	0.56	1.71 1.90
MS 374 paper pattern	1.73	2.54	1.37	1.24		2.33 2.35
MS 719 paper pattern	1.80	2.87		1.31		
MS 721 paper pattern	1.77	2.68		1.28		
MS 750 paper pattern	1.75	2.62		1.24		

[a] Altered dimensions (form MM E901e converted by Stradivari from a guitar form to a *viola d'amore* form; length considerably shortened)

Table 12.5 *Body lengths and string lengths of Stradivari's guitar forms*

Guitar, form, or paper pattern	Body length	String length	String length/ body length
"Hill" guitar	471	741	1.57
MM E901d	382	567	1.48
MM E901f	220	326.5	1.48
MS 374	496	770	1.55
MS 719	459		
MS 721	495		
MS 750	412		

wrote: "First you tune the *grande* [large guitar], as you wish, then the *mezana* [middle guitar] is voiced a little higher, that is touch the fifth string of the *grande* with the third of the *mezana*, tune the *Chitara piccola* [little guitar] by touching [its] fourth string at two [second fret], and make unison with the third open string of the *Chitara mezana*, and thus tune one fourth above."[25] In 1646, Carlo Calvi added another tuning range: "To tune four guitars in concert, first tune the third string of the *picciola Chitarra* (little guitar) to the fifth [string] of the *mezana* [middle-size guitar], and with the fourth

Table 12.6 *String lengths and body lengths of the largest Stradivari guitar and pattern and proportional lengths derived from them*

Guitar or pattern	String length; body length	8/9 string l.; 8/9 body l.	2/3 string l.; 2/3 body l.	3/4 string l.; 3/4 body l.	4/5 string l.; 4/5 body l.
"Hill" guitar	741	659	494	556	593
	471	419	314	353	377
MS 374	770	684	513	578	616
	496	440	331	372	397

[string] of the *più grande* [larger guitar] you make the unison. Play the third [string] of the other *Chitarra mezana* [second middle-size guitar] to the second string of the *grande* and make it the same. Thus the *picciola* makes a fifth with the *grande*, and the *mezana* a fourth [with the *grande*], and the other [*mezana*] the third [with the *grande*]." Though Foscarini's *mezana* guitar was not necessarily smaller than the *grande* (there is only one whole-tone difference between the two), his *piccola* guitar was a fourth higher and was presumably a smaller instrument. Calvi's *mezane* were a third and a fourth higher in pitch, and his *picciola* was a fifth higher, suggesting two, three, or possibly four different sizes of guitars.

We know from Stradivari's surviving forms and patterns that he produced guitars in different sizes. To ascertain whether these sizes bear any relation to the pitch relationships presented by Foscarini and Calvi, the string lengths of the largest paper guitar pattern and the "Hill" guitar (which is shorter than the largest pattern but more similar in size to other extant seventeenth-century guitars) were multiplied by the proportions representing a whole tone (8 : 9), major third (4 : 5), fourth (3 : 4), and fifth (2 : 3). The resulting dimensions are found in Table 12.6. The dimensions calculated in Table 12.6 do not yield any precise matches with body lengths and string lengths of the smaller forms and paper patterns (see Table 12.3); however, form MM E901d could conceivably have been tuned a third higher than a guitar having the dimensions of the "Hill" and "Giustiniani," and paper pattern MS 750 (though possibly not from Stradivari's shop) might have been tuned a whole tone higher than these extant guitars. Patterns or forms for a guitar tuned a fourth or fifth higher cannot be identified among the surviving workshop materials.

The *chitarra tiorbata*, or theorboed guitar (guitar with added diapasons having greater lengths than the fretted strings), is little known today; however, in the mid-seventeenth century a number of composers wrote for this instrument. For example, Giovanni Battista Granata includes several works for it in his *Soavi Concenti di Sonate Musicali per la Chitarra Spagnuola*

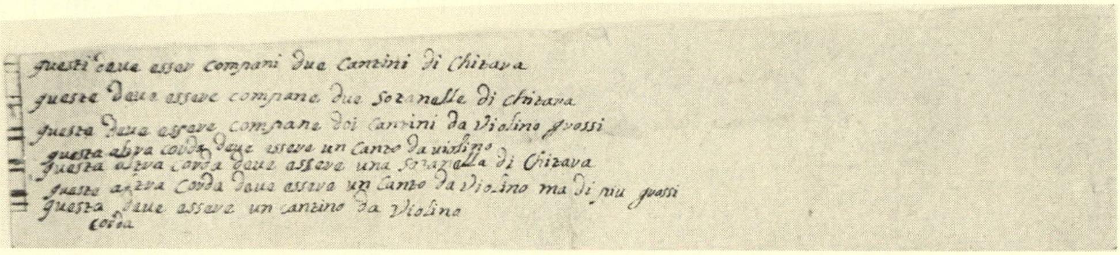

Plate 25 Stradivari neck pattern showing arrangement of strings (Cremona, Museo Stradivariano, MS 375)

(Turin, 1659); his *Preludio del terzo Tuono sopra la Chitarra Atiorbata,* written for Count Lelio Pioveni of Venice, calls for seven strings off the fingerboard. Stradivari left two neck patterns, one (MS 375) 318 mm long by 72 mm and 60 mm (widths at the juncture with the body and at the nut, respectively) inscribed "Measure of the length and width of the neck of the theorboed guitar,"[26] the other (MS 385) 921.5 mm in length and 53 mm in width, with indications for seven strings, inscribed "Measure of the length and width of the extension of the theorboed guitar and on the said extension are placed seven basses and at the top a fourth [string] of the violin and the remaining guitar [strings] total seven."[27] Form MM E901d and paper pattern MS 374 indicate that string length to neck length ratios are 2.30 and 2.12, respectively. Assuming that the *chitarra tiorbata* was constructed with a similar number (ten or eleven) of frets on the neck to Stradivari's conventional guitars, the instrument would have a fretted string length of 674–731 mm, and diapasons up to 1595–1653 mm in length. Body length would have ranged from 434 to 493 mm (using the ratios exhibited by the same form and pattern). A bridge pattern (MS 397), notched for five pairs and seven single strings, has an overall length of 165 mm and string spacing of 124 mm.

The neck pattern MS 375 is additionally inscribed on the reverse (each line next to marks for string pairs 1–5) as follows:

[1] These should be paired two of the small top strings (*cantini*) of the guitar.
[2] These should be paired two second strings (*sotanelle)* of the guitar.
[3] These should be paired two small top strings (*cantini*) of violin thickness.
[4] This should be a *canto* of a violin. / This other should be the second (*sotanella*) of a guitar.
[5] This should be the *canto* of the violin but a bit larger. / This other should be a top string (*cantino*) of a violin.[28]

From the arrangement of the descriptions on the fingerboard, it is clear that the octave strings are mounted above (see Plate 25).

The "Hill" guitar has a body length of 471 mm and a string length of 741 mm, and the paper pattern MS 374 has a body length of 496 mm and a string length of 770 mm. Both the body lengths and string lengths of these instruments are uncharacteristically long when compared with other extant seventeenth-century guitars, whose body lengths typically range from 430 to 470 mm and whose string lengths vary between 620 and 670 mm. Though the top string of the "Hill" guitar can be tuned to e^1 relative to $a^1 = 386$–415 Hz,[29] such a long string length would be precariously close to its breaking point at the higher end of this pitch range. Furthermore, the string lengths of Stradivari's violins (whose top strings were tuned an octave above that of the guitar) were about 326 mm, or considerably shorter than half the length of Stradivari's guitar strings. If one presumes that guitars and violins were tuned to the same pitch, the greater string lengths of his guitars are unexplainable. The combination of very long strings and the relatively wide string spacing afforded by the present nut and neck width is reported by one musician to be unplayable.[30] Did this large model guitar fulfill a special function or tuning (perhaps with the top string at D), or is it the errant product of a violin maker who was inexperienced in guitar design? Considering Stradivari's deserved reputation as a luthier and the plethora of guitar-associated forms and templates that have survived, it is safer to assume the former.

The surviving wood forms are all considerably shorter than the extant guitars, and guitars made on these forms were likely tuned to higher pitches. Pattern MS 719, with a body length of 459 mm (though lacking any indications of neck length or bridge position), falls within the range of typical body lengths observed in extant seventeenth-century guitars. Unfortunately, the provenance of this pattern is unclear, and there is no evidence that it was made or used by Stradivari.

Additional notes on the construction of Stradivari's guitars

Details of internal construction can be gleaned from X-ray photographs of two of the Stradivari guitars. As stated above, the necks were originally attached to the instruments by a long iron nail (about 70–80 mm long) driven through the inner top block.[31] The nail is positioned high on the top block to align with the narrow neck, which is about 22–24 mm thick at its juncture with the body. The peg heads are attached at a 10–15 percent angle to the neck by a V-joint and are veneered on the front and back surfaces; the peg-head backs include a central panel of figured maple that serves as the nameplate. The necks of the "Giustiniani" and "Hill" guitars are veneered with figured maple, with two strips of black/white/black purfling running down the side and merging with similar purfling set into the heel.

The backs of the guitars are of figured maple and are variously constructed of one piece, two pieces, and two pieces with wings. The thickness of the backs of both the "Giustiniani" and "Hill" guitars is approximately 2 mm.[32] Though the "Rawlins" currently has three bars reinforcing the back, these were likely installed at a later time to counteract distortion, as the other two guitars do not show evidence of having been fitted with back reinforcements. The multi-part backs have spacers of black/white/black purfling. All jointed boards were originally reinforced on the inside with strips of paper, as well the juncture between bottom and ribs.

The original soundboard barring probably consisted of two transverse bars, one above and the other below the sound hole. Among the three guitars there is no agreement as to the layout of the soundboard bars, very likely because the bars have been moved in the course of repair or alteration. In the "Rawlins" guitar, both bars are approximately perpendicular to the center line of the instrument; in the "Hill" guitar, the upper bar is approximately perpendicular to the center line while the lower bar is angled; in the "Giustiniani" guitar, the bars are both angled. The guitars also have a number of short triangular blocks glued along the perimeter of the soundboard; these blocks were probably used to draw the ribs into alignment when gluing on the top. (The back was glued to the rib structure while it was still affixed to the inner form, and so the triangular blocks were not required in that stage of construction.[33]) As far as can be determined, the present arrangement of these triangular blocks in the "Giustiniani" is as follows: one on either side of the upper block; one on either side of the rose; one below the rose on the right side; and three on each side between the lower block and the lower bar. The "Hill" has two on either side of the rose, angled downward and two at the lower bouts, somewhat above the bridge.

The soundboards are of quartered spruce with a central joint. The soundboard of the "Giustiniani" is reportedly approximately 1.6 mm thick[34] and that of the "Hill" about 1.5 mm thick. The roses of all three guitars are either missing, or recently fitted, or suspect. However, all three have a border around the circular opening for the rose that consists of an alternating series of ivory diamonds and squares ("Giustiniani" and "Hill") and ivory diamonds and circles ("Rawlins"). This diamond-and-circle motif can be seen in the borders of Stradivari's inlaid violins. The ivory pieces are set in a mastic of ebony filings, and bordered by strips of black/white or black/white/black purfling.

The ribs are of figured maple, approximately 1.2–1.25 mm thick in the "Giustiniani" and "Hill" guitars. The "Hill" and "Rawlins" have small plugged holes in the center of the rib at the waist, from which one may deduce that the ribs were temporarily pinned to the form during construction. Form M E901f has remnants of such wooden pegs jutting out of its perimeter along the waist.

The ribs and back were given the rich orange-colored varnish similar to that found on violins. The soundboards were probably originally unvarnished.

In conclusion, Stradivari's guitars are enigmatic. While most extant seventeenth-century guitars are richly decorated with sunken rosettes and vaulted or staved backs, his guitars are spartan in appearance, having flat backs and ribs of mildly figured maple and featuring little inlay or other decoration. The bodies and string lengths are considerably longer than most surviving seventeenth-century guitars. String lengths of 740 mm and up would appear to present difficulties for the guitarist, both in terms of string breakage and playing technique. Rather than discounting or constructing scaled-down versions of them (as has been the practice),[35] greater effort should be made to reconcile them with our understanding of late seventeenth-century repertoire and pitch. Stradivari's guitars may provide new insights into late seventeenth-century guitar timbre and performance practice. The surviving patterns and forms provide sufficient information for guitar makers to fabricate instruments of sizes not represented by extant examples.

Glossary

Included below are short definitions of guitar-specific terms and general "classical" and non-Western musical terminology that are found within the chapters in this book. It does not include many terms that are already defined within the chapters themselves. The definitions given here are for quick reference only, and for the most part explained in relation to the guitar. For longer and generally more detailed information, the reader is encouraged to consult the entries in *The New Grove Dictionary of Music and Musicians*, 2nd edn., ed. S. Sadie (London, 2001). Words in the definitions that appear in boldface can be found as entries elsewhere in the glossary.

Appoggiatura: An auxiliary note that, after creating a slight dissonance with the bass, "leans" into the main note. It was commonly used in music of the Baroque period.

Arch-top: Pioneered by the Gibson L-5 (1924), the arch-top featured two f-holes (rather than a single soundhole, as on the **flat-top** models), and a more arched soundboard, like a violin or cello.

Arpeggio: A chord that has been broken up as a series of repeated patterns, or as successive notes, rather than simultaneously.

Blue notes: In jazz or blues playing, the largely flexible third and seventh notes of the scale, which are often flattened or otherwise altered.

Chitarra battente: A wire-strung five-**course** guitar played with a quill and probably used mainly for strumming chords.

Chitarrino: Italian term used to describe the small four-**course** Renaissance guitar that flourished during the sixteenth century.

Chromaticism: The "coloring" of scales and chords with notes from outside the scale.

Comping: From the word "accompanying," its meaning in jazz denotes the use of well-chosen sparse chords when accompanying, usually not in regular or predictable strum patterns as in country, folk, or rock.

Counterpoint: Musical texture that combines independent, simultaneous lines; opposite of **homophony** and analogous to **polyphony**.

Course: The name given to the individual *pairs* of strings found on lutes and early guitars. Sometimes courses are tuned in

unison, sometimes in octaves. Even though the highest course of a lute is usually single, it is still called a "course" for practical purposes. A ten-course lute, then, would have one single course and nine pairs.

Diapasons: With regard to plucked string instruments, the term refers to added bass strings on a lute or guitar that lie off the fingerboard and are plucked only at their pre-tuned pitch (i.e., they cannot be fretted).

Diatonic: In Western harmony, the notes (and only those notes) that make up the major or minor scale. In the scale of C major, the diatonic notes are CDEFGAB(C); any **chromatic** alterations (C♯, E♭, etc.) are departures from the diatonic scale.

Diferencias: Spanish term for variations or divisions (the breaking up of long-note passages into smaller units of scales).

Dominant: The fifth degree of the scale above the **tonic**, and in Western harmony the chord that prepares, or leads back to, the arrival of the tonic.

Double stops: In a guitar solo, the playing of two notes ("doubling") simultaneously on two separate strings (e.g., a typical Chuck Berry guitar solo).

Dreadnought: Perhaps the most famous Martin guitars (designated by their numbers D-18, D-28, D-45, etc.), these large steel-string acoustics feature wide waists, sloping shoulders, and a very resonant, bassy sound, preferred by country, bluegrass, and folk players.

Flat-top: Similar to and inspired by classical guitars, steel-string flat-top guitars were introduced by Martin, featuring relatively flat soundboards and different body construction compared to the **arch-tops**.

Glissando: A slide from one specific note to another, including notes in between, or a slide for effect, as in across the keys of the piano, with no specific beginning or ending note.

Hammer-ons: Technique used (and often overused) by heavy metal guitarists, involving the picking of notes with the left-hand only though "hammering" the string against the fret with the third or fourth finger.

Heptatonic scale: Any seven-note scale.

Heterophony: A style, prevalent in Asia and in the Middle East, in which one player sings or plays a melody while another duplicates it with added embellishments and variations, or in which two players vary it simultaneously.

Homophony: Literally, "sounding together" (analogous to homorhythmic); a musical texture consisting either of melody with a chordal accompaniment that moves "in sync" with the melody or simply of a succession of chords. Almost all rock and folk music is homophonic; the music of Bach, with its layered, independent voices, or **counterpoint**, is generally not.

Intabulation (intabulating): The practice of writing music in **tablature**; or, the transcription and arrangement of music in staff notation into tablature, as was common during the sixteenth century.

Maqam: In Arab and Turkish musics, a melodic mode, distinguished by scale, pitch hierarchy, and characteristic phrases, used as a basis for improvisation and composition.

Melisma: Vocal passage, or vocalization, in which only one or two syllables of a word, or a one-syllable word, are vocalized over many notes.

Minimalism: Style in which a single rhythmic pattern, or even pulse, underlying a static harmony (often only a single chord) is extended over the entire time (or a large part) of the composition.

Monophony: Music written or improvised as a single melody, without accompaniment, and without supporting parts, e.g., Gregorian chant.

Open tunings: Guitar tunings that allow the open strings to sound as a chord (i.e., without fretting). The most common are E tuning (open strings sound an E major chord; from highest to lowest EBG♯EBE) and G tuning (open strings sound a G major chord, DBGDGD).

Ostinato: A short "obstinate" musical pattern – rhythmic, melodic, or chordal – that repeats many times in succession. The repeating guitar jabs in a reggae piece can be considered a simple type of ostinato.

Oud: Arab, fretless lute played with a plectrum or quill. The Western lute of the Renaissance, and its name, are derived from this instrument.

Pentatonic scale: Theoretically, any five-note scale. But the term is usually used to describe a particular type used in, for example, southeast Asian and African music, as well as in blues, rock, and "orientalist" classical music, that is analogous to the scale produced when playing only the black notes of the

piano, e.g. C♯–D♯–F♯–G♯–A♯, or beginning on any note and adhering to the same intervals: major second – minor third – major second – major second.

Polyphony: Musical texture characterized by independent lines and **counterpoint**. Opposite of **homophony**.

Portamento: Vocal slide from one pitch to another, generally for expressive purposes.

Pull-offs: Technique similar to **hammer-ons**, in which the note is sounded by pulling the string off the fret with the left hand, rather than plucking it with the right.

Rasgueado: Strum as opposed to picking (*punteado*).

Riff: a short, recognizable, melodic or chordal idea around which a song is based, i.e., the fuzz riff in the Stones' "Satisfaction." In this way, riffs are frequently **ostinatos**.

Rose: The intricately carved sound holes found on lutes, **vihuelas**, and early guitars.

Scordatura: The "distuning" of the guitar from its standard tuning as required by composers for specific pieces.

Serialism: Twentieth-century compositional technique involving the use of a pre-planned ordered series that controls the choices of melody, chords, and even rhythm.

Skiffle: English guitar-oriented country/folk style popularized in the 1950s by Lonnie Donegan (and profoundly influential on the young John Lennon).

Tablature: System of notation used in lute and guitar music prior to the middle of the eighteenth century, and used currently in folk and rock. In its most basic form, tablature shows where the notes are fingered on the neck of the instrument by the use of letters or numbers (0 or a = open string; 1 or b = first fret, etc.) placed on a "staff" of six horizontal lines designating the six strings of the instrument.

Tapping: An innovative electric guitar technique in which the *right* (picking) hand taps a string against the frets on the fingerboard to produce notes.

Theorbo: Long, extended-neck bass lute used mainly for accompanying between about 1600 and 1720. It was usually strung with fourteen single strings.

Tonic: In simplest terms, the central note or chord that designates the main key of the piece; it is usually the chord with which the piece begins and ends. The tonic of the Pachelbel Canon is D; the tonic of the Beatles' "Something" is C.

Tremolo: Literally, "trembling," the rapid repetition of a single note, usually as a pattern on the highest strings in twos, triplets, quintuplets, etc., sometimes in conjunction with bass notes played with the thumb.

Twelve-bar blues: What has come to be accepted as the standard blues form, it consists of three musical phrases, each four bars (or measures) in length.

Vamping: Improvised or semi-improvised repetition of a chord or melodic sequence, usually found in introductions before the soloist hits the stage or at ends of pieces, especially fade-outs.

Vihuela: The Spanish guitar-shaped version of the lute. It flourished in sixteenth-century Spain, normally had five **courses**, and was played with the fingers. The surviving repertory, all in **tablature**, is of extremely high quality.

Notes

1 Picking through cultures: a guitarist's music history

1 On the history and music of the early guitar, see James Tyler and Paul Sparks, *The Guitar and Its Music from the Renaissance to the Classical Era* (Oxford, 2002).

2 See Robert Walser, *Running with the Devil: Power, Gender, and Madness in Heavy Metal Music* (Hanover, NH, 1993); Steve Waksman, *Instruments of Desire: The Electric Guitar and the Shaping of Musical Experience* (Cambridge, MA, 1999).

3 A nanban screen showing a Japanese female musician playing a vihuela (not a lute, as stated in the catalogue), is reproduced in Michael Cooper, S.J., et al., *The Southern Barbarians: The First Europeans in Japan* (Tokyo and Palo Alto, CA, 1971), 166.

4 These documents will be published in my forthcoming article, "The Politics and Geography of Seventeenth-Century Music," in *The Cambridge History of Seventeenth-Century Music*, ed. J. Butt and T. Carter.

5 The main study of Murcia and his New World sources is Craig H. Russell's *Santiago de Murcia's "Códice Saldívar No. 4": A Treasury of Guitar Music from Baroque Mexico*, 2 vols. (Urbana and Chicago, 1995).

2 Flamenco guitar: history, style, status

1 Aside from meaning "Flemish" and denoting a musical genre from the mid-1800s, "flamenco" in Spanish was a designation for "Gypsy"; by extension, it also meant "brash" and "flamboyant."

2 It should be noted, of course, that the pitches given here and in the transcriptions below are not absolute, but relative designations referring to guitar fingerings and positions. Guitarists frequently use capos (*cejillas*) in order to adjust to the range of a singer, or to give the instrument a brighter sound. Thus, the "A Phrygian tonality" will be here referred to as such, and designated as *por medio* by guitarists, even if it is played with a capo at the fifth fret (making it D Phrygian in terms of absolute pitch).

3 Much of the information presented here derives directly or indirectly from my excellent guitar teachers Basilio Georges and Dennis Koster. I am also especially grateful to Georges and to *flamencólogo* Jay Kantor for their detailed comments on an earlier version of this text. I retain, however, full responsibility for the contents of this essay.

3 The Celtic guitar: crossing cultural boundaries in the twentieth century

1 Bob Brozman says:

The guitar can function as a portable culture translator. The guitar accompanied colonists around the world, and the colonized people often retuned to open tunings, because the European standard tuning lacks obvious logical visual and audio cues. Open tunings provide a much clearer picture of the fingerboard, enabling self-teaching. Furthermore, the diatonic European system of music is, in fact, the odd man out in world musical cultures, the rest of the world preferring the more mathematically simple and therefore natural-sounding modal approach. Open tunings not only facilitate this, but also provide drone strings, making self-accompaniment much easier. For example Open G major tuning occurs in the guitar music of: Hawaii, Mississippi, west Africa, south Africa, Philippines, India, Mexico, [and] South America.

(Personal communication, November 28, 2001)

2 I use the term "Celtic" in the interest of clarity, economy, and a realistic response to common practice, but with a caveat. The phrase "Celtic music" is mostly eschewed by players and aficionados of the traditional music of Ireland, Scotland, Brittany, and Wales, because it is essentially a marketing term invented by record retailers in order to lump together different traditional and neo-traditional musics that are, in reality, quite distinct from one another. Practitioners of "traditional music" are often wary of those who use the "Celtic music" term in an indiscriminate fashion, as such usage often comes with a set of mistaken, commerce-based preconceptions about the perceived interchangeability of these styles.

3 However, self-accompaniment, on both pipes and harp, appears to have been part of Irish traditional and art music from the

Middle Ages: the instrument called variously *crot, crouth, crowd, cruit, cruth,* and *crwth* (a simple gut-strung lyre) was associated with the performances of *rekaire,* poets who recited and chanted verses in noble courts. See Franz Jahnel, *Die Gitarre und ihr Bau* (Frankfurt, 1973), 22. In addition, in a famous, oft-cited and oft-misunderstood passage dating from 1183, the Welsh priest, folklorist, and author Giraldus Cambrensis describes Irish harpers thus: "They play the tinkling sounds on the thinner strings above the sustained sound of the thicker strings so freely," adding that he is astonished at their facility. Quoted in Ciaran Carson, *Irish Traditional Music* (Belfast, 1986), 35.

4 The thirteenth-century Scottish poet and prophet Thomas of Ercildoune (original model of the ballad hero "True Thomas"), cites the gittern, a Northern European relative of the vielle and ancestor of the guitar, in a list of instruments present at a musical event: "Harpe and fethil both thay fande / Getterne and als so the sawtrye / Lute, and rybybe, both gangande, / And all manere of mynstralsye." Cited in John Purser, *Scotland's Music: A History of the Traditional and Classical Music of Scotland from Earliest Times to the Present Day* (Edinburgh, 1992), 62. In his useful *Rotunda Music in Eighteenth-Century Dublin* (Dublin, 1992), 79, Brian Boydell cites a newspaper announcement regarding music-making in that city:

The Governors have at great Expense, increased their Number of Performers to a full and compleat Band, having written to London for a Woman Singer, and building a new Orchestra in the Garden, and intend to entertain the Publick with continual Variety of new Italian and German Musick, and some Instruments quite unknown in this Kingdom. On Wednesday the 4th inst a song by Master Passerini, accompanied on the Guitar by Mr Claget; and on Friday next a Duet on two Clarionets.

Both "English guitars" (wire-strung citterns) and "Spanish guitars" (with six gut strings in the fashion of the modern instrument) were available for sale to a middle-class urban Dublin clientele by 1746; Boydell's *A Dublin Musical Calendar 1700–1760* (Blackrock, 1988) mentions the stock of music printer and seller Dennis Connor, which included "flutes, concert flutes, guitars, violins, and hautboys" (259). However, the art- and light-music idioms of Dublin city life were and remained far removed from the folk music idioms of the rural South and West, and the modern guitar only becomes part of those latter idioms in the twentieth century. For more on the social and cultural contexts and associations for cittern and guitar in eighteenth-century Britain, see David Johnson, *Music and Society in Lowland Scotland in the Eighteenth Century* (Oxford, 1972), 23–27.

5 Guitars are depicted in English and Spanish settings in paintings by Watteau (1684–1721; *La Gamme d'Amour*), Bayeu (1746–93; *Dance on the Banks of the Manzaneros,* Museo Municipal, Madrid), and Ollivier (*An English Tea Party at a Salon,* showing the child Mozart in 1776 playing trio music for a noble audience), but these tell us nothing about the rural traditions of the far West. See Tom and Mary Ann Evans, *Guitars: Music, History, Construction, and Players From Renaissance to Rock* (New York, 1979), 145–50.

6 James Cowdery, in his *The Melodic Tradition of Ireland* (Kent, Ohio, 1990), 23, mentions Francis O'Neill's 1913 citation of the guitarist John Dunne (*Irish Minstrels and Musicians.* Dublin, 1973, 217), active in Ireland in the late nineteenth century, but O'Neill offers little additional information beyond Dunne's name.

7 These included the independent companies Celtic, Emerald, Gaelic, and New Republic, followed later by the large multi-stylistic corporations Columbia and Victor. See Gearóid Ó hAllmhuráin, *A Pocket History of Irish Traditional Music* (Dublin, 1998), 106.

8 Ibid., 107.

9 Aibhlin Dillane and Geraldine Cotter, "Piano," in *The Companion to Irish Traditional Music,* ed. Fintan Vallely (Cork, 1999), 298.

10 Ibid., 295. The term "pure drop" is derived from Irish rural idiom, and originates as a reference to pure and high-quality *poitín,* the spirit distilled from potatoes, barley, or oats. By extension, it refers to the expression of a powerful, unadulterated traditional quality in food, drink, or the arts.

11 However, Ciaran Carson, in his *Last Night's Fun: In and Out of Time with Irish Music* (San Francisco, 1998), accurately describes the more typical limitations of guitarists in this music, and the typical response to those limitations: "Or some guitar-player, oblivious to protocol, after footering and tuning, will start up a three-chord accompaniment in the wrong key in the middle of someone's unaccompanied song. Someone else will comment on the player's marvellous 'accomplishment'" (136).

12 For more on guitarists and pianists in the New York studios, see Ó hAllmhuráin, *Pocket*

History, 108, and also Harry Bradshaw's liner notes to *The Tunes We Like to Play on Paddy's Day* (The Flanagan Brothers), Viva Voce 007 (1996), 2–8.

13 Ethnomusicologist Philippe Varlet, personal communication, 11/27/00. See also *From Galway to Dublin: Early Recordings of Irish Traditional Music* [Rounder ROUN1087], 1993.

14 See Ciaran Carson, *Irish Traditional Music* (Dublin, 1986), 52, and Ó hAllmhuráin, *Pocket History*, 102.

15 Ó hAllmhuráin, *Pocket History*, 103.

16 Piano played in a "vamping" (chording) style was an essential part of the céilí band sound, but plucked strings were used infrequently. Exceptions which "prove the rule" would include the great tenor banjo player Mike Flanagan on recordings with his brothers Joe and Louis (cited earlier), and the occasional guitar, tenor banjo, or banjo-mandolin player improvising chords in support of the mainstay piano.

17 Ó hAllmhuráin, *Pocket History*, 128.

18 Ibid., 130.

19 Sean Og Potts; anecdote quoted in National Public Radio special program, *The Boy in the Gap*, first aired March 1991.

20 Seán Ó Riada, *Our Musical Heritage* (Portlaoise, 1982), 74.

21 Ironically, many of the traditional players who heard, or even played in, Ó Riada's ensembles found his ideas peculiar, and anything but traditional: one elderly player, hearing Ceoltóiri Chualann on Irish radio, said "Aye; them're the ones who keep startin' and stoppin' the tunes in the middle, right?" James Kelly, personal communication, July 1998.

22 For those players without experience in playing in this tuning, a good introduction is in Andy Ellis, "DADGAD for Dummies: A Lesson with Fingerstyle Wizard Martin Simpson," *Guitar Player* (September, 2000), 61–65.

23 See Simon's uncredited borrowing of Carthy's arrangement of the traditional song "Scarborough Fair," from the album *Parsley, Sage, Rosemary, and Thyme* from 1966, in Evans, *Guitars: Music, History, Construction, and Players*, 330–31.

24 For good and clear examples of Moynihan's early and influential bouzouki style, consult the trio Sweeney's Men (*Tracks of Sweeney*, Castle Music America); for Finn's consult his duet record with fiddler Frankie Gavin (*Frankie Gavin and Alec Finn*, Shanachie).

25 For Planxty, which featured Lunny on bouzouki and Andy Irvine on mandolin, consult the eponymous "black album" *Planxty* (Shanachie, originally released 1972); for De Danann, which featured Finn and later Moynihan on bouzoukis, consult *The Best of De Danann* (Shanachie; compilation); for Altan, which featured Sproule's DADGAD playing and Ciaran Curran on "cittern" (a bouzouki variant), consult *Altan* (Green Linnet, 1987); for the Bothy Band, which featured Lunny on bouzouki and Mícheál Ó Dohmnaill on DADGAD guitar, consult *After Hours: Live in Paris* (Green Linnet 3016).

26 Matt Molloy, quoted in the liner notes to *Music at Matt Molloy's* (Real World CAROL 2324-2, 1993). For good examples of McGlynn's accompanimental prowess, consult this album; for Cahill's, consult the *Live in Seattle* recording (Green Linnet, 1999) with duet partner and fiddler Martin Hayes.

4 African reinventions of the guitar

1 Eric Charry, "Plucked Lutes in West Africa: An Historical Overview," *Galpin Society Journal* 49 (1996), 3–6.

2 Andrew L. Kaye, "The Guitar in Africa," in *The Garland Encyclopedia of World Music*, vol. I: *Africa*, ed. Ruth M. Stone (New York, 1998), 351.

3 Ibid.

4 Titles from the Original Music label are hard to find these days, but they are worth looking for, as they contain some of the best examples of older palm wine and highlife music. Recent *juju* recordings by King Sunny Ade and his main rival Chief Commander Ebenezer Obey are readily available. And there are new plans to release much of Ade's back catalog. Ade's group in particular demonstrates mastery at layering relatively simple guitar parts to create rich, orchestral textures.

5 John Collins, "Post War Popular Band Music in West Africa." *African Arts* 10 (1977), 53–60, cited in Christopher Alan Waterman, *Juju: A Social History and Ethnography of an African Popular Music* (Chicago and London, 1990), 46.

6 Cynthia Schmidt, "Kru Mariners and Migrants of the West African Coast," *The Garland Encyclopedia of World Music*, vol. I: *Africa*, 376.

7 A CD called *African Elegant, Sierra Leone's Kru/Krio Calypso Connection* (Original Music) gathers together rare recordings of this early afropop form.

8 Rogie's *Dead Men Don't Smoke Marijuana* (Real World), recorded shortly before the

guitarist's death in 1994, is a fine example of the genre.

9 John E. Collins, "Jazz Feedback to Africa," *American Music* 5 (1987), 176–93, cited in Kaye, "The Guitar in Africa," 353.

10 Eric Charry, *Mande Music* (Chicago and London, 2000), 243.

11 Ibid., 251.

12 This field work formed the basis for my book *In Griot Time: An American Guitarist in Mali* (Philadelphia, 2000).

13 The *ngoni* is a four- or seven-string spike lute, a likely ancestor of the banjo, and the favored composer's instrument in Mali. The *kora* is a twenty-one-string bridge-harp constructed from a large calabash. It is favored by Mande *jelis* in Gambia and Guinea-Bissau. The *balafon* is a xylophone with wooden slats, around twenty in the case of the heptatonic *jeli* version. It is the favored *jeli* instrument in Guinea.

14 Eyre, *In Griot Time*, 56–57.

15 Examples 4.2–4.5 in this article are reproduced from articles by Banning Eyre by kind permission of *Guitar Player* magazine.

16 Gerhard Kubik, *Africa and the Blues* (Jackson, MS, 1999), 197.

17 Ibid., 189–96.

18 Ibid., 69.

19 A good example can be heard on *In Griot Time: String Music from Mali* (Stern's Africa, 2000), "Wild Goose Chase."

20 Gary Stewart, *Rumba on the River: A History of the Popular Music of the Two Congos* (New York and London, 2000), 3.

21 Kazadi wa Mukuna, "The Changing Role of the Guitar in the Urban Music of Zaire," *Journal of the International Institute of Traditional Music* 36 (1994), 62–63.

22 Ibid., 67.

23 Lokassa's and Syran's quotes first appeared in Banning Eyre, "Super Soukous," *Guitar Player* (February, 1997), 75–84.

24 Mukuna, "The Changing Role of the Guitar," 69.

25 Christopher Ballantine, *Marabi Night* (Johannesburg, 1993), 14.

26 Thomas Turino, *Nationalists, Cosmopolitans, and Popular Music in Zimbabwe* (Chicago and London, 2000), 234–35.

27 Nollene Davies, "The Guitar in Zulu Maskanda Tradition," *Journal of the International Institute of Traditional Music* 36 (1994), 118–19.

28 Ibid., 119.

29 Ibid., 121.

30 Turino, *Nationalists*, 223–310.

31 Ibid., 234–35.

32 Damping techniques are found in a number of African guitar styles. In Cameroon's bikutsi music, not covered in this chapter, guitarists actually weave a strip of foam rubber through the strings right at the bridge. This allows them to play freely and hard, producing only percussive, damped notes, never a ringing tone.

33 Banning Eyre, "Zimbabwe Roots Guitar," *Guitar Player* (December, 1994), 117–24.

34 The release simply called *Salegy!* by the band Jaojoby (Xenophile, 1996) provides an introduction.

35 These guitarists can be heard on compilations available on the German Feuer und Eis label, the British GlobeStyle label, and on Shanachie Records' World Out of Time series. The Shanachie release *The Moon and the Banana Tree: New Guitar Music from Madagascar* (1996) is particularly rich.

36 Ian Anderson, "Gitara Gasy!" *Folk Roots* 178 (1998), 22–31.

37 Ibid., 27.

6 A century of blues guitar

1 W. C. Handy, *Father of the Blues* (New York, 1974), 74.

2 Ibid.

3 Ibid.

4 Perry Bradford, *Born With the Blues* (New York, 1965), 14.

5 Johnny Shines, interview with author, Watsonville, California, January 23, 1989, published in *Blues Guitar: The Men who Made the Music*, ed. Jas Obrecht, 2nd edn. (San Francisco, 1993), 20.

6 Johnny Shines, interview with the author, Watsonville, California, January 23, 1989.

7 B. B. King, interview with the author and Billy Gibbons, 1991, published in *Rollin' & Tumblin': The Postwar Blues Guitarists*, ed. Jas Obrecht (San Francisco, 2000), 338.

8 Ibid., 340.

9 Interview with the author, published in "Ry Cooder: Talking Country Blues," *Guitar Player* (July, 1990), 85.

10 *Blues Guitar*, ed. Obrecht, 23.

11 Ibid., 20.

12 Ibid., 28.

13 *Rollin' and Tumblin'*, ed. Obrecht, 414.

14 *Blues Guitar*, ed. Obrecht, 2.

15 Introduction to his "Good Morning Blues," recorded in New York, June 19, 1940, reissued on *Good Morning Blues* (BCD 113 [1990]).

16 Bob Yelin, "Jazz Guitar Wouldn't be the Same Without George Barnes," *Guitar Player* (February, 1975), 26.

17 *Rollin' and Tumblin'*, ed. Obrecht, 6.

18 Ibid., 2.

19 Ibid.

20 "Muddy Waters," interview with Jim O'Neal in *Living Blues* 64 (April, 1985), 25.

21 "Country Blues" and "I Be's Troubled," 78s recorded for the Library of Congress, Stovall, Mississippi, August 24–31, 1941; available on *Muddy Waters: The Complete Plantation Recordings*, MCA, 1993.

22 *Rollin' and Tumblin'*, ed. Obrecht, 154.

23 Interview with author, in ibid., 6.

24 Ibid., 73

25 1993 interview with author, in *Blues Guitar*, ed. Obrecht, 257.

26 1994 interview with author, in *Rollin' and Tumblin'*, ed. Obrecht, 432.

27 Ibid., 436.

28 Ibid., 11.

29 James Rooney, *Bossmen: Bill Monroe and Muddy Waters* (New York, 1971), 137.

30 *Rollin' and Tumblin'*, ed. Obrecht, 12.

31 Ibid.

32 Jas Obrecht, "Filthy, Filthy, Filthy: Keith Richards Comes Clean on Distortion and the Meaning of Music," in *The Rolling Stones: Inside the Voodoo Lounge* (San Francisco, 1994), 62.

33 Ibid.

34 Interview with author, in *Rollin' and Tumblin'*, ed. Obrecht, 290.

35 Rooney, *Bossmen*, 145.

36 Ibid., 145.

7 The turn to noise: rock guitar from the 1950s to the 1970s

1 One can find reference to "Rocket 88" as the first rock and roll record in Philip Ennis, *The Seventh Stream: The Emergence of Rocknroll in American Popular Music* (Hanover, NH, 1992), 233; and in David McGee's remarks on *Blue Flames: A Sun Blues Collection* (Rhino, 1990), contained in the *Rolling Stone Album Guide*, ed. Anthony DeCurtis and James Henke with Holly George-Warren (New York, 1992), 824.

2 Phillips's account of the incident is cited in Robert Palmer, "The Church of the Sonic Guitar," in *Present Tense: Rock & Roll and Culture*, ed. Anthony DeCurtis (Durham, NC, 1993), 22.

3 Robert Bowman and Ross Johnson, "Train Kept a Rollin': A Conversation with Paul Burlison of the Rock 'n' Roll Trio," *Journal of Country Music* 3 (1987), 17.

4 Ibid.

5 Ibid., 17–18.

6 I have detailed some of these developments at length in my book *Instruments of Desire: The Electric Guitar and the Shaping of Musical Experience* (Cambridge, MA, 1999). See especially Chapter 4, "Racial Distortions:

Muddy Waters, Chuck Berry, and the Electric Guitar in Black Popular Music," 113–66.

7 Jacques Attali, *Noise: The Political Economy of Music*, trans. Brian Massumi (Minneapolis, MN, 1985), 19.

8 Samuel Floyd, *The Power of Black Music: Interpreting Its History from Africa to the United States* (New York, 1995), 28.

9 Gil Rodman offers perhaps the most insightful reading of Presley's television appearances, concentrating upon the Berle performance while debunking the common assumption that it was on the Ed Sullivan show that Presley made his biggest mark. Rodman, *Elvis After Elvis: The Posthumous Career of a Living Legend* (London, 1996), 146–58.

10 Ibid., 27–28.

11 Waksman, *Instruments of Desire*, 152.

12 Ibid., 162–65. Also see Timothy Taylor, "His Name Was in Lights: Chuck Berry's 'Johnny B. Goode,'" *Popular Music* 1 (1992), 27–40.

13 For a detailed account of the careers of Paul and Atkins, respectively, see the relevant chapters of *Instruments of Desire*, "Pure Tones and Solid Bodies: Les Paul's New Sound" (36–74) and "Mister Guitar: Chet Atkins and the Nashville Sound" (75–112).

14 Dan Forte, "Duane Eddy: The Return of the King of Twang," *Guitar Player* (June, 1984), 78.

15 Link Wray, *Rock Guitarists* (Saratoga, CA, 1978), 169.

16 Dan Forte, "The Ventures: Still Rockin' After All These Years," *Guitar Player* (September, 1981), 95.

17 Ray Minhinnett and Bob Young, *The Story of the Fender Stratocaster: Curves, Contours and Body Horns* (San Francisco, 1995), contains an interview with Dale on his relationship with Fender (73–74). For further background on the Fender guitar company, see Richard Smith's authoritative *Fender: The Sound Heard 'Round the World* (Fullerton, CA, 1995); Forrest White, *Fender: The Inside Story* (San Francisco, 1994); and Tom Wheeler, *American Guitars: An Illustrated History* (New York, 1992), which is the best overall history of guitar manufacturing in the United States.

18 Patrick Ganahl, "Dick Dale: The Once and Future King of the Surf Guitar," *Guitar Player* (July, 1981), 38.

19 Chris Welch, "Magnificent Seven," *Melody Maker* (September 9, 1967), 8.

20 Waksman, *Instruments of Desire*, 245. Also see Iain Chambers, *Urban Rhythms: Pop Music and Popular Culture* (New York, 1985), 31–37.

21 Jann Wenner, "Eric Clapton," in *The Rolling Stone Interviews: Talking with the Legends of Rock and Roll, 1967–1980*, ed. Ben Fong-Torres (New York, 1981), 28.

22 Steve Rosen, "Jeff Beck," *Rock Guitarists*, 11.

23 The story of Guy's discovery of feedback is best told in Jas Obrecht, "Buddy Guy," in *Blues Guitar: The Men Who Made the Music*, ed. Jas Obrecht, 2nd edn. (San Francisco, 1993), 205.

24 It was only later in the 1960s that Townshend turned to the Hiwatt amplifiers with which he would later become identified. In the middle of the decade, though, the guitarist was a dedicated user of Marshall amps. Moreover, by the account of Ken Bran, the engineer who oversaw the technical details of the Marshall workshop, the first 100-watt Marshall amplifier was produced for Townshend to use with the Who. John Seabury, "In Search of Volume: Guitar Amplification in the '60s," in *The Electric Guitar: An Illustrated History*, ed. Paul Trynka (San Francisco, 1995), 84.

25 Quoted in Dave Marsh, *Before I Get Old: The Story of the Who* (New York, 1983), 75.

26 Matt Resnicoff, "Godhead Revisited: The Second Coming of Pete Townshend," *Guitar Player* (September, 1989), 83.

27 Noel Redding and Carol Appleby, *Are You Experienced? The Inside Story of the Jimi Hendrix Experience* (New York, 1996), 44.

28 Douglas Hall and Sue Clark, *Rock: A World Bold as Love* (New York, 1970), 25.

29 Waksman, *Instruments of Desire*, 172.

30 Quoted in John Sinclair, *Guitar Army: Street Writings/Prison Writings* (New York, 1972), 9.

31 Susan Hiwatt, "Cock Rock," in *Twenty Minute Fandangos and Forever Changes: A Rock Bazaar*, ed. Jonathan Eisen (New York, 1971), 143.

32 For a more complete discussion of Page as guitar hero, and his use of the violin bow in performance, see Waksman, *Instruments of Desire*, 237–44.

33 Robert Walser, *Running with the Devil: Power, Gender, and Madness in Heavy Metal Music* (Hanover, NH, 1993), 63–65.

34 Robert Duncan, *The Noise: Notes from a Rock and Roll Era* (New York, 1984), 37.

35 Ibid., 46–47.

8 Contesting virtuosity: rock guitar since 1976

1 Reprinted in Jon Savage, *England's Dreaming: Anarchy, Sex Pistols, Punk Rock, and Beyond* (New York, 1992), 280. Dick Hebdige also discusses the diagram and its message in *Subculture: The Meaning of Style* (London, 1991), 112.

2 Quoted in John Lydon with Keith and Kent Zimmerman, *Rotten: No Irish, No Blacks, No Dogs* (New York, 1994), 79.

3 Ibid., 78.

4 Dan Forte, "Johnny and Dee Dee Ramone: Two Punks with an Axe to Grind," *Guitar Player* (April, 1985), 8.

5 Ibid., 9.

6 Robert Walser, *Running with the Devil: Power, Gender, and Madness in Heavy Metal Music* (Hanover, NH, 1993), 42–43.

7 The above description borrows liberally from Robert Walser's extended analysis of "Eruption" in *Running with the Devil*, found on 68–75. For a hands-on discussion of two-handed technique, see Edward Van Halen, "My Tips for Beginners," *Guitar Player* (July, 1984), 52–60.

8 For instance, Dan Amrich, writing in *Guitar World* magazine, proclaimed that with "Eruption" Van Halen "personally reconfigured the technical and aural parameters of his instrument – all in one minute, 42 seconds flat." Amrich, "Atomic Punk," reprinted in *Guitar World Presents Van Halen* (Wayne, NJ, 1997), 3.

9 Dan Hedges, *Eddie Van Halen* (New York, 1986), 3.

10 Jas Obrecht, "Eddie Van Halen: Young Wizard of Power Rock," *Guitar Player* (April, 1980), 98. For a more extended discussion of Van Halen's career in light of punk rock, see my essay "Into the Arena: Edward Van Halen and the Cultural Contradictions of the Guitar Hero," in *Guitar Cultures*, ed. Andrew Bennett and Kevin Dawe (London, 2001), 117–34.

11 "Randy Rhoads Stumbles into the Spotlight," *Guitar World* 3 (May 1982), 53.

12 Ironically, Van Halen himself resisted the lionization of classical music, even as his music opened the way toward its widespread use. Recounting his early experiences studying classical music, for instance, he declared about reading music that "all it's good for is to learn how to play songs that have been written. And I told you the reason I didn't like the violin was that I didn't like the songs we were supposed to play. I guess I was just a snot-nosed kid, and I didn't want to waste the time doing it." Steven Rosen, "The Life and Times of Van Halen," in *Guitar World Presents Van Halen*, 26.

13 Some of the most interesting comments in this regard came from another fleet-fingered metal guitarist, Vivian Campbell, who proclaimed in a 1985 interview that "the trouble amongst guitar players especially is

that they think it's always against the clock. Competition's a wonderful, healthy thing, but it can get the better of you . . . I don't give a flying fuck if I don't play as fast as Yngwie Malmsteen. Sometimes it would be nice, but I'm happier doing what I do." Jas Obrecht, "Vivian Campbell: Dio's Fire and Brimstone," *Guitar Player* (February, 1985), 25.

14 Joe Lalaina, "Yngwie Malmsteen: Like Him or Not, He Demands Your Attention," *Guitar World* 1 (January 1986), 25. Commenting upon Malmsteen's tendency toward such statements, Robert Walser astutely observed that the guitarist "exemplifies the wholesale importation of classical music into heavy metal," not only in his playing style and points of musical reference but in "the social values that underpin these activities." Walser, *Running with the Devil*, 98.

15 Chris Jisi, "Crossover Dream," *Guitar World* 10 (November 1988), 38.

16 Jas Obrecht, "Neil Young: In the Eye of the Hurricane," *Guitar Player* (March, 1982), 55.

17 James Rotondi, "Is Shred Dead?" *Guitar Player* (August, 1993), 34.

18 Ibid., 32.

19 Joe Gore, "Jennifer Batten: Storming the Boy's Club," *Guitar Player* (July, 1989), 96.

20 This is not to say, of course, that women have not made significant headway in finding a voice within rock over the past two decades. Yet for all the rhetoric about "women in rock" that has been put forth, certain lines seem to remain rather firmly in place. Since the late 1970s, punk has been the creative space in which the greatest number of female instrumentalists (as opposed to singers) have found a space; the rise of the "Riot Grrl" movement in the early 1990s was in many ways the culmination of a long process of women taking hold of electricity. But, given the punk opposition to virtuosity, this has also meant that the majority of women rockers remain outside the sphere of virtuosic musicianship in its most flamboyant, visible forms, whether by exclusion or by purposeful resistance.

21 Tricia Rose, *Black Noise: Rap Music and Black Culture in Contemporary America* (Hanover, NH, 1994), 81–82.

22 Ibid., 82.

23 Simon Reynolds, *Generation Ecstasy: Into the World of Techno and Rave Culture* (Boston, 1998), 41.

24 Ibid., 102.

25 Ibid., 383.

26 Greg Rule, "The Chemical Brothers: Stompbox Techno," *Guitar Player* (August, 1997), 25.

27 Rose, *Black Noise*, 78.

9 The guitar in country music

1 Bill Malone, *Country Music, U.S.A.*, rev. edn. (Austin, 1985), 10.

2 Timothy Scheurer, *Born in the U.S.A: The Myth of America in Popular Music from Colonial Times to the Present* (Jackson, 1991), 26, 54.

3 It should be noted as well that folk singers like Woody Guthrie are considered folk, while artists such as Gordon Lightfoot or Bob Dylan are considered "folk revival."

4 Despite its seemingly traditional sound, bluegrass music was actually a manufactured genre emerging during the 1940s with the music of Bill Monroe and others. The traditionalism is built into the music and the use of acoustic instruments locates a mid-twentieth-century genre in the traditionalism of the past.

5 Malone, *Country Music*, 154.

6 Both six- and twelve-string acoustic guitars are tuned identically. The twelve-string guitar has six courses with two tuned in unison and four tuned in octaves. Though predominantly a folk instrument, the twelve-string guitar is played by one country artist. Dan Seals, a former member of the pop-vocal duo England Dan and John Ford Coley, plays a twelve-string guitar left-handed and upside down.

7 Guitar manufacturers offer several models of acoustic guitars to suit any application. Martin, Gibson, Washburn, Ovation, and the Japanese manufacturer Takamine have an entire complement of guitars available ranging from the smaller parlor guitars or 000 models to the larger Dreadnought and jumbo styles. In addition, all of these manufacturers offer "electrified" acoustic guitars that are equipped with a pick-up imbedded in the bridge to facilitate the use of an amplifier. The "electrified" acoustic guitar allows the player to compete at the same sound level as other electrified instruments, external miking not being required.

8 Here, a twelve-string guitar is employed with the lowest three strung only with the octave strings.

9 Folk singer John Prine uses the same finger-style as Merle Travis, as does Mike Meldrum from the Canadian country-punk band the Law.

10 It is unclear who first coined the term "Nashville Sound" but it refers to three things: first, the period of time when the country music establishment was trying to recover a section of their market lost to rock and roll; second, the de-emphasizing or omission of pedal steel guitar and fiddle and adoption of pop elements like back-up singers and string sections; third, the particular production techniques that were used by producers Owen

Bradley and Chet Atkins in an altruistic attempt to make country music more popular. Sometimes called "country-pop," "middle-of-the-road," or "countrypolitan," it was designed to reach new listeners and retain the old ones. See Joli Jensen, *The Nashville Sound: Authenticity, Commercialization, and Country Music* (Nashville and London, 1998); Bill C. Malone, *Southern Music American Music* (Lexington, 1979), 127–28; and Bill Ivey, "Commercialization and Tradition in the Nashville Sound," in *Folk Music and Modern Sound,* ed. William Ferris and Mary Hart (Jackson, 1982), 129–41.

11 Donald D. Kilolani Mitchell and George S. Kanahele, "Hawaiian Steel Guitar: Origins and Development," *Guitar Player* (July, 1980), 32.

12 Ibid., 36.

13 "Dobro" has become the term used to define an acoustic guitar with a metal resonating cone in place of a sound hole. Resonator guitar is the traditional name and these were first developed by John Dopyera, who started the National Stringed Instrument Company in California during the mid-1920s. Resonator guitars are constructed of aluminum and began as a search for a louder acoustic guitar that would compete with the horns and rhythm sections of jazz bands of the 1920s. Dopyera left National in 1928 and developed a more affordable wood body guitar with a resonating cone. He introduced his invention in that same year under the name "Dobro"® – a combination of Dopyera and Brothers. Dobro merged with National in 1932 after much legal wrangling and, after World War II, National ceased making the Dobro guitar. Dopyera family members formed the Original Musical Instrument Company in 1967 and acquired the brand name Dobro® in 1970. Since 1993 Dobros have been manufactured by Gibson Musical Instruments, who obtained O.M.I. in that year. Further information can be found at www.nationalguitars.com and www.gibson.com.

14 Buddy Emmons, in *Definitive Country: The Ultimate Encyclopedia of Country Music and its Performers,* ed. Barry McCloud et al. (New York, 1995), s.v. "Steel Guitar," 767. Buddy Emmons is a prominent steel guitarist appearing on numerous recordings. He pioneered the development of the pedal steel guitar through his own company Sho-Bud Guitars of Nashville with friend Shot Jackson (the name Sho-Bud is constructed from the first names of the partners, Shot and Buddy) and his own brand of instruments that bear his name.

15 Slide guitar is related to steel guitar by virtue of the presence of a bar to fret the notes on the strings instead of the fingers. Slide guitar is most often associated with blues, owing to the fact that many pioneer blues artists used cut-off wine bottle necks as a slide, hence the name "bottleneck guitar." Periodicals like *Guitar* and *Guitar Player* often feature "lessons" on slide guitar technique.

16 The terms "fills," "licks," and "riffs" are present in the lexicon of popular music. "Fills" and "licks" are the same thing: snippets of melody played after melodic lines in a kind of call and answer manner. "Riffs" are longer melodic fragments usually in the introduction or between verses, a kind of instrumental signature for the song.

17 Other models were used as well, like the Gretsch Country Gentleman, made famous by guitarist/producer Chet Atkins, and the Gibson Les Paul played by Charlie Daniels.

18 Guitar amplifiers have become big business. Manufacturers come and go but there are a few that have remained the premier choices for many guitarists. Fender, Marshall, Peavey, Mesa-Boogie, Line 6, and Soldano are some of the more popular amplifier manufacturers. Magazines like *Guitar Player* and *Guitar World* constantly feature articles, reviews, and buyers' guides with a focus on amplifiers and their respective tone. The choice of guitar amplifier is analogous to the choice of automobile one would drive. There is a car for every personality and an amplifier for every guitarist.

19 Rich Kienzle, "The Electric Guitar in Country Music: Its Evolution and Development," *Guitar Player* (November, 1979), 30.

20 Ibid.

21 Ibid., 32.

22 Since the inception of glue-on nails, many country guitarists use artificial fingernails.

23 For those guitarists wishing to truly emulate the pedal steel, a mechanical device can be incorporated into the electric guitar that raises the pitch of the B string one whole step. The so-called "B-bender" is activated by a strap pin or bridge lever. By pulling down on the guitar neck or pushing with the heel of the picking hand, the string is raised to the requisite pitch.

24 "Natural positions" refers to the manner in which the notes of the major pentatonic scale lie on the fretboard. This positioning allows the first and third fingers of the fretting hand to perform the majority of the fretting. Similar techniques can be found among guitarists of all genres.

10 Radical innovations, social revolution, and the baroque guitar

1 Joan Carles Amat, *Guitarra española y vandola en dos maneras de guitarra, castellana y cathalana de cinco órdenes*, intro. by Monica Hall, facsimile edn. of Joseph Bró edn. of Amat, between 1761 and 1766 (Monaco, 1980). It is probable that Amat's book was first issued in 1586, rather than 1596; see the entry by Craig H. Russell for "Amat, Joan Carles" in *The New Grove Dictionary of Music and Musicians*, 2nd edn., ed. Stanley Sadie (London, 2001), vol. I, 443.

2 "El bueno, y practico Pintor tiene aparejados todos los colores que son necessarios para pintar, de las quales está á su alvedrio si quiere pintar, ò un hombre, ò un león, ò un buey; de la mesma manera nosotros hasta aqui avemos aparejado todos los puntos, que son como materia, y como los colores del Pintor, de los quales se pueden formar toda manera, y suerte de tonos, saltando del uno al otro. Puedense con estos puntos hazer vacas, passeos, gallardas, villanos, italianas, pabanillas, y otras cosas semejantes, por doze partes; y lo que es de maravillar (lo que à muchos parecerá impossible) que con estos puntos puede qualquier a juntar, a acomodar por las dichas doze partes, todo lo que se tañe, y pueda tañer, con qualquier instrumento de musica." Amat, *Guitarra española*, Chapter 7, 23–24. All translations in this article are by the author.

3 Girolamo Montesardo, *Nuova inventione d'intavolatura per sonare li balletti sopra la chitarra spagniuola* (Florence, 1606). For a thorough discussion of Montesardo and the development of early guitar styles, see Richard Hudson, *Passacaglio and Ciaccona: From Guitar Music to Italian Keyboard Variations in the 17th Century*, Studies in Musicology, 37 (Ann Arbor, 1981), 17–25, 303.

4 Benedetto Sanseverino, *Intavolatura facile delli passacalli, ciaccone, saravande, spagnolette, fulie, pavaniglie, pass'e mezzi, correnti, & altre varie suonate* (Milan, 1620). See Hudson, *Passacaglio and Ciaccona*, 16, 304; and Richard T. Pinnell, *Francesco Corbetta and the Baroque Guitar With a Transcription of His Works*, 2 vols. (Ann Arbor, 1980), vol. I, 33–35.

5 Giovanni Ambrosio Colonna, *Intavolatura di chitarra spagnuola* (Milan, 1637). See Hudson, *Passacaglio and Ciaccona*, 303; and Pinnell, *Francesco Corbetta*, vol. I, 36–40. Giovanni Battista Abatessa, *Corona di vaghi fiori overo nuova intavolatura di chitarra alla spagnola* (Venice, 1627).

6 Foriano Pico, *Nuova scelta di sonate per la chitarra spagnola* (Venice, 1628?). See Pinnell's

Francesco Corbetta, vol. I, 48 n. 34 and his discussion on 41–43. Also see Hudson, *Passacaglio and Ciaccona*, 304. One of the most important treatments of the *alfabeto falso* occurs in Francesco Corbetta's first publication, *De gli scherzi armonici* (Bologna, 1639). See Pinnell, *Francesco Corbetta*, vol. I, 52–55.

7 Pietro Millioni and Lodovico Monte, *Vero e facil modo d'imparare a sonare et accordare da se medesimo la chitarra spagnuola* (Venice, 1678), 6.

8 Stefano Pesori, *Lo Scrigno armonico* (Mantua, 1640). Pesori, *I concerti di chitarriglia* (Verona, n.d. [post 1640]). Examination of the two sources reveals that Pesori frequently took the plates originally used in publishing *Lo Scrigno armonico* and then reused them for his subsequent *I concerti di chitarriglia*. He even cut out the original dedications and pasted in new ones so as to get more mileage out of the same plates. Giovanni Paolo Foscarini, *Il primo, secondo, e terzo libro della chitarra spagnola*, book 2 publ. in Macerata, 1629. *Li Cinque libri della chitarra alla spagnola* [Rome, 1640]; available in facsimile with an introduction by Paolo Paolini, Archivum Musicum, no. 20 (Florence, 1979). For a thorough discussion of Foscarini, see Hudson, *Passacaglio and Ciaccona*, esp. 53–55 and Chapter 3, "Passacaglio and Ciaccona in the Variation Pieces of Foscarini," 95–169.

9 For a thorough discussion of Corbetta, including this specific publication, the definitive work is Pinnell's *Francesco Corbetta*.

10 For discussions of the physical aspects of the five-course baroque guitar and its common tunings, consult Tom and Mary Evans, *Guitars: Music History, Construction and Players from the Renaissance to Rock* (New York, 1977), 24–39, 136–51; James Tyler, *The Early Guitar: A History and Handbook*, Early Music Series, no. 4 (London, 1980); Eloy Cruz, *La casa de los once muertos: historia y repertorio de la guitarra* (Mexico City, 1993), esp. 32–35; Pinnell, *Francesco Corbetta*, esp. vol. I, 20–21; Cristina Azuma Rodrigues, "Les musiques de danse pour la guitare baroque en Espagne et en France (1660–1700), Essais d'étude comparative," 2 vols., Ph.D. diss., Université Paris-Sorbonne, 2000, esp. 46–47, 59–60.

11 The effect is similar to the so-called "Nashville" tuning of a modern twelve-string, in which the lower octaves of the bass strings are removed, leaving only the higher octaves.

12 Nina Treadwell, "The Guitar *Passacalles* of Santiago de Murcia (ca. 1685–1740): An Alternative Stringing," *Musicology Australia* 15 (1992), 67–76, esp. 72.

13 Pietro Millioni, *Quarta impressione del primo, secondo et terzo libro d'intavolatura di chitarra spagnola* (Rome, 1627). Foriano Pico similarly describes this ornament. Foriano Pico, *Nuova scelta di sonate per la chitarra spagnola* (?1628). Cited in Pinnell, *Francesco Corbetta*, vol. I, 42–43, 48, nn. 31 and 34.

14 Pinnell, *Francesco Corbetta*, vol. I, 42.

15 Francesco Corbetta, *La Guitarre royalle dediée au Roy de la Grande Bretagne* (1671), available in facsimile (Geneva, 1975); a complete study and transcription available in Pinnell, *Francesco Corbetta*, vol. I, 147–78 and vol. II, 193–331.

16 Corbetta, *La Guitarre royalle*, fols. 71r–73r, cascading runs found particularly on fol. 72v. For a complete transcription, see Pinnell, *Francesco Corbetta*, vol. II, 296–97.

17 Francisco Gueráu, *Poema harmónico compuesto de varias cifras de la guitarra española* (Madrid: Manuel Ruiz de Murga, 1694), fol. 5r; facsimile edn. with an intro. by Brian Jeffery (London, 1977). Also see Janis Stevenson, "A Transcription of *Poema Harmónico* by Francisco Guerau for Baroque Guitar," M.A. thesis, San Jose State University, 1974.

18 "Estas condiciones, y otras que yo ignoraré, pide la Guitarra al que desea tocarla con algun primor: y aunque todas son necessarias para el buen orden, lo que mas hermosea, y causa mas harmonia, es la continuacion del Trino, Mordente, Extrasino, y harpeado; que aunque en la verdad, si la Musica es buena, y la tocas á compás, y el instrumento está templado, sonará bien; no obstante, usando destos afectos, que son alma de la Musica, verás la diferencia que vá de uno á otro." Gueráu, *Poema harmónico*, fol. 5.

19 Corbetta, *La Guitarre royalle*, 3, 5, 7–9. See Pinnell, *Francesco Corbetta*, vol. I, 164–65.

20 See Robert Strizich, "Ornamentation in Spanish Baroque Guitar Music," *Journal of the Lute Society of America* 5 (1972), 18–39; Tyler, *The Early Guitar*, esp. 83–102; and Azuma Rodrigues, "Les musiques de danse pour la guitare baroque," vol. I, 65–70.

21 Robert de Visée, *Livre de guittarre dedié au Roy* (Paris: Bonneüil, 1682) and *Liure de pieces pour la gvittarre dedié au Roy* (Paris, 1686); both available in facsimile (Geneva, 1973). For the most definitive recent research on de Visée, including a study of his ornamentation and baroque guitar technique, see the collaborative effort of Hélène Charnassé, Rafael Andia, and Gérard Rébours, *Robert de Visée: Les Livres de Guitare (Paris 1682 et 1686); La guitare en France à l'époque baroque, transcription de la tablature et interprétation*

(Paris, 1999). Nicolas Derosier, *Les Principes de la guitarre* (Amsterdam, 1690) and *Nouveaux principes pour la guittare* (Paris, 1699).

22 Santiago de Murcia, "Códice Saldívar No. 4" (c. 1732). Available in facsimile with some commentary by Michael Lorimer, *Saldívar Codex No. 4*, vol. I: *The Manuscript* (Santa Barbara, CA, 1987). Available in facsimile with an introduction, commentary, and complete transcription by Craig H. Russell, *Santiago de Murcia's "Códice Saldívar No. 4": A Treasury of Guitar Music From Baroque Mexico*, 2 vols. (Urbana and Chicago, 1995); see the "Cumbées" on fols. 43r–44v, reproduced and transcribed in vol. II, 47–48, 188–91.

23 See, for example, the guitar books of Angelo Michele Bartolotti, *Libro P[rim]o di chitarra spagnola* [Florence, 1640], and his *Secondo libro di chitarra* (Rome, c. 1655); both books available in facsimile with an introduction by Claude Chauvel (Geneva, 1984). See his Prelude in D minor in the *Secondo libro*, 69–70, esp. 70, and the allemande on 75.

24 Corbetta, *La Guitarre royalle*. Giovanni Battista Granata, *Soavi concenti di sonate musicali per la chitarra spagnuola* (Bologna, 1659), M.837 in Madrid, Biblioteca Nacional; available in facsimile, with an introduction by James Tyler (Monaco, 1979). Nicola Matteis, *The False Consonances of Mvsick or Instructions for the Playing a True Base Upon the Guitarre* [London, 1682]; available in facsimile with an introduction by James Tyler (Monaco, 1980). Santiago de Murcia, *Resumen de acompañar la parte con la guitarra* (Antwerp and Madrid, 1714 [approbation dated 1717]), R.5048 in Madrid, Biblioteca Nacional; also available in two facsimile editions, one with an introduction by Monica Hall (Monaco, 1980), and another with an introduction by Gerardo Arriaga (Madrid, 1984); a complete translation and transcription is available in two doctoral dissertations – Craig H. Russell, "Santiago de Murcia: Spanish Theorist and Guitarist of the Early Eighteenth Century," 2 vols., Ph.D. diss., University of North Carolina at Chapel Hill, 1980; and Monica Hall, "The Guitar Anthologies of Santiago de Murcia," 2 vols., Ph.D. diss., Open University [England], 1983. Nicolao Doizi de Velasco, *Nuevo modo de cifra para tañer la guitarra con variedad y perfeccion* [Naples, 1640], R.4042 in Madrid, Biblioteca Nacional. François Campion, *Traité d'accompagnement et de composition* (Paris, 1716), and his *Addition au traité d'accompagnement et de composition* (Paris, 1730); both volumes available in

facsimile (Geneva, 1976). Gaspar Sanz, *Instrvccion de mvsica sobre la gvitarra española* (Zaragoza, 1674 and 1697), R.14513 in Madrid, Biblioteca Nacional; available in at least three facsimile editions: (1) with an introduction by Luis García Abrines (Zaragoza, 1979); (2) (Geneva, 1976); and (3) with an introduction by Rodrigo de Zayas, Series "Los Guitarristas," Colección Opera Omnia (Madrid and Seville, [1985]). A complete transcription of Sanz's *Instrucción* is available both in Rodrigo de Zayas's edition and in the most recent contribution by Robert Strizich, *The Complete Guitar Works of Gaspar Sanz*, transcription and translation by R. Strizich (Saint-Nicolas, Québec, 2000).

25 James Tyler lists over eighty separate publications from the early Baroque as well as several dozens of manuscripts devoted to song accompaniments as opposed to solo instrumental playing in the Appendix to his *The Early Guitar*, 140–54.

26 Girolamo Montesardo, *I lieti giorni di Napoli, concertini italiani in aria spagnuoa à due, e tre voci con le lettere dell'alfabeto per la chitarra* (Naples, 1612). For a thorough discussion of this work, see Jean L. Kreiling, "*I lieti giorni di Napoli*: Girolamo Montesardo as Monodist," unpublished paper for James Haar's MU337/1 at the University of North Carolina at Chapel Hill, December 1983. Montesardo was a singer at San Petronio in Bologna before accepting the post of *maestro di cappella* at Fano in 1608.

27 Giovanni Girolamo Kapsberger, *Libro primo di villanella a 1, 2, et 3 voci* (Rome, 1610) does not use *alfabeto* symbols – not surprisingly, given that Montesardo's use of *alfabeto* chords had not yet appeared. Kapsberger's second and third books of *villanelle* (Rome, 1619, 1623), however, do insert the *alfabeto* chords into the score. See Kreiling, "*I lieti giorni*," 10. For further examples, see Paolo d'Aragono, *Canzonette a tre voci* (Naples, 1616), Andrea Falconieri, *Libro primo di villanella* (Rome, 1616), and Filippo Vitali, *Arie a 1.2.3. voci da cantarsi nel chitarrone chitarra Spagnuola, & altri stromenti di Filippo Vitali, Libro Quarto* (Venice, 1622).

28 Giovanni Battista Abatessa, *Cespuglio di varii fiori overo intavolatura de chitarra spagnola* (Orvieto, 1635).

29 Giovanni Casalotti's "Vilanelle di più sorte con l'intavolatura per sonare e cantare sù la chitarra spagnola," British Library, Add. MS 36, 877.

30 For a thorough discussion of Ms. 2804, see Hudson, *Passacaglio and Ciaccona*, 57.

31 Corbetta, *La Guitarre royalle*, 83–98; Henry Grenerin, *Livre de guitarre et autres pieces de*

musique (Paris, 1680); facsimile edition available (Geneva, 1977), 71–89.

32 The definitive study of the small theatrical genres and entr'actes of the era is Emilio Cotarelo y Mori, *Colección de entremeses, loas, bailes, jácaras y mojigangas desde fines del siglo XVI á mediados del XVIII* (Madrid, 1911). For a copiously researched study in English of Spanish theatre, see Louise K. Stein, *Songs of Mortals, Dialogues of the Gods: Music and Theatre in Seventeenth-Century Spain* (Oxford, 1993). See also Russell, *Santiago de Murcia's "Códice Saldívar No. 4"*, vol. I, 17–18; and Craig H. Russell, "Spain in the Enlightenment," in *The Classical Era: From the 1740s to the End of the 18th Century*, ed. Neal Zaslaw, Man and Music, vol. V (London, 1989), 350–67, esp. 356–60.

33 See Louise Kathrin Stein, "El 'Manuscrito Novena': Sus textos, su contexto histórico-musical y el músico Joseph Peyro," *Revista de Musicología* 3 (1980), 197–234, esp. 233–34.

34 The virtuoso baroque guitarists Eloy Cruz, Gabriel Camacho, and Isabelle Villey have been concertizing prodigiously in Mexico, playing "folkloric" versions of old Baroque pieces and relating them to the "classically oriented" versions that are notated in baroque guitar books from the past. Also see the ground-breaking article by Antonio Corona Alcalde, "The Popular Music from Veracruz and the Survival of Instrumental Practices of the Spanish Baroque," *Ars Musica Denver* 7 (1995), 39–68.

35 Possible collaborations between Francisco de Castro and Santiago de Murcia – all of them dating from the first decades of the eighteenth century – include: *El inglés hablador, Los cuatro toreadores, Amor buhonera, El amor sastre, La noche buena, El destierro de hoyo, Pagar que le descalabran*, and *Juego de magister*. See Russell, *Santiago de Murcia's "Códice Saldívar No. 4"*, vol. I, 18, 54, 59–60, 72, 79, 95, 111, 136.

36 The most recent and compelling research on Gueráu has been done by Mallorcan scholars Mosen Antoni Gili, Joan Parets i Serra, and Antoni Pizà, all of whom delivered major addresses on "350 anys dels naixament de Francesc Garau i Femenia (1649–1722)" at the *VI Trobada de Documentalistes Musicals*, held in Artá, Mallorca, October 1999. Their lectures will appear in the published acts of that conference, which are forthcoming. Also see Gerardo Arriaga, "Francisco y Gabriel Gueráu, músicos mallorquines," *Revista de Musicología* 7 (1984), 253–99; and Russell, *Santiago de Murcia's "Códice Saldívar No. 4"*, vol. I, 120–22.

37 Pinnell, *Francesco Corbetta,* vol. I, 121.

38 Ibid.

39 For an examination of de Visée's settings of Lully and role at the French court, see Charnassé, Andia, and Rébours, *Robert de Visée,* esp. 15–17, 21–26, 62, 86–90.

40 For a discussion of the importance of French dance in Hispanic cultures in the late Baroque, see Craig H. Russell, "Imported Influences in 17th and 18th Century Guitar Music in Spain," in *Actas del Congreso Internacional "España en la Música de Occidente",* vol. I (Madrid, 1987), 385–403; Russell, "Lully and French Dance in Imperial Spain: The Long Road from Versailles to Veracruz," *Proceedings of the Society of Dance History Scholars Fourteenth Annual Conference,* ed. Christina L. Schlundt (Riverside, CA, 1991), 145–61; Russell, "New Jewels in Old Boxes: Retrieving the Lost Musical Heritages of Colonial Mexico," *Ars Musica Denver* 5 (1995), 13–38; Russell, "The *Eleanor Hague Manuscript:* a Sampler of Musical Life in Eighteenth-Century Mexico," *Inter-American Music Review* 14 (1995), 39–62; and Russell, "El manuscrito Eleanor Hague: una muestra de la vida musical en el México del siglo XVIII," *Heterofonía* 116–17 (1997), 51–97. Several books are indispensable in the study of French "noble danse," including Wendy Hilton, *Dance of Court and Theater: The French Noble Style 1690–1725,* ed. Caroline Gaynor, labanotation by Mireille Backer (Princeton, 1981); Meredith Ellis Little and Carol Marsh, *La Danse Noble: An Inventory of Dances and Sources* (New York, 1992); and Anne L. Witherell, *Louis Pécour's 1700 "Recüeil de dances",* Studies in Musicology, no. 60 (Ann Arbor, 1981).

41 For an extensive and perceptive study of French dance – as well as Spanish dance – and their direct influence on the repertoire for the baroque guitar, refer once again to Azuma Rodrigues, "Les musiques de danse pour la guitare baroque."

42 Murcia, *Resumen de acompañar,* esp. 57–81.

43 The advertisement is the last two unnumbered plates appended to the back of Raoul-Auger Feuillet and Louis Pécour, *Recüeil de dances composées par M. Pécour ... et mises sur le papier par M. Feuillet* (Paris, 1709).

44 For a thorough treatment of these dances and the ways they are distinguished, see Maurice Esses, *Dance and Instrumental "Diferencias" in Spain During the 17th and Early 18th Centuries,* 3 vols. (Stuyvesant, New York, 1992) vol. I: *History and Background, Music and Dance.* Also see Russell, *Santiago de Murcia's "Códice Saldívar No. 4",* vol. I, esp. 12–17.

45 Madrid, Biblioteca Nacional, Ms M.811: "Libro de diferentes cifras de guitarra [sic] escojidas de los mejores avtores año de 1705."

46 "Passacalles por la L," in Sanz, *Instrucción de música,* book 3, plate 9. "Passac[alles] de la L," in "Libro de diferentes cifras," 51–55. The fingering for the "L" shape that is indicated in the title produces a C minor harmony.

47 "Passacalles por la +," in Sanz, *Instrucción de música,* book 3, plate 5. "Passac[alles] de 3° tono," in "Libro de diferentes cifras," 39–42. The fingering for the "+" shape that is indicated in the title produces an E minor harmony.

48 "Muchos ay señora mía que se burlan de la guitarra y de su son. Pero si bien consideran hallaran que la guitarra es un instrumento el más favorable para nuestros tiempos que jamas se bió. Por que si el día de oy se busca el ahorro de bolsa y de la pena, la guitarra es un theatro para cantar, tañer, dançar, saltar, y correr, baylar, y zapatear." Preface to Luis Briçeño, *Metodo mvi facilissimo para aprender a tañer la gvitarra a lo español* (Paris, 1626); available in facsimile (Geneva, 1972). For a discussion of Briçeño and his role at the French court, see Richard Pinnell with Ricardo Zavadivker, *The Rioplatense Guitar,* vol. I: *The Early Guitar and Its Context in Argentina and Uruguay* (Westport, CT, 1993), 130.

49 "Perdónesele Dios a Vicente Espinel, que nos traxo esta novedad y las cinco cuerdas de la guitarra, con que ya se van olvidando los instrumentos nobles." Quoted in Pinnell, *Rioplatense Guitar,* 159.

50 See Pinnell, *Francesco Corbetta,* vol. I, 77, 84, 86, 93–95, 117, 122–23, 131–35, 139–41, 147–50, 179–83.

51 See Arriaga, "Francisco y Gabriel Gueráu, músicos mallorquines," and Russell, *Santiago de Murcia's "Códice Saldívar No. 4",* vol. I, 115–16, 120–31.

52 For example, the numerous pamphlets issued by Spanish publisher Pablo Minguet y Yrol in the mid 1750s – under the title *Reglas y advertencias generales que enseñan el modo de tañer todos los instrumentos mejores [Rules and General Advice that Teaches the Way to Play All the Best Musical Instruments]* – all place on their title pages the bold claim "that any amateur will be able to learn easily and with great facility [these instruments and rules] and without having a teacher (para que qualquier aficionado las pueda comprehender con mucha facilidad, y sin maestro)."

53 For numerous excellent iconographic depictions of the baroque guitar in various social contexts, consult Tom and Mary Evans, *Guitars*, esp. 136–51.

54 "Se vuol ballare, signor contino, il chitarrino le suonerò," Figaro's *cavatina* in Scene 2 of Act I.

55 Modern historian Richard Pinnell has masterfully shown the extent to which the guitar was an indispensable part of life in South America, Central America, and other regions within the orbit of Spanish influence. His scholarship meticulously chronicles each step of development from the first explorers up to more recent times, and – significantly – he explores the various ethnic and social implications of this encounter between cultures. Pinnell and Zavadivker, *Rioplatense Guitar*, esp. 163 ff. Much information is found in Gabriel Saldívar y Silva and Elisa Osorio Bolio de Saldívar, *Historia de la música en México: Épocas precortesiana y colonial* (Mexico City, 1934/rpt. 1987). Robert Stevenson's monumental studies of music in the Americas in the 1500s and 1600s continue to be the definitive contributions in the field. See Stevenson, *Music in Aztec and Inca Territory* (Berkeley and Los Angeles, 1968); *Music in Mexico: A Historical Survey* (New York, 1952); and *The Music of Peru: Aboriginal and Viceroyal Epochs* (Washington, DC, 1960).

56 Pinnell and Zavadivker, *Rioplatense Guitar*, 179.

57 Ibid., 169–75.

58 Ibid., 181–87.

59 The Aguirre manuscript is in the possession of the Gabriel Saldívar family in Mexico City. For information concerning the Aguirre manuscript consult: Gabriel Saldívar y Silva, *Bibliografía mexicana de musicología y musicografía*, 2 vols. (Mexico City, 1991), esp. vol. I, 81–87; Russell, "New Jewels in Old Boxes"; Stevenson, *Music in Aztec and Inca Territory*, 234–35; Robert Stevenson, "La música en el México de los siglos XVI a XVIII," in *La Música de México: I. Historia, 2. Periodo Virreinal (1530 a 1810)*, ed. Julio Estrada, Instituto de Investigaciones Estéticas (Mexico City, 1986), 41–43; and José Antonio Guzmán Bravo, "La música instrumental en el Virreinato de la Nueva España," also in *La Música de México. I. Historia, 2. Periodo Virreinal (1530 a 1810)*, 120.

60 These genres are found in the following locations in the Aguirre manuscript: *tocotín*: "tocotin por 3 y 4 rasgado y Punteado," fols. 14v–15r; [tocotín de] dos vozes," fol. 15r; "tocotin por P y + Punteado. dos vozes," fol. 15r–v. *corrido*: "Corrido," fol. 27r, "Otro

[corrido] Por arriba," fol. 27r. *guasteco*: "El Guasteco por 1 y +," fol. 22v. *chiqueador*: "Chiqueador de la Puebla Por 1," fol. 19v; "Chiqueador por 4 y alacran rasgado," fol. 20r; "Balona de Bailar chiqueadora por + y P. rasgada y Punt[ea]da," fol. 25v.

61 "*chiqueadores* = (1) Rodajas de carey que usaban antiguamente las mejicanas como adorno. (2) (Méjico) Rodajas de papel, como de un centimetro de diámetro, que, untadas de sebo u otras substancias, se pegan en las sienes para curar el dolor de cabeza." María Moliner, *Diccionario de uso del español*, 2 vols. (Madrid, 1979), vol. I, 609.

62 *chiqueadores* = (American) headache plasters. *chiquear* = (American) to pamper, to mollycoddle, to flatter. Ramón García-Pelayo y Gross et al., *Larousse Diccionario Moderno español–inglés, English–Spanish* (Paris, 1976), 271.

63 These genres are found in the following locations in the Aguirre manuscript: *panama*: "Panama," fol. 29r; *porto rico*: "Puerto rico de la Puebla por 1 y 2 rasg[ue]da y p[untea]da," fol. 19r; "Portorrico por 3 y 4 rasg[uea]do y Pun[tea]do," fol. 19v; "Portorrico Por 4 y alacran rasg[uea]do," fol. 20r; "Portorrico por P. y + rasg[uea]do," fol. 20r; "Portorrico por + rasg[uea]do," fol. 20r; "Portorrico de los negros por 1 y 2 rasg[uea]do," fol. 20r; "El mismo [portoricco] Por 4 y alacran," fol. 20v.

64 "El Coquis Por 2 y 3 rasg[uea]do y Punt[ea]do," fol. 21r. "*coquí* = (Cuba, Puerto Rico; 'Hylodes martinicensis'). Reptil pequeño, al que se aplica ese nombre por el sonido de su grito." Moliner, *Diccionario de uso del español*, vol. I, 764.

65 "Morisca por 6 y 7 rasg[ue]ada," fol. 12v. "*morisco* (see "*moro*") = (1) Natural del África Septentrional frontera con España, donde estaba la provincia romana llamada Mauritania, de la que el Marruecos que fue español es una parte. (2) Por extensión, musulmán. (3) Se aplica a los musulmanes que invadieron España y vivieron en ella entre los siglos VIII y XV, y a sus cosas." Moliner, *Diccionario de uso del español*, vol. I, 456. "*morisco* = Moorish. The term *morisco* is applied to the Spanish Moors who, during the Reconquest (711–1492), accepted Christianity." *Larousse Diccionario Moderno*, 623.

66 "Zarambeques, o Muecas" on fols. 45r–46r and "Cumbées" on fols. 43r–44v of Murcia's "Códice Saldívar No. 4."

67 Eugenio Salazar in the mid-1500s equates the *cumbé* and *guineo*. See Russell, *Santiago de Murcia's "Códice Saldívar No. 4"*, vol. I, 70–71,

and nn. 241, 242, 243, 244 on 219–20. The dramatist Francisco de Castro uses the terms *guineo* and *zarambeque* interchangeably in his charming *Pagar que le descalabran* (pre-1713). See Russell, *Santiago de Murcia's "Códice Saldívar No. 4"*, vol. I, 79, and nn. 276, 277, 278 on 225. Recently, Rolando Pérez Fernández has authored two important studies directly related to the *cumbés*: "El chuchumbé y la buena palabra," *Son del sur* 3 (November, 1996), 24–36, and 4 (June, 1997), 33–46; and *La música afromestiza mexicana* (Xalapa, Mexico, 1990), esp. 59–64.
68 "[Las palabras] son en sumo grado Escandalosas obcenas, y ofensibas de Castos Oydos, y se an cantado, y cantan acompañadolas con Baile no menos Escandaloso, y obceno – acompanado con acciones demostraciones y meneos desonestos, y probacativos de Lascibia, todo ello en grabe ruina, y Escandolo á la Almas del Pueblo Christiano." Archivo General de la Nación. Inquisición, tomo 1297, expediente 3, fol. 19r.

11 Perspectives on the classical guitar in the twentieth century

1 The Naxos label, classical music's largest, is currently in the middle of a comprehensive CD retrospective of the guitar repertoire that so far numbers eighty.
2 Andrés Segovia, *Segovia: An Autobiography of the Years 1893–1920*, trans. W. F. O'Brien (New York, 1976), 6.
3 Emilio Pujol, *Tárrega, Ensayo Biográfico* (Lisbon, 1960), quoted in Frederic V. Grunfeld, *The Art and Times of the Guitar* (London, 1969), 286.
4 Segovia, *Segovia*, 59.
5 "Llobet had serious misgivings which prevented him from securing compositions from the great composers who were his friends – Debussy, Ravel, Fauré, Falla, and Granados. He believed that the guitar was not resonant or strong enough to be heard in the more important and large concert halls of Europe, a belief that was shared by Tárrega and his disciples." See Charles Postelwate, "Andrés Segovia: A Living Legend," *American String Teacher* (Winter, 1981), 29–30.
6 One measure of the willpower of Segovia is that he insisted on playing a Wigmore Hall recital in 1937 just a few hours after learning that his thirteen-year-old son had been accidentally electrocuted at an aqueduct.
7 Segovia, *Segovia*, from the book jacket.
8 Postelwate, "Andrés Segovia," 31.
9 Peter Mennin, former president of the Juilliard School, summed up this criticism

when he was interviewed by Allan Kozinn of the *New York Times*: "What I don't understand is why Segovia went after composers like Turina, Ponce and Torroba rather than composers like Stravinsky or Webern – the truly great, or at any rate, much more significant composers of his day. He had an opportunity to seek out first-class music from first-class composers, but instead, he developed a literature that is not very substantial musically." Quoted in Brian Hodel, "Twentieth-Century Music and the Guitar: Part I: 1900–1945," *Guitar Review* 117 (Summer, 1999), 12–13.
10 The composer Joaquin Nin-Culmell set out to write a piece for Segovia, and, as he reports, "He said, 'Send your piece to me and I'll fix it.' Of course no composer is willing to accept that kind of statement!" *Guitar Review* 99 (Fall, 1994), 2.
11 See Peter E. Segal, "The Role of Andrés Segovia in the Shaping of the Literature of the Classical Guitar," Ph.D. diss., Temple University, 1994, 39–45.
12 Naxos is producing one with various artists, and guitarists Antonio Lopez and Gérard Abiton are recording Ponce projects on Soundset and Mandala, respectively.
13 Brian Hodel, "Villa Lobos and the Guitar," *Guitar Review* 72 (Winter, 1988), 22.
14 Richard D. Stover, *Six Silver Moonbeams: The Life and Times of Agustín Barrios Mangoré* (Clovis, CA, 1992).
15 Richard D. Stover, "Agustín Barrios Mangoré, Part II: Emerging Genius," *Guitar Review* 99 (Fall, 1994), 33.
16 Eleftheria Kotzia, "Wish you Were Here: Ida Presti," *Classical Guitar* 19/9 (May 1992), 1.
17 For Bream's own feelings about this topic, see his conversation with Victor Coelho in "Julian Bream in 1990," *The Lute Society Quarterly* (July, 1991).
18 Graham Wade and Gerard Garno, *A New Look at Segovia: His Life and His Music*, 2 vols. (Pacific, MO, 1997), vol. II, 55.
19 See Julian Bream, "Toru Takemitsu: An Appreciation," *Guitar Review* 105 (Spring, 1996), 2.
20 Hans Werner Henze, *Royal Winter Music – First Sonata on Shakespearean Characters for Guitar* [GA 467] (Mainz, 1976), introduction.
21 Many extended techniques and notations are covered in John Schneider's *The Contemporary Guitar* (Berkeley and Los Angeles, 1985).
22 Gareth Walters, "A Conversation with John Williams [Part II]," *Guitar Review* 92 (Winter, 1993), 10.

23 Jim Tosone, "A Prodigal Son Returns: Eliot Fisk in Conversation," *Guitar Review* 107 (Fall, 1996), 18–19.

24 Wade, *Segovia*, vol. II, 90.

25 In my case, I found the classical guitar through a Segovia concert, but having come from playing fairly advanced piano music I felt a paucity in the repertoire. I immediately got a piece from my father, a composer, thus beginning my life of working with composers, but I also clearly remember picking up Bream's *20th-Century Guitar* and listening breathlessly as one fine piece after another floated by.

26 Perhaps the editions of Sor's *Estudios* most clearly embody the old and new. Segovia's edition of twenty of the studies remains a kind of rite of passage for young guitar students. However, in publishing a facsimile edition of the complete works of Sor, Brian Jeffery in 1981 said "[Segovia's edition of Sor] does not reach the minimum standards of editing which were current at the time this book was first published, let alone today" (*Soundboard*, 1981). Later, it was revealed that Segovia worked in part from a Napoleon Coste version of those pieces, and some of the note and tempo changes in fact derived from Sor's friend Coste. The Segovia edition is now published with notes showing the original tempo markings of Sor, but the fact is that Segovia's edition remains immensely valuable. It reveals, perhaps more than any source, the technical thinking of Segovia, and also modernizes many of the technical issues – remember that Sor basically avoided the right-hand ring finger, an idea that is no longer possible with today's repertoire, and was hardly even put into practice by Sor's own contemporaries.

27 Jim Tosone, "A Conversation with John Williams," *Guitar Review* 97 (Spring, 1994), 6.

28 As Brian Hodel, who has lived for many years in Brazil, remarks:

This is a music as much centered on the nylon-stringed classical or Spanish guitar as on any particular music genre. Elements of European classical guitar tradition participate in it, along with those of jazz and myriad native styles, urban and rural, traditional and commercially conceived. Many classical guitarists from Brazil began by playing popular music, later returning to it in arrangements for their repertoires. Brazilian popular – and sometimes traditional ("folk") – guitarists often study classical guitar methods and pieces as part of their largely informal training. Many Brazilian jazz guitarists play the nylon-stringed instrument with great facility and some can play steel-stringed electric guitars with classical right-hand technique.

("The Brazilian Guitar," *Guitar Review* 84 [Winter, 1991], 12)

29 Mention should be made here of Maria Luisa Anida, the Argentinian guitarist who played duos with Llobet, but who was discouraged from touring by him because she was a woman.

30 Reprinted in *Guitar Review* 32 (Fall, 1969), 3.

12 Antonio Stradivari and baroque guitar making

1 Prior to 1969, the date on the pegbox of this guitar was thought to read 1680, but a closer examination revealed the last figure to be an "8" rather than a "0"; see David D. Boyden, *Catalogue of The Hill Collection of Musical Instruments in the Ashmolean Museum, Oxford* (Oxford, 1969), 45.

2 Gianpaolo Gregori, "La harpe et les guitares d'Antonio Stradivari," *Musique, Images, Instruments: Revue française d'organologie et d'iconographie musicale* 3 (Paris, 1997), 17–19, 30–31.

3 "Belchior Dias a fez em. / 1X^a nomes de dez.^{ro} 1581."

4 Antonio Corona-Alcalde, "The Viola da Mano and the Vihuela, Evidence and Suggestions about their Construction," *The Lute: The Journal of the Lute Society* 24, part 1 (1984), 11–13.

5 Joël Dugot, "Un nouvel exemplaire de *vihuela* au musée de la musique?", *Luths et luthistes en Occident, actes du colloque organisé par la cité de la musique. 13–15 mai 1998* (Paris, 1999), 307–17.

6 Michael Prynne, "A Surviving Vihuela de Mano," *The Galpin Society Journal* 16 (May, 1963), 22–27; Pierre Abondance, "La Vihuela du Musée Jacquemart-André: restauration d'un document unique," *Revue de Musicologie* 66, no. 1 (1980); Antonio Corona-Alcalde, "The Vihuela and the Guitar in Sixteenth-Century Spain: A Critical Appraisal of Some of the Existing Evidence," *The Lute: The Journal of the Lute Society* 30 (1990), 3–24; Dugot, "Un nouvel exemplaire de *vihuela*." Richard Bruné feels the Jacquemart-André instrument is not authentic because it is "proportionally corrupt, musically impossible, and does not have a provenance beyond its acquisition around 1880 – a time of extensive musical instrument fakery." Personal communication.

7 According to Egberto Bermudez, Pierre Abondance considers the Quito instrument to be a guitar. Egberto Bermudez, "The Vihuela: The Paris and Quito Instruments," in *The Spanish Guitar*, exhibition catalog (New York and Madrid, 1991), 38. Richard Bruné views the instrument as "an anachronistic New World creation." Personal communication.

8 Measurements of the vihuela body lengths and string lengths are taken from Dugot, "Un nouvel exemplaire de *vihuela*," 317. The author examined the vihuela from the Musée Jacquemart-André when it was on loan to the Metropolitan Museum of Art in 1991–92. Measurements of the Belchior Dias guitar were kindly supplied by the Royal College of Music.

9 Juan Bermudo, *Declaración de instrumentos musicales* (Osuna, 1555), Chapter 60, fol. 93v; Chapter 64, fol. 95r; Chapter 65, fol. 96r; Chapter 86, fol. 109r. For a new translation, see Dawn Astrid Espinosa, "Juan Bermudo, 'On Playing the Vihuela' from *Declaración de instrumentos musicales (Osuna, 1555)*," *Journal of the Lute Society of America* 28–29 (1995–96), 22, 36–39, 127–30.

10 Bermudo, *Declaración*, chapter 65, fol. 96r; Espinosa trans., 40.

11 Ibid., chapter 65, fol. 96r; Espinosa trans., 41.

12 Bartolomeo Lieto, *Dialogo quarto di musica* (Naples, 1559/rpt. Lucca, 1993), unpaginated; Corona-Alcalde, "The Viola da Mano and the Vihuela," 8.

13 Pablo Nassarre, *Escuela musica, segun la practica moderna*, vol. I (Zaragoza, 1724), 461.

14 Ibid., 461–62:

There are two principal parts: the body and the place of manipulation, which is commonly called the neck. The woods of which the body is made must be strong and solid, as with all the other instruments, except the top, which should always be of *pino avete* for the reasons stated. The lower extreme is semicircular in form, as is the upper part, with the difference that in the middle of it originates the neck. A straight line is not formed by the two angles of the sides, for they curve toward the middle of the body [forming the waist].

The acoustical proportions, which should have the same [numerical] figures as the shape, are as follows: The greatest width of the extreme lower part of the body must be doubled to equal the length, and the upper extreme width, which should be smaller in width [than the lower part], must be in a proportion of *sexquiquarta* (5 : 4) of the lower.

The measurement of the two extremes should be in proportion to the length of the entire body. The depth of the body should be *dupla sexquialtera* (5 : 2) of the width of the two extremes; and speaking practically, the width of the lower bout should be half of the whole body length, which is *dupla* (2 : 1). The upper bout should have a width of four parts, having five below, so that it may have a fifth part less than the lower; for the measure of the middle, it should be one-third the length, it should be one part wide, which is the *tripla* (3 : 1). For the depth of the sides, of five parts, in which the lower-bout width is divided, take only two; the same applies to the upper-bout width, which divided in five parts, gives two in depth, so that both are *dupla sexquialtera* (5 : 2). This is everything with respect to the body. That which is played at the place of manipulation, called the neck, can have a length with allows one to form six to eight stops. These instruments have the distinction that all of the stops which are formed on the neck are semitones.

15 Michael Praetorius, *Syntagma Musicum II: De Organographia Parts I and II*, trans. and ed. David Z. Crookes (Oxford, 1986), 59.

16 Marin Mersenne, *Harmonie Universelle: The Books on Instruments*, trans. Roger Chapman (The Hague, 1957), 137.

17 The technical drawing made by Stephen Barber (obtained from the Ashmolean Museum) has rectified this problem, but as such, it does not accurately represent the instrument in its present state.

18 Gregori, "La harpe et les guitares d'Antonio Stradivari," 25–26.

19 Luisa Cervelli, *La Galleria Armonica; Catalogo del Museo degli strumenti musicali di Roma* (Rome, 1994), 273.

20 Dimensions of the guitars were obtained from the following sources: "Hill" guitar, a technical drawing supplied by the Ashmolean Museum; "Rawlins" guitar, staff of The Shrine to Music Museum, Vermillion, SD; "Giustiniani" guitar, Gianpaolo Gregori, *La Chitarra "Giustiniani" Antonio Stradivari 1681* (Cremona, 1998), 25–27.

21 Ignazio Alessandro Cozio di Salabue, *Carteggio*, transcribed by Renzo Bacchetta (Milan, 1950), 420–21.

22 Andrea Mosconi and Carlo Torresani, *Il Museo Stradivariano di Cremona* (Milan, 1987), 20–21.

23 Stewart Pollens, *The Violin Forms of Antonio Stradivari* (London, 1992), 24–28.

24 See Mosconi and Torresani, *Il Museo Stradivariano di Cremona*.

25 Giovanni Paolo Foscarini, *Li cinque libri della chitarra alla spagnola* (Rome, 1640), unpaginated. See under "Modo d'accordar più Chitare per sonar di concerto."

26 "Misura della Longezza e Largezzo del manico della Chitara Tiorbata"

27 "Misura della longezza e largezza della tratta di Citara Tiorbata et in su la detta tratta ge vanno susa sette bassi e Questa in Cima deve essere una Quarta da violino e il restando deve da chitara tutte sette."

28 "Questi deve esser compani due Cantini di Chitara / queste deve essere compane due Sotanelle di chitara / queste deve essere compane doi Cantini da Violino grossi / queste altra corda deve essere un Canto da violino / questa altra corda deve essere una sotanella di Chitara / questa altra corda deve essere un Canto da Violono ma di più grossi / questa deve essere un cantino da violino / corda."

29 The author has experimentally determined that gut strings of 0.40–0.57 mm diameter and 74.4 cm in length can be tuned up to e^1 at $a^1 = 440$ Hz. Such a high pitch would, however, be highly precarious.

30 The lutenist and guitarist Lynda Sayce commissioned Edward Fitzgibbon to construct a full-scale copy of the "Hill" Stradivari guitar. She reports that it was necessary to reduce the string spacing and neck width to render the copy playable. The lute and guitar maker Stephen Barber contends that the string spacing is, in fact, usable. He feels the "Hill" guitar may have been designed for continuo playing, though he admits he makes his copies with 670–80 mm string lengths, with ten frets on the neck.

31 Gregori, *La Chitarra "Giustiniani"*, 26.

32 Ibid., 25.

33 I would like to thank Richard Bruné for suggesting the function of the triangular blocks.

34 Gregori, *La Chitarra "Giustiniani"*, 25–26.

35 As indicated above, Stephen Barber's technical drawing of the "Hill" guitar (obtained from the Ashmolean Museum) depicts a scaled-down instrument with a 690 mm string length (a few original dimensions are mounted on the drawing for reference). Presumably, the drawing was scaled to facilitate the construction of "comfortable" instruments for modern use.

Select bibliography

The literature on the guitar is immense, and ranges from doctoral dissertations on specific early traditions to "how-to" tips in popular journals and magazines. For a very thorough bibliography (though not for rock), see the article "Guitar" in *The New Grove Dictionary of Music and Musicians*, 2nd edn. (2001). The following gives only essential books and articles in English that are considered authoritative, available at any good university library, and in some cases definitive on the history, performance, and construction of the guitar. References to more specific books, articles, and websites are listed within the bibliographies and notes contained in these studies, and, of course, in the notes to the chapters in this book.

General
Bennett, Andy and Kevin Dawe. *Guitar Cultures* (Oxford, 2001).
Denyer, Ralph. *The Guitar Handbook: A Unique Source Book for the Guitar Player – Amateur or Professional, Acoustic or Electric, Rock, Blues, Jazz or Folk* [with a foreword by Robert Fripp]. New York, 1999.
Evans, Tom and Mary Evans. *Guitars: Music, History, Construction, and Players from Renaissance to Rock* (New York, 1979).
Gill, C. *Guitar Legends: The Definitive Guide to the World's Greatest Guitar Players.* London, 1995.
Grunfeld, Frederic V. *The Art and Times of the Guitar.* London, 1969.
Morrish, J., ed. *The Classical Guitar: A Complete History.* London, 1997.
The New Grove Dictionary of Music and Musicians. 2nd edn. Ed. Stanley Sadie, s.v. "Guitar." London, 2001.
Stimpson, Michael, ed. *The Guitar: A Guide for Students and Teachers.* Oxford, 1988 [includes articles by Brian May, Paco Peña, David Russell, Alphonso Johnson, John Ethridge].
Turnbull, Harvey. *The Guitar from the Renaissance to the Present Day.* New York, 1974.
Wheeler, Tom. *The Guitar Book: A Handbook for Electric and Acoustic Guitarists.* New York, 1974.

Early and classical guitar
Coelho, Victor, ed. *Performance on Lute, Guitar, and Vihuela: Historical Practice and Modern Interpretation.* Cambridge, 1997, esp. Chapters 7–9.
Heck, Thomas. "Guitar-Related Research in the Age of the Internet: Current Options, Current Trends." *Soundboard* 25 (1998), 61–68.
Schneider, John. *The Contemporary Guitar.* Berkeley and Los Angeles, 1985.
Tyler, James. *The Early Guitar: A History and Handbook.* Oxford, 1980.
Tyler, James and Paul Sparks. *The Guitar and its Music from the Renaissance to the Classical Era.* Oxford, 2002.

Rock, country

Covach, John and Graeme Boone. *Understanding Rock*. New York and Oxford, 1997.

Green, Douglas. "The Guitar in Early Country Music." In *The Guitar Player Book*, by the editors of *Guitar Player* magazine. New York, 1978, 281–83.

The Guinness Encyclopedia of Popular Music. Ed. Colin Larkin. London, 1995 [vol. VI, pp. 4633–4708, contains a very extensive bibliography of hundreds of items].

Kienzle, Rich. "The Electric Guitar in Country Music: Its Evolution and Development." *Guitar Player* (November, 1979), 30–41.

Van Halen, Edward. "My Tips for Beginners." *Guitar Player* (July, 1984), 52–60.

Waksman, Steve. *Instruments of Desire: The Electric Guitar and the Shaping of Musical Experience*. Cambridge, MA, 1999.

Walser, Robert. *Running with the Devil: Power, Gender, and Madness in Heavy Metal Music*. Hanover, NH, 1993.

Blues and jazz

Jazz Guitarists: Collected Interviews from Guitar Player Magazine. Introduction by Leonard Feather. Saratoga, CA, 1975.

Kubik, Gerhard. *Africa and the Blues*. Jackson, MS, 1999.

Obrecht, Jas, ed. *Blues Guitar: The Men who Made the Music*. 2nd edn. San Francisco, 1993.

   Rollin' & Tumblin': The Postwar Blues Guitarists. San Francisco, 2000.

Palmer, Robert. "The Church of the Sonic Guitar." In *Present Tense: Rock & Roll and Culture*. Ed. Anthony DeCurtis. Durham, NC, 1992, 13–38.

Summerfield, Maurice J. *The Jazz Guitar: Its Evolution and Players*. Gateshead, 1978.

Wyman, Bill. *Bill Wyman's Blues Odyssey*. New York, 2001.

World music

Becker, Judith. "Kroncong, Indonesian Popular Music." *Asian Music* 7 (1975), 14–19.

Eyre, Banning. *In Griot Time: An American Guitarist in Mali*. Philadelphia, 2000.

Kanahele, George. *Hawaiian Music and Musicians: An Illustrated History*. Honolulu, 1979.

Kaye, Andrew L. "The Guitar in Africa," in *The Garland Encyclopedia of World Music*, vol. I: *Africa*. Ed. Ruth M. Stone. New York, 1998.

Manuel, Peter. *Popular Musics of the Non-Western World: An Introductory Survey*. New York and Oxford, 1988.

Sevilla, Paco. *Paco de Lucía: A New Tradition for the Flamenco Guitar*. San Diego, 1995.

World Music: The Rough Guide. Ed. Simon Broughton et al. London, 1994.

Instruments

Bacon, Tony and Paul Day. *Complete History of Fender Electric Guitars* (1992).

Gruhn, George and W. Carter. *Acoustic Guitars and Other Fretted Instruments: A Photographic History*. San Francisco, 1993.

Minhinnett, Ray and Bob Young, *The Story of the Fender Stratocaster: Curves, Contours and Body Horns.* San Francisco, 1995.

The New Grove Dictionary of Music and Musicians. 2nd edn. Ed. Stanley Sadie, s.v. "Guitar." London, 2001.

Wheeler, Tom. *American Guitars: An Illustrated History.* New York, 1992.

Trynka, Paul, ed. *The Electric Guitar: An Illustrated History.* San Francisco, 1995.

General index

Index of song and album titles